EMERGING HUMANITY

Multi-Ethnic Literature
for
Children and Adolescents

EMERGING HUMANITY

Multi-Ethnic Literature
for
Children and Adolescents

Ruth Kearney Carlson
California State College—Hayward

Illustrations by Louise Noack Gray
Photos by Ernest Jaco

WM. C. BROWN COMPANY PUBLISHERS
Dubuque, Iowa

Copyright © 1972 by Wm. C. Brown Company Publishers

Library of Congress Catalog Card Number: 76—181743

ISBN 0—697—06197—3

Printed in the United States of America

This book is respectfully dedicated to all individuals who comprise minority groups and who have played a part in the symphony of American culture, and particularly to the memory of Nina and Oscar Carlson who have made their contribution to our land.

CONTENTS

The author of this book assumes that a better understanding of much ethnic literature can help teachers to live better the ideals of those ancient Náhautl poets who felt that their destiny was "to humanize people" and "to make their hearts strong."

The book is organized in two parts. The first section consisting of Chapters, One, Two, and Three includes some mention of many types of ethnic literature. There is a discussion of novels of several ethnic groups including ones about Polish, Japanese, Armenian, and Jewish people, as well as some examples of stories about black, American Indian, and Mexican-American characters. Chapter One clarifies some definitions and values for understanding various types of ethnic literature. Chapter Two is principally concerned with some basic criteria for selecting good ethnic literature and some examples of good and poor literature in relation to these criteria. Chapter Three discusses some teaching ideas which may help children, adolescents, and adults to interpret ethnic literature.

The second part of this book focuses upon four particular ethnic groups and their literature. Chapter Four links the African heritage and culture to that of black Americans living on this continent. Chapter Five is concerned with black literature in the pluralistic society of the United States. Chapter Six gives an Indian heritage of folk tale and song. Chapter Seven discusses the basic conflicts of persons in the American Indian ethnic groups who are struggling between two worlds—one of Indian traditions and old accustomed ways and the white man's world of technocracy, bureaucracy, and duplicity. The final chapter is about the Mexican-American, his rich cultural heritage, and his resentment at being considered a hyphenated American.

In her poem *Dark Testament,* an eloquent black poet pleads for a "song of hope and a world where I can sing it."* May readers of this volume help others to sing a song of hope for man so that people can be humanized and the heart can be filled with a humane feeling for all mankind.

*Pauli Murray, *Dark Testament and Other Poems,* Comstock Hill, Norwalk, Connecticut 1970, p. 22.

PART ONE

The Brazier
of Humanity

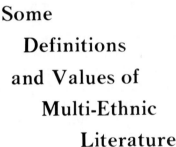

CHAPTER ONE

Some
Definitions
and Values of
Multi-Ethnic
Literature

One of the greatest values of all good literature is a momentary glimpse of the glow of humanity when one experiences the problems and purposes, the hates and hurts, and the values, dignities, and human worth of another human being who is both similar to and different from oneself. G. Robert Carlsen beautifully expresses this "reverence for life" in the words:

> No matter where human life is found, no matter what pressures it is submitted to, no matter what the reactions to those pressures, the individual, that brazier of life, is valued because though the light he casts is small, he is still a part of the large creative force of the universe. This regard for human worth is perhaps one of the greatest themes in man's literature and storytelling.[1]

This sense of compassion for our fellow men is only one of the numerous

1. G. Robert Carlsen, "The Way of the Spirit and the Way of the Mind," *Elementary English* 40 (February 1963): 146.

values of reading and experiencing multi-ethnic literature. The author of this book hopes to help children and young adolescents to understand better the problems of cultural minorities so that the contributions of members of such minority groups to the mainstream of American culture can be appreciated.

Definitions of Multi-Ethnic Literature

As used in this book, multi-ethnic literature refers to the literature of a minority ethnic group which differs from typical white Anglo-Saxon middle-class values and characteristics of persons living in the United States. In some countries of the world, such as parts of Africa or India, white Anglo-Saxons are considered as a minority group. Carey McWilliams in *Brothers Under the Skin* defines an ethnic group as "a people living competitively in relationship of superordination or subordination with respect to some other people or peoples within the same area or region."[2]

In the words of Rose, in his book *They and We, Racial and Ethnic Relations in the United States,* "Groups whose members share a unique social and cultural heritage passed on from one generation to the next are known as *ethnic groups.*"[3] Such groups have distinctive patterns of family life, language, religion, or customs which differentiate them from others. Some ethnic groups are distinguished by race as their forebears are from Italian, Irish, or Mexican lineage. Others, like the Jews, are more frequently differentiated by differences in religion and are often designated as a "people."

Some Metaphors About Newcomers

In 1909, an English author, Israel Zangwell, created the colorful metaphor of "The Melting Pot" in his play by this title. In this drama he depicted America as a gigantic crucible, a great melting pot into which thousands of humans—Celts and Latins, Slavs and Teutons, Greeks and Syrians, and black and yellow persons were amalgamated into an American who was supposed to combine the greatest virtues of all persons. Newcomers were asked to abandon their older ways of life and be merged or culturally fused into new beings.[4]

2. Carey McWilliams, *Brothers Under the Skin,* Rev. ed. (Boston: Little, Brown and Company, 1964), page 113.
3. Peter I. Rose, *They and We, Racial and Ethnic Relations in the United States* (New York: Random House, 1968), p. 11.
4. *Ibid.,* p. 54.

Six years later, the concept of cultural pluralism evolved. Horace M. Kallen saw strengths in *diversity* as opposed to the absorption and fusion of immigrant groups. In an article published in *The Nation* on February 18, 1915 entitled "Democracy versus the Melting Pot," Kallen developed the image of an America as "a multiplicity in a unity, an orchestration of mankind."[5]

Most of the recent multi-ethnic books for children and adolescents published during the past few years ignore the "melting pot" metaphor with its amalgamation of peoples. Instead they suggest the metaphor of an orchestra or a mosaic of separate ethnic groups offering diversity and variety contributing to a national heritage benefiting from the contributions of different groups. However, education for better intergroup relations in the United States has some distance to go before the majority of citizens value the separate identity, individualities, and contributions of racial, ethnic, or religious groups. In a recent "tell-it-like-it-is" approach to some of the books being written for children and adolescents, readers learn about a society where prejudice and discrimination deny the rights of individuals. Problems of civil rights, bigotry, housing, education, employment, religion, and social ostracism appear in various novels, dramas, stories, and poems. Some of the more recent writings of young black poets and novelists is frequently tinged with bitterness and irony as authors struggle to depict the black experience.

Values of Multi-Ethnic Literature

Librarians, teachers, curriculum consultants, and others concerned with the education of children have variant opinions concerning the values of a planned multi-ethnic literature curriculum for young readers. Dangers of exploitation, propagandizing, didacticism, and mediocrity are given. Many teachers, such as those cited in *The Short Changed Children of Suburbia,* are in a quandry and fear social living experiences in the school. In most instances facile generalizations about countries and peoples are taught, but many teachers lack the expertise to help children understand differences and similarities between races, religions, and cultural traditions.

Teachers and librarians also fear the wrath of parents who accuse them of advocating love for so-called inferior persons on the social ladder of a middle-class dominated society.

Before citing several values of reading literature about minorities, certain principles should be established.

5. *Ibid.,* p. 56.

Multi-Ethnic Literature Should Not Be the Total Reading Program

Multi-ethnic literature should not comprise the total literature program. The Chinese, Japanese, or Mexican child should not merely read novels about his own people. He should not be denied an exposure to such classics as *Alice in Wonderland, Charlotte's Web,* or *Wind in the Willows.* He should enjoy such imaginative fantasies as *The Borrowers* or *The Hobbit.* He should chant the lyrical tunes of poetry by Eleanor Farjeon and Rachel Field. An adolescent reader should enjoy poetry by Robert Frost as well as the poems by Langston Hughes and Juan Ramón Jimínez. A young reader's literary diet should be a smorgasbord of numerous attractive offerings, not the repetitive flavor of a few literary themes and scenes.

Each Minority Reader Should Have an Opportunity to Read about His Own Heritage

Although minority literature should not be the total reading program for the young reader, neither should it be neglected or ignored. As teachers and librarians become more and more immersed in literature for the Negro, Mexican-American, and Indian child, they should remember the adage of "the right book for the right child." A Chinese or a Filipino adolescent reader may be interested in reading a few novels about Afro-American or Spanish characters, but occasionally he needs to be directed to a book about his own people and heritage.

Books Presenting Persons as Negative Stereotypes Should Be Avoided

One of the greatest dangers of reading a large number of books about minority peoples is that of the negative stereotypes seen in many stories and novels. All Mexican-Americans are not Catholic migrants who are poverty-stricken persons following the crops from farm to farm. All Negroes do not live in Harlem or in the slums in poverty-stricken squalor eating soul food and rejecting law and order. All Indians do not wear moccasins and live wretchedly on Indian reservations in filth and ignorance. By the same reasoning, neither do all white Anglo-Saxon middle-class teachers and employers cruelly reject persons from various ethnic groups who have different mores or customs.

In an illuminating article entitled "The Dawning of the Age of Aquarius for Multi-Ethnic Children's Literature," David K. Gast depicts nine approaches to children's literature which are evident. Many of these same approaches could also apply to adolescent literature. These include: (1) the invisible man approach, (2) the noble savage approach, (3) the white man's burden approach, (4) the minstrel-show approach, (5) the queer customs approach, (6) the multi-ethnic Dick and Jane approach, (7) the reversed stereotype approach, (8) the "tell-it-like-it-is" approach, and (9) the remanufactured past approach.[6]

Most of these approaches are clearly indicated in their titles. The *reversed stereotype approach* consists of overdoing the social or political status of a minority person in order to avoid a negative stereotype. For instance, in order to avoid the image of a Negro being employed as a garbage collector or as a house servant, authors tend to do a "stereotype switch" placing all of their Negro characters in secure middle-class jobs such as the professions of medicine and law.

Gast also cautions against the "remanufactured past approach." Scholars are assiduously questing information on black, Mexican, or Indian soldiers, financiers, doctors, and congressmen who have made contributions to American history. Gast warns against a too-hastily contrived, out-of-context appendix to history in which minority persons become better known than their white counterparts.

Multi-Ethnic Literature Should Avoid Focusing Upon Differences at the Expense of Similarities

Teachers and librarians presenting literature to young readers should avoid focusing upon the differences of ethnic groups. Too many Jewish novels depict particular Jewish religious holidays when white gleaming tablecloths adorn tables and candles glow during a religious observance peculiar to persons of the Jewish faith. Too often Japanese holidays such as the Festival of the Dolls or Kite Days are portrayed rather than scenes showing a Japanese-American child living comfortably on his strawberry farm or as the daughter or son of a Japanese banker in San Francisco or Los Angeles. Authors of books designed for the primary age child are particularly prone to emphasize differences rather than similarities between persons. June Handler, in an article entitled "Books for Loving" appearing in the May 1970 issue of *Elementary English,* discusses some approaches to considering differences in general. Some of these include: (1) differences in ways of acting cannot be equated with physical differences; (2) people are more alike than different; (3) every individual in his uniqueness can contribute something to the world; (4) a person's difference may make him more appealing and important.[7]

6. David K. Gast, "The Dawning of the Age of Aquarius for Multi-ethnic Children's Literature," in *Elementary English* 47 (May 1970): 661-665.
7. June Handler, "Books for Loving," *Elementary English* 47 (May 1970): 687, 688, 692.

Multi-Ethnic Literature Studied by Children Should Usually Meet the Criteria of Good Children's Literature

Ordinarily, literature books should not be selected for children purely on the basis of their themes and the characterizations of minority peoples. Such literature should usually meet the criteria of all good literature for children such as distinctive language, good characterization, a clear-cut plot, imaginative conceptions, natural, appropriate dialogue, an honesty and sincerity of purpose, and other criteria which will be elaborated later. However, occasionally, there might be a few exceptions to this principle. Sometimes an author writes a biography which adds to the cognitive knowledge store about a minority figure. This biography might be accepted tentatively through the application of less rigorous standards than ordinarily would be required. Later, as a more definitive biography or novel is created, the mediocre book can be abandoned.

Sometimes, reviewers reject a biography or novel on valid grounds when such writing is not considered good literature meeting certain prescribed criteria. However, occasionally an imaginative teacher can utilize such literature creatively and effectively in ways to fill the gaps of knowledge. For instance, some reviewers have criticized *Forten, the Sailmaker: Pioneer Champion of Negro Rights,* by Douty, and have stated that it has an uninteresting writing style and a wooden dialogue. However, Douty has made use of basic firsthand documentary material. Some of the content can be used in docudramas or musical plays presented as part of a history unit. Also, such a book as *Forten, the Sailmaker* is enhanced by an additional biography such as *I, Charlotte Forten, Black and Free* by Polly Longsworth.

One reviewer was critical of the carnival-like aspect of sections of *No Promises in the Wind* by Irene Hunt. Yet, this book vividly depicts characteristics of the depression of the thirties. The conflict between a Polish son, Jack Grondowski, and his father during the unemployment of his father, gives insight and compassion for the jobless. This book may seem contrived in places, but it vividly depicts the conflicting loyalties of a family and a desperate struggle to survive under the crushing force of poverty. Some books fill a particular niche even though they do not meet all of the criteria of good literature for children.

Enlightened Intergroup Education Is a Necessary Adjunct to the Successful Teaching and Interpretation of Multi-Ethnic Literature

Teachers, librarians and parents who are interpreting multi-ethnic literature and considering ways of involving young readers in such writing about other minority persons need much work in reading about successful

Mexican Bulletin Board stimulates bullfighting stories.

practices in intergroup education. The book *The Shortchanged Children of
Suburbia* offers several suggestions for an action program for schools and
communities. A helpful volume which outlines steps in ethnic assimilation
and differences between the "We and They" is *Why Can't They Be Like
Us?: Facts and Fallacies About Ethnic Differences and Group Conflicts in
America* by Andrew M. Greeley.

A third volume which is particularly helpful in ways of using intergroup materials in the classroom is one by Jean Dresden Grambs entitled
Intergroup Education, Methods and Materials. This book focuses upon
the needs for intergroup education, suggests some promising practices, and
offers an extensive annotated bibliography of instructional materials and
techniques which can be used.

In addition to learning some techniques of teaching ethnic materials,
some teachers and librarians also need more assistance in the interpretation
of the values of multi-ethnic literature to parents. Other communication
media such as radio, television, motion pictures, and advertising billboards,
and circulars are constantly bombarding people with propaganda and half-

truths. Special meetings or study groups need to be organized so that parents can be helped in ways to understand more accurately the values of
some of the newer literature being written for children and adolescents.
Sometimes, teachers and parents need to examine attitudes of children and
adults through studying such topics as race awareness and prejudice. A
few sources include: *Race Awareness in Young Children* by Mary Ellen
Goodman, *Prejudice and Your Child* by Kenneth B. Clark, and *Prejudiced
—How Do People Get That Way?* by William Van Til. An older book
which offers suggestions of ways teachers can diagnose feelings and bring
them into the open is *Feelings Are Facts* by Margaret M. Heaton. This
author is concerned with social and school situations which lower the self-
esteem of children and adolescents. Walter Loban offers some practical
suggestions and classroom procedures which enhance social sensitivity for
teachers of secondary school literature in his booklet *Literature and Social
Sensitivity.* He indicates that imitation and identification are two relevant
factors used in educating readers to gain social sensitivity. Therefore he
suggests that several forms of dramatization including role playing and
sociodrama can be used in developing some feelings of social consciousness.

A book of short stories and excerpts from novels which shows examples of prejudice in people of many cultures is *Prejudice: 20 Tales of
Oppression and Liberation,* which has been edited by Charles R. Larson.
These tales range from "Beggar My Neighbor" by Dan Jacobson, who was
born in Johannesburg, South Africa in 1929, to "Our Story of Ah Q" by
Lusin, which is the pseudonym of Shu-jên Chou who lived from 1881-
1936. The editor states in his introduction that "no culture holds a
monopoly on prejudice."[8]

Another enlightening book is *The Dark and Tangled Path: Race in
America,* edited by David D. Anderson and Robert L. Wright. This interesting group of readings commences during the colonial period with writings
by William Bradford, John Winthrop, and Cotton Mather, and concludes
with "A Testament of Hope" by Martin Luther King, Jr. An article by
Nathan Hare entitled "Brainwashing of Black Men's Minds" is particularly
illuminating as it calls attention to some negative words appearing in the
language of white America which are destructive to the self-image of the
black man. These are such terms as "blackball," "blacklisted," "black
market," and "dark mood." Nathan Hare also explains that the word
"black" was used by the English to describe a free man of color while
"negro" was used to designate a black slave.[9] Another enlightening

8. Charles R. Larson, ed., *Prejudice: 20 Tales of Oppression and Liberation* (New
York: New American Library, 1971), p. xii.
9. Nathan Hare, "Brainwashing of Black Men's Minds," in *The Dark and Tangled
Path: Race in America,* edited by David D. Anderson and Robert L. Wright (Boston:
Houghton Mifflin Company, 1971), p. 333.

article in this collection is "Folklore of the South and Racial Discrimination" by James M. Lacy. This states that the child is introduced to racial prejudice quite early when he learns that a Negro is called "a coon," "darky," "nigger," "burr-head," and hears that nuts are called "nigger toes," and that a jingle says "catch a 'nigger' by the toe."[10]

Values of Reading and Teaching Multi-Ethnic Literature

Relevance

One of the most significant values of multi-ethnic literature is its relevance to the child or adolescent who is a member of a minority culture. A Japanese child living in a pearl diver's family reads *Kumi and the Pearl* by Patricia Miles Martin and feels that the little novel is relevant to him. A Chinese immigrant in San Francisco, who is struggling with a new language, can smile at the pictures in *Chinese Mother Goose Rhymes,* compiled by Robert Wyndham. An older adolescent who is a good reader and interested in both Mexican and Indian cultures may enjoy such an historical novel as *The Quetzal Feather* by Frances Riker Duncombe, or an Indian novel such as *House Made of Dawn* by N. Scott Momaday.

A black child who wants a relevant book in the "tell-it-like-it-is" approach may be interested in *The Soul Brothers and Sister Lou* by Kristin Hunter, and many older adolescents can identify with Malcolm X in the *Autobiography of Malcolm X* and with Claude Brown in *Manchild in the Promised Land.*

Gaining An Identity With One's Own Culture

Multi-ethnic literature offers a minority reader a sense of identity with his own cultural heritage. A younger black child reviewing the pictures in *Oh Lord I Wish I Was a Buzzard* by Polly Greenberg may identify with the plight of the small worker who is picking cotton but longs to be anywhere but at work in a cotton field. The child's thoughts are fanciful and the language is rhythmical. A Jewish boy may be amused by the antics of Schlemiel and others in *When Schlemiel Went to Warsaw and Other Stories,* translated by Isaac Beshevis Singer and Elizabeth Shub, with pictures by Margot Zemach. A small Filipino boy who is proud of his people may enjoy *Lagalag the Wanderer,* with the story and pictures by Carol Fenner. An older adolescent may identify with Kino, the fisherman and his wife Juana, in *The Pearl* by John Steinbeck, or with Shebah in *A Navajo Saga* by Kay and Russ Bennett.

10. James M. Lacy, "Folklore of the South and Racial Discrimination," in *Tangled Path,* ed. Anderson and Wright, p. 29.

Gaining a Positive Self-Concept

Multi-ethnic literature helps to improve the self-concept of an ethnic minority child who finds no place for himself in a white middle-class society. A small child reading *A Letter to Amy* by Ezra Jack Keats admires the pictures of Peter and Amy. The message is a slight one, but a birthday party is a rather universal custom, and most small tots like Amy hope to be invited to one. A more difficult book for older adolescent pupils is *Pioneer in Blood Plasma: Dr. Charles Richard Drew* by Robert Lichello. Although this fictionalized biography is a somewhat eulogistic depiction of the Negro scientist who was dedicated to his profession, a black adolescent youth who reads it might feel it is possible that he too might become a research scientist or teacher. A slight little novel for younger pupils, *Salt Boy* by Mary Perrine, illustrated by Leonard Weisgard, might make an Indian Navajo child prouder of his tribal heritage. Salt Boy practices roping his mother's sheep and is rebuked by his father for his playfulness until an accident arises and he saves a lamb from drowning.

Cultural Contributions of Ethnic Groups

Numerous literature books highlight cultural contributions of minority persons, and readers of such books learn to appreciate these contributions. Cultural differences should be accepted and added to the heritage of all children. Ordinarily, nonfiction books depict cultural contributions. For instance, two books about the Indians as music makers and singers are *American Indians Sing* by Charles Hofmann, drawings by Nicholas Amorosi, and *Indian Music Makers,* written and illustrated by Robert Hofsinde. Shirley Glubok has written *The Art of Ancient Mexico,* designed by Gerard Nook with special photography by Alfred H. Tamarin. Persons interested in the history of jazz can read *Cool, Hot and Blue: a History of Jazz for Young People.* This is the story of the New Orleans and Chicago schools and the emergence of swing, bop, and rock'n'roll music, with an informative explanation of individual musical styles.

Historical Concepts in an Interesting Framework

Minority literature contributes information necessary for understanding historical concepts. Many current literature books are adding new footnotes to American and world history. Little known facts about achievements and characteristics of minority peoples enliven the study of history. For instance, *The Wrath of Coyote* by Jean Montgomery relates the tale of Kurtola of the Miwok people who resents the Spaniards and the cruelty, disease, and death brought by the soldiers and missionaries to the California shores. *Dark Venture* by Audrey White Beyer describes the capture and enslavement of a twelve-year-old African in the year of 1795. *Sophia*

Scrooby Preserved by Martha Bacon, illustrated by David Omar White, describes the life of a young slave who comes to live with a Connecticut family, which fosters her desire for education and musical training. Two interesting black autobiographies for intermediate grade and teen-age readers are *The Slave Who Bought His Freedom: Equiano's Story,* adapted by Karen Kennerly, and *In Chains to Louisiana: Solomon Northup's Story* adapted by Michael Knight. The first autobiography is one by Equiano, later renamed Gustavus Vasa. He was stolen from his Ibo tribe in West Africa by black tribesmen and later crossed the waters in a slave ship. The second autobiography relates how Soloman Northup, a freeman of a freed slave, was kidnapped at the age of thirty-three in 1841. He had to live in the Louisiana bayous and suffer great degradation and hardship in his forced enslavement.

Folk Lore and Folktales Around the World

Ethnic literature offers a sense of identity with people of the world through oral folk literature and recorded folktales. Afro-American literature provides a wealth of folk tales representing almost any country of Africa. *When the Stones Were Soft: East African Fireside Tales* by Eleanor B. Heady includes sixteen East African folktales retold from traditional material from Kenya, Tanzania, and Uganda. In each case Mama Semamingi gathers the village children around a campfire while she tells a tale. Some tales from Russia are included in *Arcturus the Hunting Hound and Other Stories* by Yuri Kazakov. These are set in the forests, plains, and villages in the uplands of Siberia. One tale is about a sixteen-year-old boy who longs to translate into music the sounds and sights of the forest he loves. *Latin American Tales: From the Pampas to the Pyramids of Mexico* by Genevieve Barlow offers some background about the people creating the tale. For instance, "The Enchanted Palace" is a story told by the Tehuelche Indians of Patagonia. One learns that these Indians existed on guanacos, ostrich eggs, armadillos, wild potatoes, and roots before the Spaniards brought sheep so that they could eat lamb and have wool for clothing.

Geographical Concepts and Customs

Numerous geographical and natural history concepts are gleaned from books about different cultural groups living in various regions. A recent book, *Along Sandy Shores* by Ann Nolan Clark, gives glimpses of the desert of the southwest. *Gussuk Boy* by Aylette Jenness is the story of Aaron who is interested in the Eskimos as individuals and in their way of life. *Akavak: An Eskimo Journey,* written and illustrated by James Houston, is the stark, dramatic tale of young Akavak who sets out alone with his grandfather and crosses the high mountains on the journey to his great-uncle's home. A mature novel for young adults by the same author is *The White Dawn*. This is a tale of Eskimos living in far northeastern Canada who are known as the Sea-Ice people of Baffin Island. Here they lived in contentment, fishing and hunting seal and walrus, until the arrival of three shipwrecked sailors, Billy, Daggett, and the Portagee. The men are treated kindly by Sarkak and his people, but the hospitable, primitive Eskimos undergo great culture-shock as they suffer the impact of an alien culture which makes the life of the Sea-Ice people more strange and complicated.

Man's Humanity to Man

A study of multi-ethnic literature offers a greater sense of social sensitivity to pupils reading books about various people. They learn to feel that all men are human beings who should be considered as individuals, not stereotypes. Such a book is *Our Eddie* by Sulasmith Ish Kishor. Eddie is the older son of a large family of English Jews, the Raphaels. They suffer poverty because Papa, headmaster of a Hebrew school, helps other needy persons. Papa suffers a nervous breakdown and is tyrannical in his behavior toward Eddie. It takes the death of Eddie to cause Papa to become more understanding of others in the family. Another similar type of story about a Jewish family is *Ruthie* by Norma Simon. This is a realistic story about a family living in Brooklyn during the depression. Ruthie is depressed and worried when her mother is hospitalized, and she is forced to live with the Felds who are older and more strict about religious observances. In *Bimby* by Peter Burchard, one senses crucial events in the life of a young slave on the Georgia coast just prior to the Civil War. Bimby has not recognized the cruelty of a slave's life until the day that his friend, Ole Jesse, is killed. Bimby then talks with his mother. He learns that his own father also was killed when he sought his freedom from slavery. Both Bimby and his mother realize that life without freedom is empty.

An Understanding of Sociological Change

Pupils reading examples of multi-ethnic literature gain a background for understanding sociological change. Many nonfictional books for adolescents in grades seven and eight offer cognitive and affective materials which help readers to understand some of the complex social forces evident in this era. The volume *The Bitter Choice: Eight South Africans' Resistance to Tyranny* by Colin and Margaret Legum includes chapters about Alan Paton, Nelson Mandela, Albert Lutuli, Robert Sobukwe, Beyers Naudé, Nana Sita, Dennis Brutus, and Michael Scott who are men of varied racial, cultural, and economic backgrounds. Such problems as

apartheid, violence, guerilla warfare, partition, and international intervention are considered. A second book for readers in junior high school grades
is *Marching Toward Freedom: the Negro in the Civil War, 1861-1865.* This
book concerns the Negro's role in the Civil War and his loyalty and
courage. Quotations from original sources are used. A third book for the
same age group is *Tear Down the Walls! A History of the American Civil
Rights Movement* by Dorothy Sterling. This book briefly surveys the
African beginnings of black Americans, the slave trade, the abolitionists
and the Civil War. It includes such Negro leaders as Carver, Douglass, and
Du Bois, and considers some of the current pressures such as problems of
legislation, school integration, riots, and voter-registration drives.

Intercultural Relations

A study of multi-ethnic literature often helps both teachers and pupils
to improve their intercultural relations. Intergroup relations can be fos-
tered through reading, discussing, and role playing episodes which help to
eliminate prejudices and avoid negative stereotyping of ethnic groups.
Blood Brothers by Doris Anderson recounts the adventure of a Norwegian
family migrating from Minnesota to the British Columbia wilderness in
1895. Nels meets Quata and they become blood brothers, but Quata's
tribe and the medicine man are suspicious of newcomers who might take
their land and disturb their cultural patterns. The problem of searching
for an identification of an Indian boy in a white man's world is sensed in
Half Breed by Evelyn S. Lampman. Twelve-year-old Hardy comes to look
for his white father in the Oregon Territory as his mother has just married
another Crow. Hardy finds that his father has disappeared, but he remains
alone in his cabin until his father's sister, Aunt Rhody, arrives. Hardy
does not enjoy the local Indians and finds little acceptance by the whites
living in this Territory. When his father returns from his wanderings, he
rejects his son because he can not face responsibility. The half-breed boy
longs for his familiar Crow village but feels a certain amount of affection
and responsibility for his aunt; so he remains with her and finds some
degree of happiness.

Another book which can be used effectively in classroom discussions
is *The Lucky Ones: Five Journeys Toward a Home,* compiled by Elizabeth
Jane Coatsworth. The author tells of five refugee families in different parts
of the world. It includes the story of a fatherless Chinese boy in Hong
Kong who manages to attend school and that of a Tibetan family who
follow the Dalai Lama on a long trek to India. Stories also depict displaced Watusi in refugee communities in Tanzania and Algerians in
Morocco. A poignant tale is the one about a Hungarian family in Austria
which must be separated because the son who has contacted tuberculosis
cannot emigrate to Australia.

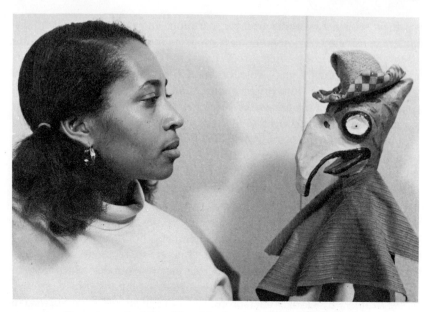

Puppet used while telling Mexican stories to Chicano and
Anglo-American students.

A book of a different type which is also provocative is *Member of
the Gang* by Barbara Rinkoff. Leroy is a leader of the gang, and Woody
hangs around him because he wants to be accepted by his peers. Some
fellows play hookey from school and get away with it; so Woody agrees to
be front man for a store robbery. One of the boys is knifed in the fight;
Woody stays with him and is picked up, tried, and placed on probation.
The probation officer is black and Woody resents his authority, but
gradually he is helped to understand that there is little future in being
tough.

Raising the Aspiration Level

Many selections of various multi-ethnic literature books can help to
raise the aspiration level of nonachieving children of a minority group.
Some librarians, teachers, and social workers are using minority literature
as a means of encouraging pupils to raise their hopes and goals. In an
article entitled "Books As An Aid in Preventing Dropouts" appearing in
the February 1969 issue of *Elementary English,* Helen F. Faust suggests
numerous novels and biographies which may assist children in believing
in their own capacities and may help them in imaginatively satisfying themselves in an adult role. Her article supplies both the reading and interest
levels of several books which can be used in this way. She frequently

mentions several books at different reading levels. For instance, *She Wanted to Read* by Ella Kaiser Carruth is a biography about Mary Bethune who wants to read and sit at the "banquet table of books." Two other biographies about the same Negro educator are *Mary McLeod Bethune* by Catherine C. Peare and *Mary McLeod Bethune* by Emma C. Sterne. Another book which Faust recommends is *Annuzza, A Girl of Romania.* This is a novel written at about a seventh-grade reading level and concerns a peasant girl of a Carpathian Mountain village who is forced to work in the maize fields although she longs to get an education. Her father is prone to drunkenness and frequently loses his temper. He resents her desire to study and reminds her that she is a peasant girl and will always be one. Finally, she achieves her goal of an education. A similar book is *Dobry* by Monica Shannon. Although his mother does not understand his desire to become an artist, his understanding grandfather recognizes that persons should be individuals and use their own unique talents. One of the most impelling novels about a desire for an education is *I Will Try* by Legson Kayira, the tale of a boy growing up in a small African village. He refuses to accept the inevitability of poverty, ignorance, and disease. He leaves his village with a Bible, a copy of *Pilgrim's Progress,* and the words, "I Will Try" sewn across his shirt. He travels long distances at great sacrifices before he reaches the west coast of the United States where he achieves his dream of an education which will enable him to help his people at Malaw. This is a book for adolescents.

Bibliotherapy and Therapy through the Use of Literature

In recent years considerable interest has arisen in the planned use of literature as therapy—a means of working out individual problems. Although novels, biographies, and poetry do offer possibilities if used therapeutically, such use of literature should be considered with caution. Few teachers and librarians have enough psychological knowledge to handle problems arising when particular books are used with individual children having deep-seated emotional psychoses. Not all multi-ethnic books are concerned with psychological problems, but many books about minority people do reveal such problems. Caroline Shrodes has written a doctoral dissertation on this subject entitled "Bibliotherapy: a Theoretical and Clinical Experimental Study." Matilda Bailey has discussed novels for younger children in "Therapeutic Reading," which appears in *Readings About Children's Literature,* edited by Evelyn R. Robinson.

A highly technical book for physicians and adults is *Poetry Therapy: The Use of Poetry in the Treatment of Disorders,* edited by Jack J. Leedy. Some multi-ethnic poetry has therapeutic possibilities. A current trend of multi-ethnic literature books seems directed more to a children's problems approach than it does to literature. Such a book is the one entitled *It's Wings That Make Birds Fly: The Story of a Boy.* The book is illustrated with beautiful photographs and is based on taped conversations with Harlem children, particularly on those of one child, Otis. Otis is depicted with warmth, dignity, and poignant comments concerning his need for acceptance in spite of his broken and shifting home life. Another different type of book is *Who Look at Me* by June Jordan which is illustrated with twenty-seven paintings and helps the Negro child to identify with his black experiences in a manner of saying "I am black, alive, and looking back at you."

Literature as a Means of Illumination for the Individual Child

Much excellent imaginative literature should provide illumination on the significance of being. Few teachers or librarians can personally direct the processes which lead to the "aha stage of discovery" as this is the intuitive stage of thinking when a reader's personal background experiences and anticipated future roles are illumined through direct involvement with a book. This is when a character or hero strikes the right chord in a reader's being. Some of these experiences come about through unexpected events. A student teacher gave a Spanish-American child a copy of *Martin de Porres, Hero* by Claire H. Bishop. A little later, after the child had avidly read this novel about a sixteenth century saint of Lima, Peru, he stated that the book had made all the difference in the world to him; now he was no longer discouraged. Teachers and librarians cannot prepare children for moments of illumination, but they can surround readers with a rich storehouse of books raising thought provoking questions about social justice and the priceless heritage of minority peoples. Also, each of us can read as much multi-ethnic literature as possible and study reviews of such writing in order to provide information and help to readers.

Multi-ethnic literature helps to humanize man. Children who feel that their cultural heritage is being trampled upon or denied, and other children and adolescents who have little understanding of the mores of various ethnic groups can learn much from the reading of ethnic literature.

Summary

In this chapter the author has stated certain definitions of ethnic literature. Also, the Kallen metaphor of an American society as "a multiplicity in a unity, an orchestration of mankind" rather than the melting pot metaphor has been preferred.

Certain principles concerning the reading of multi-ethnic literature in the classroom have been stated. Multi-ethnic literature should not be the total reading diet, but each minority child or adolescent should have an opportunity to read some books about his own heritage. Books presenting characters as negative stereotypes should be avoided. Ethnic literature should not focus upon differences at the expense of the similarities of persons. In most instances only the best examples of multi-ethnic literature should be studied in the classroom.

The author has stated that an enlightened study of intergroup education is a necessary adjunct to the successful teaching and interpretation of much ethnic literature.

Multi-ethnic literature has several values. Ethnic literature is often more relevant to the child or adolescent reader since it is often a means of gaining an identity with one's own culture. Much ethnic literature is helping readers to gain a more positive self-concept. Such books offer examples of the cultural and historical contributions of various ethnic groups. Folk tales of various world countries help readers to gain a world viewpoint, and they offer many geographical and linguistic concepts. Many ethnic books depict examples of man's humanity and inhumanity to others. Some novels and nonfiction books offer a better understanding of social change and intercultural relations. Some ethnic literature helps to raise the aspiration level of young readers or adolescents. A few talented teachers and librarians have successfully used ethnic literature in bibliotherapy. Perhaps one of the greatest contributions of ethnic literature is the "shock of recognition" which comes to a reader when a passage in a good novel or a poem adds a new dimension to the self. The self is expanded so that the child or adolescent student does not grow up with the "armored and concluded mind" depicted by Muriel Rukeyser.[11]

11. John Ciardi, "The Shock of Recognition," *Journal of the American Association of University Women* 47, no. 1 (October 1953): 13.

Reaction—Questions and Projects

In order to obtain the most beneficial help from a professional book, one should react to ideas of the author. In some instances this may be a violent disagreement with cognitive or affective concepts. Sometimes the reader may agree with some ideas but wish to extend them through involving himself in further research thus "hitchhiking" on to an idea and extending it further. Reaction questions are designed to *involve* the reader in an action type of activity.

1. What are some ethnic groups which are significant in your neighborhood? Select an ethnic group and review literature which might be appropriate in overcoming prejudicial ideas about such a group. Visit a local children's book store or library, or review descriptions of books or periodicals in such a source as *Children's Catalog, School Library Journal, Bulletin of the Center for Children's Books* of the University of Chicago Graduate Library School, or others. Discuss how such books might be used effectively.

2. Make a study of prejudice or stereotypes in your classroom or library study group. Develop some ways of measuring prejudice and then find a few novels which might overcome these prejudicial ideas. Does prejudice exist?

3. The author distinguishes between several historical approaches toward the assimilation of newcomers or American minority groups in the cultural and social history of the United States, such as "ethnic islands," "the melting pot," and "cultural pluralism." Can you develop an original metaphor or image which describes structural societal changes of the present? Create the metaphor and develop the idea in a paragraph or essay.

4. Select some books about one ethnic group which present strong negative stereotypes of a particular race or people. Indicate ways these stereotypes are evident in the context of the books. Choose a book about a minority hero which seems to present few negative stereotypes. Or select some recent novels on Black, Mexican-American, or Indian literature which present the "reversed stereotype." Or select a book for children or adults which aptly illustrates the "remanufactured past" approach as described by David K. Gast.

5. Choose a book for primary-grade children which overemphasizes differences between people. Indicate how the teacher or librarian might help children realize that people are more alike than different and that the uniqueness of an individual of a minority group might contribute something to a middle-class Caucasian culture.

6. Select a book from a collection of multi-ethnic books which, although it violates several of the principles of good literature for children, offers some valuable understanding about a minority history or cul-

ture which needs to be illuminated. Indicate how this book might be used beneficially with children or young adolescents.

7. Survey some materials which might be used in intergroup education such as movies, slides, flat pictures, films, and recordings. After reviewing this material, suggest how it might be used, or advance arguments why such material should not be studied.

8. Is it true that feelings are facts?" Develop some techniques by means of which you can survey feelings of minority and white Anglo-Saxon children who might be reading books about minority peoples.

9. The author has enumerated several values of studying multi-ethnic literature. What are some problems or disadvantages inherent in reading too much of this type of writing?

10. The use of multi-ethnic novels and stories as a means of raising the aspiration level of "dropouts" or "tuned-out students" has been suggested. Discover some books which might be used as a means of raising the achievement level of nonachieving Caucasian as well as students from minority groups.

11. Charles R. Larson, who is the editor of *Prejudice: 20 Tales of Oppression and Liberation* indicates that "no culture has a monopoly on prejudice and prejudice is likely to appear when conditions are right."[12] Read some of the tales in this collection or in another book and indicate some conditions which cause prejudice to appear.

BIBLIOGRAPHY

BOOKS FOR PRIMARY CHILDREN (GRADES K to 4)

FENNER, CAROL. *Lagalag, The Wanderer*. New York: Harcourt, Brace and World, 1968.

GREENBERG, POLLY. *Oh Lord, I Wish I Was a Buzzard*. New York: Macmillan Company, 1968.

HEADY, ELEANOR B. *When the Stones Were Soft: East African Fireside Tales*. New York: Funk and Wagnalls Co., Inc., 1968.

KEATS, EZRA JACK. *A Letter to Amy*. New York: Harper and Row, Publishers, 1968

WEINER, SANDRA. *It's Wings That Make Birds Fly: A Story of a Boy*. New York: Pantheon Books, 1968.

WYNDHAM, ROBERT. *Chinese Mother Goose Rhymes*. New York: World Publishing Company, 1968.

BOOKS FOR INTERMEDIATE CHILDREN

ANDERSON, DORIS. *Blood Brothers*. New York: St. Martins Press, 1967.

BARLOW, GENEVIEVE. *Latin American Tales: From the Pampas to the Pyramids of Mexico*. Chicago: Rand, McNally & Company, 1966.

12. Charles R. Larson, *Prejudice: 20 Tales of Oppression and Liberation* (New York: New American Library, a Mentor Book, 1971), p. xii.

BISHOP, CLAIRE H. *Martin de Porres, Hero.* Boston: Houghton Mifflin Co., 1954.

BURCHARD, PETER. *Bimby.* New York: Coward-McCann, 1968.

CARROLL, LEWIS. *Alice in Wonderland and Other Favorites.* New York: Washington Square Press, 1960.

CARRUTH, ELLA KAISER. *She Wanted to Read: The Story of Mary McLeod Bethune.* New York: Washington Square Press, 1969.

CLARK, ANN NOLAN. *Along Sandy Shores.* New York: Viking Press, 1969.

CROWELL, ANN. *A Hogan for Bluebird.* New York: Charles Scribner's Sons, 1969.

ERNO, RICHARD B. *Billy Lightfoot.* New York: Crown Publishers, 1969.

GLUBOK, SHIRLEY. *The Art of Ancient Mexico.* New York: Harper & Row, Publishers, 1968.

GRAHAME, KENNETH. *Wind in the Willows.* New York: Grossett and Dunlap, 1967.

HEADY, ELEANOR B. *When the Stones Were Soft: East African Fireside Tales.* New York: Funk and Wagnalls Co., 1968.

HOFMANN, CHARLES. *American Indians Sing.* New York: The John Day Co., 1967.

HOFSINDE, ROBERT. *Indian Music Makers.* New York: William Morrow and Company, 1967.

HOUSTON, JAMES. *Akavak: An Eskimo Journey.* New York: Harcourt, Brace & World, 1968.

HUNT, IRENE. *No Promises in the Wind.* Chicago: Follett Publishing Company, 1970.

HUNTER, KRISTIN. *The Soul Brothers and Sister Lou.* New York: Charles Scribner's Sons, 1968.

ISH-KISHOR, SULAMITH. *Our Eddie.* New York: Pantheon Books, 1969.

JENNESS, AYLETTE. *Gussuk Boy.* Chicago: Follett Publishing Company, 1967.

KAZAKOV, YURI. *Arcturus the Hunting Hound and Other Stories.* Translated from the Russian by Anne Terry White. New York: Doubleday and Company, 1968.

MARTIN, PATRICIA MILES. *Kumi and the Pearl.* New York: G. P. Putnam's Sons, 1968.

NORTON, MARY. *The Borrowers.* New York: Harcourt, Brace and World, 1952, 1953.

PEARE, CATHERINE O. *Mary McLeod Bethune.* New York: Vanguard Press, 1951.

PERRINE, MARY. *Salt Boy.* Boston: Houghton Mifflin Company, 1968.

RINKOFF, BARBARA. *Member of the Gang.* New York: Crown Publishers, 1968.

SEUBERLICH, HERTHA. *Annuzza, A Girl of Romania.* Chicago: Rand, McNally & Co., 1962.

SHANNON, MONICA. *Dobry.* New York: Viking Press, 1934.

SIMON, NORMA. *Ruthie.* New York: Meredith Press, 1968.

SINGER, ISAAC BESHEVIS, AND SHUB, ELIZABETH. trans. *When Schlemiel Went to Warsaw and Other Stories.* New York: Farrar, Straus & Giroux, 1968.

STERNE, EMMA G. *Mary McLeod Bethune.* New York: Alfred A. Knopf, 1957.

WHITE, E. B. *Charlotte's Web.* New York: Dell Publishing Co., 1967.

BOOKS FOR ADOLESCENTS

BACON, MARTHA. *Sophia Scrooby Preserved*. Boston: Atlantic-Little, Brown & Company, 1968.

BENNETT, KAY AND RUSS. *A Navajo Saga*. San Antonio: The Naylor Company, 1969.

BEYER, AUDREY WHITE. *Dark Venture*. New York: Alfred A. Knopf, 1968.

BOECKMAN, CHARLES. *Cool, Hot and Blue: A History of Jazz for Young People*. New York: Robert B. Luce, 1968.

BROWN, CLAUDE. *Manchild in the Promised Land*. New York: New American Library, a Signet Book, 1965.

COATSWORTH, ELIZABETH JANE, comp. *The Lucky Ones: Five Journeys Toward a Home*. New York: Macmillan Company, 1968.

DOUTY, ESTHER M. *Forten the Sailmaker*. Chicago: Rand McNally and Company, 1968.

DUNCOMBE, FRANCES RIKER. *The Quetzal Feather*. New York: Lothrop, Lee & Shepard Company, 1967.

JORDAN, JUNE. *Who Look at Me*. New York: Thomas Y. Crowell Company, 1969.

KAYIRA, LEGSON. *I Will Try*. New York: Bantam, 1966.

KENNERLY, KAREN. *The Slave Who Bought His Freedom: Equiano's Story*. New York: E. P. Dutton & Co., 1971.

KNIGHT, MICHAEL. *In Chains to Louisiana, Solomon Northup's Story*. New York. E. P. Dutton & Co., 1971.

LAMPMAN, EVELYN S. *Half Breed*. New York: Doubleday and Company, 1965.

LARSON, CHARLES R., ed. *Prejudice: 20 Tales of Oppression and Liberation*. New York: New American Library, 1971.

LEGUM, COLIN AND MARGARET. *The Bitter Choice: Eight South African's Resistance to Tyranny*. New York: World Publishing Company, 1968.

LICHELLO, ROBERT. *Pioneer in Blood Plasma: Dr. Charles Richard Drew*. New York: Julian Messner, 1968.

LONGSWORTH, POLLY. *I, Charlotte Forten, Black and Free*. New York: Thomas Y. Crowell Company, 1970.

MALCOLM X. *The Autobiography of Malcolm X*. New York: Grove Press, 1966.

MCPHERSON, JAMES M. *Marching Toward Freedom: The Negro Child in the Civil War*, 1861-1865. Edited by John A. Scott. New York: Alfred A. Knopf, 1968.

MOMADAY, N. SCOTT. *House Made of Dawn*. New York: The New American Library, a Signet Book, 1969.

MONTGOMERY, JEAN. *The Wrath of Coyote*. New York: William Morrow and Company, 1968.

STEINBECK, JOHN. *The Pearl*. In *The Pearl* and *The Red Pony*. New York: The Viking Press, Compass Book Edition, 1965.

STERLING, DOROTHY. *Tear Down the Walls: A History of the American Civil Rights Movement*. New York: Doubleday and Company, 1968.

TOLKIEN, J. R. R. *The Hobbit* or *There and Back Again*. rev. ed. New York: Ballantine Books, 1966.

PROFESSIONAL AND ADULT BOOKS

ANDERSON, DAVID D., AND WRIGHT, ROBERT L., eds. *The Dark and Tangled Path: Race in America.* Boston: Houghton Mifflin Company, 1971.

BURMA, JOHN H. *Mexican Americans in the United States, A Reader.* New York: Harper and Row, Publishers, distributed by Canfield Press, 1970.

CAHN, EDGAR S. *Our Brother's Keeper: The Indian in White America.* New York: New Community Press, 1969.

CIARDI, JOHN. "The Shock of Recognition." In *Journal of the American Association of University Women* 47, no. 1 (October 1953): 13.

CARLSEN, G. ROBERT. "The Way of the Spirit and the Way of the Mind." *Elementary English* 40 (February 1963): 146.

CLARK, KENNETH B. *Prejudice and Your Child.* 2nd ed. enlarged. Boston: Beacon Press, 1963.

COLLIER, JOHN. *Indians of the Americas, The Long Hope.* New York: The New American Library, Mentor Book, 1947.

DINNERSTEIN, LEONARD, AND JAHER, FREDERIC COPLE. *The Aliens: A History of Ethnic Minorities in America.* New York: Appleton-Century-Crofts, 1970.

FAUST, HELEN F. "Books as an Aid in Preventing Dropouts." *Elementary English* 46 (February, 1969): 191-198.

GAST, DAVID K. "The Dawning of the Age of Aquarius for Multi-Ethnic Children's Literature." In *Elementary English* 47 (May 1970): 661-665.

GLAZER, NATHAN, AND MOYNIHAN, DANIEL PATRICK. *Beyond the Melting Pot. The Negroes, Puerto Ricans, Jews, Italians and Irish of New York City,* 2nd ed., Cambridge, Massachusetts and London, England: The Massachusetts Institute of Technology Press, 1970.

GOODMAN, MARY ELLEN. *Race Awareness in Young Children.* rev. ed. New York: Collier Books, 1968.

GRAMBS, JEAN DRESDEN. *Intergroup Education, Methods and Materials.* Englewood Cliffs, New Jersey: Prentice Hall, 1968.

GREELEY, ANDREW M. *Why Can't They Be Like Us? Facts and Fallacies About Ethnic Differences and Group Conflicts in America.* Institute of Human Relations Press, The American Jewish Committee, 1969.

HANDLER, JUNE. "Books for Loving." *Elementary English* 47 (May 1970): 687, 692.

HEATON, MARGARET M. *Feelings are Facts.* New York: The National Conference of Christians and Jews, 1957.

HOUSTON, JAMES. *The White Dawn: An Eskimo Saga.* New York: Harcourt, Brace, Jovanovich, 1971.

HUTHMACHER, J. JOSEPH. *A Nation of Newcomers: Ethnic Minorities in American History.* New York: Dell Publishing Co., 1967.

INFORMATION CENTER ON CHILDREN'S CULTURES. *Latin America.* An Annotated List of materials for children selected by a committee of librarians, teachers and Latin American specialists in cooperation with The Center for Inter-American Relations, 331 East 38th Street, New York, New York 10016; Information Center of Children's Cultures, United States Committee for UNICEF, 1969.

LEEDY, JACK J. *Poetry Therapy, The Use of Poetry in the Treatment of Disorders.* Philadelphia: J. B. Lippincott Co., 1969.

LOBAN, WALTER. *Literature and Social Sensitivity.* Urbana, Illinois: National Council of Teachers of English, 1954.

MACIA, YSIDRO RAMON. "The Chicano Movement." In *Wilson Library Bulletin,* March 1970.

MCWILLIAMS, CAREY. *Brothers Under the Skin.* Rev. ed. Boston: Little, Brown and Company, 1964, p. 113.

————. *The Mexicans in America: A Student Guide to Localized History.* New York: Teachers College Press, Columbia University, 1968.

MIEL, ALICE, AND KIESTER, EDWIN, JR. *The Shortchanged Children of Suburbia: What Schools Don't Teach About Human Differences and What Can Be Done About It.* New York: Institute of Human Relations Press, the American Jewish Committee, 1967.

ROSE, PETER I. *They and We, Racial and Ethnic Relations in the United States.* New York: Random House, 1968, p. 11.

SAMORA, JULIAN, ed. *La Raza: Forgotten Americans.* Notre Dame, Indiana: University of Notre Dame Press, 1966.

SENIOR, CLARENCE. *The Puerto Ricans: Strangers-then-Neighbors.* Published in cooperation with the Anti-Defamation League of B'nai B'rith. Chicago: Quadrangle Books, 1965.

STEINER, STAN. *La Raza, The Mexican Americans.* New York: Harper and Row, Publishers, 1970.

————. *The New Indians.* New York: Dell Publishing Company, 1968, p. 158.

TEBBEL, JOHN, AND RUIZ, RAMÓN EDUARDO. *South by Southwest, The Mexican-American and His Heritage.* Garden City, New York: Doubleday and Company, Zenith Books, 1964.

VAN TIL, WILLIAM. *Prejudiced—How Do People Get That Way?* Anti-Defamation League of B'nai B'rith, 1968 Revised Edition.

VASQUEZ, RICHARD. *Chicano.* New York: Doubleday and Company, 1970.

WAGLEY, CHARLES, AND HARRIS, MARVIN. *Minorities in the New World: Six Case Studies.* New York: Columbia University Press, Paperback edition. 1964.

CHAPTER TWO

Griots and
Reality Mirrors:
Some Criteria
of Good
Multi-Ethnic Literature

In *Sundiata: An Epic of Old Mali,* by D. T. Niane, a learned griot, Mamadou Kouyaté, depicts the power and place of the storyteller in the culture of Mali. It was the griot who eloquently related the exploits of kings and chieftains and the rise and fall of monarchies and kingdoms. Children and adults sat under bamboo trees at the foot of griots to learn the wisdom of the ages. In this chapter some of the mysteries of his storytelling power will be examined, and the qualities of good literature will be outlined. Someone should help the child encounter the true experiences of a minority person struggling to find his identity as a thinking human being in a strange society where he represents an outnumbered group. Good multi-ethnic literature can be one means of helping a child of a minority culture find his identity and a positive self-image.

Qualities of Good Multi-Ethnic Literature

Ethnic literature should have the qualities of all good literature. Perhaps the most important element of a good story or novel is its power to engage the imaginative attention of the reader or listener. A multi-ethnic book should have a significant theme and basic problems presented in a realistic style. Characters must be interesting ones representing real individuals, not stereotypes, in order for the reader to identify with them. Plots for younger children should be straight forward and direct with few pages of lengthy discussion. As children become more mature readers, they can learn to understand some of the hidden meanings and symbolism used by an author. For instance, adult readers can savor the indirectness of approach used by such a talented Nigerian author as Chinua Achebe who enhances his ideas through the use of Ibo proverbs in his novels, such as *Arrow of God* or *Things Fall Apart.* Younger children, however, are annoyed by digressions which take away from the directness of the tale. For instance, in chapter two of *Arrow of God* one reads: "Wisdom is like a goatskin bag; every man carries his own. Knowledge of the land is like that."[1] A mature reader may find his perceptions heightened through puzzling over the meanings of the words; a child will probably skip over the words to read the events of the story.

When Mamadou Kouyaté identifies himself as a griot in *Sundiata: An Epic of Old Mali* by D. T. Niane, he indicates that his word is pure and free from untruths. One of the most significant attributes of good literature is its sincerity and truth. Unfortunately, much ethnic literature about Negroes, American Indians, Mexican-Americans, Orientals, and Jewish people becomes distorted and false through ignorance or prejudice of authors and publishers. Mrs. Dharathula H. Millender has depicted some of the tragic false images implanted in the minds of readers in her illuminating article entitled "Through a Glass Darkly."[2] Although most of her indictments against authors and publishers concern literature about the Negro people, many of her criticisms are valid for the Mexican-American, American Indian, or Oriental.

Stereotyping of persons through art and story line is evident in most literature about the Negroes prior to 1930. In many instances Negro characters are presented as caricatures or jokes, as persons being superstitious and afraid, and as ones being lazy, docile, and unambitious. A plantation novel designed for young children by Ellis Credle entitled *Across the Cotton Patch* depicted some black twins, "Atlantic" and "Pacific," who were not even real human beings, which was evident by their names.

1. Chinua Achebe, *Arrow of God* (Garden City, New York: Doubleday and Company, Anchor Books, 1969), p. 17.
2. Dharathula H. Millender, "Through a Glass Darkly," in *The School Library Journal,* December 1967.

Changes in Literary Styles of Ethnic Books

In 1917 Estelle Margaret Swearington copyrighted the novel *Pickaninny*. This is just one example of the stereotyped type of novel which was written by many authors at that period in American history.

The title of the novel, *Pickaninny,* offers an image of a stereotyped child-hero, since this is a patronizing and contemptuous term for a Negro baby or child who is visualized as running around on Southern cotton or tobacco plantations with his mammy.

The novel opens with the first chapter entitled "The Hunted Blackling" in which epithets are shouted at the little orphan who lived in an orphan asylum. One hears such terms as "nigger, nigger," "blackberry," "kinky-headed coon," "stove polish," "black baby," and others. Some of the artificial dialect of a black child is used.

In addition to the title and the style of the language, Pickaninny is depicted as a caricature of a child who is not a real human being. For instance, when he is confronted by a mob of fellow orphans chanting epithets at him, his hands are described as "little black claws" stuck in front of his face.

This book has a patronizing attitude of the white Anglo-Saxons towards the black Pickaninny. Persons are kindly toward the little child as they would be toward a dog or a kitten. One does not have honest sympathy for Pickaninny as he becomes a monkey caricature of a child dancing around on a string to ingratiate himself with those who offer kindness and physical comfort. It is interesting to study the craftmanship of this book as an example of changes which ethnic literature have undergone during the last fifty years.

In considering criteria, some persons are currently tending to indicate that an author's ethnic identity should be a criteria for selection.

The Controversy Over the Black Experience

During the past few years, considerable controversy has arisen concerning the authorship of books about the "black experience." Some black authors and speakers argue that no one but a black person can write about the "black experience." Other critics, both white Anglo-Saxon and black scholars, indicate that it is possible for creative artists to write imaginative novels in which Afro-Americans or African characters play predominant roles. A logical response to the argument concerning authorship should be that all literature written by either black or white authors should be judged on its merits, not according to the skin color of the author.

Some arguments have arisen concerning the selection of *Sounder* by William H. Armstrong as a Newbery award winner. Some black critics have criticized this choice because Mr. Armstrong is not a black author and therefore, he can not really comprehend the "black experience." Approaches to literary study may become racist propaganda if skin color and race become the principal criteria of good literature. Literature is an imaginative human experience which should be characterized by both *humanity* and *artistry*. If an author merely records a ghetto environment in the style of a television camera, such literature may be biased, inartistic, and unimaginative. All children and adolescents need the best possible types of good literature regardless of the racial heritage of an author. Some readers can mistakenly misinterpret the intent of an author, but the very complexity and stylistic qualities of a book may offer many interpretations. *Sounder* can be interpreted as the story of the great hound dog and the plight of a poor black sharecropper who was impelled to steal ham and sausage for his hungry wife and children. But *Sounder* can also be interpreted as the personification of the plight of poverty-stricken persons in all sections of the world who are suffering from malnutrition and abuse. Or, again, *Sounder* can be a depiction of man's determination to survive with patience and courage. The novel can also be a simple explication of a coon dog's unflagging devotion to his master. Most good novels have many themes, and astute readers of *Sounder* can read the book from several viewpoints.

The Artistry of a Novel

Numerous books, such as *The Art of Reading a Novel* by Philip Freund and *How to Read a Novel* by Caroline Gordon, suggest various ways in which an interpretive reader can be developed. M. Agnella Gunn indicates at least ten high-level reading skills which are significant in developing an imaginative approach toward good literature. These are ones such as recognizing the difference between *denotation* and *connotation;* ways to recognize *plot* and *theme;* techniques of *interpreting characters* through clues, inferences, values, character changes, and their causes; a study of various aspects of *setting* such as physical setting, values, time, and work done; the *arrangement of the form* of a literary piece such as the organization pattern in time sequence or flash back; an appreciation of the *mood or feeling* of a story and how the author produces the mood; a knowledge of *stylistic elements* such as form, sentence structure, or a choice of words; a recognition of the "tone of voice" of the writer, such as seriousness, satire, or humor; the *point of view* of the character or the one who is telling the story; and the *figures of speech* which offer subtle levels of meaning through symbols, parables, fables, or stories within a story.[3]

The development of critical, appreciative readers of ethnic literature requires all of these skills, but such learning does not take place through a minute dissection of the elements of one particular novel. A reader gradually acquires such interpretive skills under the guidance of an artist-teacher who helps the learner at the critical point at which optional learning can take place.

Some Interpretations of Sounder

The author of *Sounder* uses the unusual technique of not giving proper noun names to the characters. Only Sounder, the coon dog, has a name. Other characters are delineated, such as the father, the boy, the three children, the white man, the mother, deputies, the sheriff, and the teacher, or the man with the white beard. Immature readers can be encouraged to speculate upon some of the reasons which might have caused the author not to use common names for his characters.

Sometimes, children and young adolescents need some clues to ways of interpreting various artistic methods of characterization. The mother in *Sounder* is gradually depicted as one who is imbued with a strong religious faith; but she has many superstitious beliefs. Armstrong develops much of the characterization of the mother through various Biblical allusions. The boy likes to listen to the mother tell about David the boy, or King David, and he enjoys hearing about Joseph in many roles, such as that of the slave boy, the prisoner, the dreamer or as a "big man in Egypt."[4] And in time of great defeat and suffering, the boy in *Sounder* is to fight back through the inspiration of the story of David and Goliath.[5]

Sometimes, the mood or tone of a novel is unified through the singing of a song or the chanting of a bit of verse. In *Sounder* the mother often hums a tune or sings a song softly when she is worried. The mood or tone of a story is reenforced through a repetitive use of certain phrases or snatches of a song.

Another theme in *Sounder* is one of aching loneliness, the loneliness of a boy who deeply longs for the companionship of the father and the

3. M. Angella Gunn, "What's Important in Developing Young Readers of Literature?" *New Directions in Reading,* edited by Ralph Staiger and David A. Sohn (New York: Bantam Books, 1967), p. 111.
4. William H. Armstrong, *Sounder.* (New York: Harper & Row, Publishers, 1969), p. 81.
5. *Ibid.,* p. 89.

friendly love of the coon dog, Sounder. Or again, there is the loneliness of the mother sitting in her lonely cabin awaiting the return of her imprisoned husband who has been placed on a chain gang. Armstrong manages to portray loneliness through several different devices. The author indicates that "loneliness was always in the cabin, except when the mother was singing or telling a story about the Lord."[6] During many lonesome evenings, the boy hears his mother softly hum or sing the words, "you gotta walk that lonesome valley."[7]

Young readers can be encouraged to note fresh imagery, similes, metaphors, and expressions in a novel such as *Sounder*. Older adolescent readers can also note examples of figurative language in such a novel as *Jubilee* by Margaret Walker. It is important to note the appropriateness of a simile within the context and tone of an artistic piece of work. Some metaphors which are appropriate to one setting seem artificial in another context.

In most instances, Armstrong in *Sounder* utilizes his similes and images in an appropriate, pictorial style. For instance, the opening part of Chapter Two commences as follows:

> The road which passed the cabin lay like a thread dropped on a patchwork quilt. Stalk land, fallow fields, and brush land, all appeared to be sewn together by wide fence row stretches of trees.[8]

The imagery of the road enhances the feeling of poverty and despair which lay in poor argicultural workers. An unusual example of personification used freshly by Armstrong are the words "now the sun had lost its strength."[9] Such a fresh use of language raises this novel above the commonplace.

Much of the "tell-it-like-it-is" style of literature ends abjectly with little hope or prospect of a better world to be faced by protagonists mired in the "sloughs of despond."

Marion Edman discusses this problem of tortured doubts in her illuminating article "Literature for 'Children Without' " which appears in *A Critical Approach to Children's Literature*. The question is whether or not a culturally-deprived, or slum-culture child gains more from reading about the "real, raw problems of life" in an exciting and challenging context, or whether such pain and vulgarity should be minimized. Claude Brown, author of *Manchild in the Promised Land,* ponders about the problem of lower and middle-class values. Should middle-class values be superimposed on persons living in a lower class, or should lower-class persons be

6. *Ibid.,* p. 31.
7. *Ibid.,* p. 37, 69.
8. *Ibid.,* p. 17.
9. *Ibid.,* p. 66.

encouraged to imitate middle-class values?[10] Edman quotes reports of four negative aspects of the child's self-image which are: "a sense of failure, alienation from people, a feeling of being treated unfairly, and finally, hopelessness concerning the future." Although Claude Brown faces many hopeless difficulties in Harlem he states that "Everybody I knew in Harlem seemed to have some kind of dream."[11]

Sounder is written in a terse, taut style with a feeling of a Greek tragedy lingering over most of the novel. Little happiness is enjoyed by the man, the boy, or the mother who are the principal characters. *Sounder* does, however, have something which offers hope to a lonely, sad boy. Even though the boy suffers many disappointments, he is going to have an opportunity to go to school and to learn to read: the teacher will help him to open the doors to a better world.

Such novels as *Sounder* and *Jubilee* manage to lead the reader to a deeper understanding of hidden human motivations, discouragement, and tragedy beneath the surface layer of plot and story. Books for younger pupils often need to be evaluated by considering the quality of illustrations and their relationship to the basic story fabric.

Criteria for Picture Books

In recent years, art has become such an important part of a child's book that illustrations are carefully studied as a source of negative stereotyping in art. Two controversial books are *Harriet and the Promised Land* by Jacob Lawrence and *O Lord, I Wish I Was a Buzzard* by Polly Greenberg. Ethel Richard reviews these two books with respect to their social consciousness in an issue of *Inter-racial Books for Children.* She states that *Harriet and the Promised Land,* by an outstanding artist, offers a beautiful symmetry of text and illustration. However, in her estimation, the art is too sophisticated for young black children who sometimes resent and reject the book. They object to the "deathlike skulls" or bony appearance of the heads and the agony demonstrated in the "stark-white teeth." Also, parts of the body, particularly the hands, are presented in grotesque shapes and disproportionate sizes. However, this reviewer points out that New York City blacks seem to like the book.

The second picture book *Oh Lord, I Wish I Was A Buzzard* has moderately stylized pictures using a combination of tempera, water color,

10. Claude Brown, *Manchild in the Promised Land* (New York: The Macmillan Company, 1965), p. 414.
11. Marion Edman, "Literature for 'Children Without'," in *A Critical Approach to Children's Literature,* The Thirty-First Annual Conference of the Graduate Library School, August 1-3, 1966 (Chicago and London: University of Chicago Press, 1967), p. 39.

crayon, and pen and ink. The text is poetic and is based on the experiences of children which were formerly dictated and published in mimeographed form as part of the 1965 Mississippi Head Start Program. Some persons have objected to the use of *buzzard* in the wish, but scholarly folklorists such as Richard Dorson indicate that the subject of a buzzard has appeared in numerous Negro oral folk tales

Many picture books written about Mexican or Mexican-American characters present negative stereotyped figures. One of these is *The Story of Pancho and the Bull with the Crooked Tail,* written and illustrated by Berta and Elmer Hader. This has a delightful story line, but the characters are depicted as Mexican bandits with droopy mustaches, wearing typical sombreros, and looking at persons like a caricatured cartoon.

These three mentioned illustrated books present a dilemma for teachers and librarians. They could be cast aside on the not-recommended

First grade children dramatizing "The Bull With a Crooked Tail."

list and discarded as unworthy examples of ethnic literature. However, each one of these books is beautifully written and has potential for developing the imaginations of pupils by providing good stimuli for creative thinking and writing. Some adults have criticized *Oh Lord, I Wish I Was A Buzzard,* but the content is wistful and childlike. Children in this Mississippi Head Start program could not relate to *Little Bear,* but they knew about hound dogs, partridges, and buzzards; so the book tells about the experience of the rural black child in the delta. An imaginative teacher could carry these wishes further and have pre-school children create wishing books of considerable originality. *Harriet and the Promised Land* has an effective rhythm which can be used in creating verses for a song or creative dance. Two student teachers at California State College in Hay-

Another scene from "The Bull With a Crooked Tail."

ward used *The Story of Pancho and the Bull with a Crooked Tail* in creative dramatics with a group of students who were mostly Mexican-Americans. Neither one of these teachers focused attention on the illustrations. One teacher rewrote the whole story as a play in couplets and quatrains. Then children took part in the play during the oral participation work of their reading groups. The other student teacher rewrote the story as a modified operetta with scenery and costumes. Children made serapes out of wrapping paper and paint, and some actors and actresses wore Mexican costumes which they obtained from home. These experiences indicate that persons have mixed emotions about these picture books. However, instead of completely rejecting them, some consideration might be given on ways to use such books in a creative classroom experience, such as in the making of roller movies, recreating images in puppet plays, or in painting murals or friezes illustrating dramatic moments of stories.

American Indian Ethnic Literature

Jeffrey Newman has written a provocative article entitled "Indian Association Attacks Lies in Children's Literature" which appears in *Interracial Books for Children* published in 1969. The author states that approximately a hundred new children's books concerning Indian people, plus many reprints, flood the market each year. Many of these books present distorted, outdated concepts which illustrate ethnocentricism of the worst kind. Authors frequently present an American Indian character according to Anglo-American standards. The reviewer criticizes historians of United States history who have followed a double standard in writing about Indian-white relationships. Frequently, such authors relate incidents revealing the cruelty of an Indian warrior toward a white man, but often these same historians fail to tell the story of white violence, cruelty, and broken promises. In 1969 the Association on American Indian Affairs reviewed children's books about American Indians in preparation for the publication of a *Preliminary Bibliography of Selected Children's Books About Indians*. The final list included sixty-three books although more than 200 books were read by expert reviewers who were compiling the list. Nearly two out of three books were rejected because of "inaccurate, unrealistic, ethnocentric statements about the Indian." A more extensive list based on a review of many more books about Indians was published in 1970. Three basic criteria were used in compiling these lists. These were: (1) a consideration of whether authors offered a realistic picture of American Indians without being patronizing, sentimental, and emotional; (2) whether authors gave an accurate and honest picture of the problems of Indians; (3) whether authors of books about contemporary

Indians were sensitive to the problems inherent in being Indian in the United States today.

Ann Nolan Clark who has created such novels as *Secret of the Andes, In My Mother's House,* and *Tia Maria's Garden,* has had numerous experiences as a teacher among the Zuni, Navajo, Pueblo, and other Indian households and tribes of the Southwest. In her recent book, *Journey to the People* this author discusses five qualities which are more significant than plot, suspense, and style in writing novels or tales about an Indian character. A book about Indians must have a *quality of sincerity and honesty.* If an author is creating an Indian as a character, he must depict certain characteristics which Indians have in common. An Indian shares his respect for the glories of the ancients in an Indian World. Just as a boy from Mali, in Africa, quietly saturates himself with deeds of ancient royal kings, many Indians also have respect for the ancients.

A second quality of a good story about an ethnic group is that of *accuracy,* and this should be true for books about Indians as well as for those about Mexican-Americans and Negroes. A writer must check and re-check his information, but he must not include in his plot so much detail that the central emotional thread of the story is lost in a maze of facts and figures. A Negro author may spend years going through archives of Lloyds of London to discover the name of a particular slave ship on which a Negro slave came to America, but the final version of the biography may include all of these significant details in one terse, explicit sentence.

Clark indicates in her *Journey to the People* that a good novel should have a *quality of reality.* Dramatic, suspenseful events may add to the interest of a book, but sometimes real events do not have a dramatic quality. For instance, many episodes in *And Now Miguel* by Joseph Krumgold seem quiet and uneventful, but gradually a quiet sequence of events leads to the growth in the maturity of Miguel Chavez. Three books about African people by Reba Paeff Mirsky, *Thirty-One Brothers and Sisters, Seven Grandmothers,* and *Nomusa and the New Magic* do not have many violent dramatic scenes, but one looks at life in a different culture and gradually learns in the last book how Nomusa struggles between the old ways and the new ones as she watches the witch doctor's magic and the work of Buselapi who has studied nursing.

A fourth quality of good literature which Clark and other authors have outlined is that of *imagination*—the ability of an artist to make original pictures as he writes his story or novel. For instance, *Dwellers of the Tundra: Life in an Alaskan Eskimo Village* by Aylette Jenness is a somewhat serious book based on the experiences of the author and her husband in an Eskimo village. Older readers in grades six through ten can imaginatively identify themselves with these people feeling the impact of white cultures on the old ways of the Eskimos. One learns about food, hunting, recreation, the tundra, ecology, and education in a setting depicted with imaginative word pictures. Such a volume as *Mill Child: The Story of Child Labor in America* by Ruth Holland, which is written for young adolescents, vividly depicts the children of poor immigrant families who worked for long hours under deplorable working conditions. Through the book the reader can imaginatively identify with the problems of a child laborer at that time.

A fifth quality outlined by Clark as well as by several literary critics is one of *appreciation*. One certainly learns more about beauty when he notes how an Indian boy appreciates the earth, the sunburst bronze sunset, the blowing sands of the mesa, or the majestic view from a mountain top. This appreciation or sensibility is often seen in the personification of objects chanted by a Pima child who says that she is "a pima basket formed of nature's materials" and "once was a willow by the running water with arrow weeds."[12] This same sense of identity with man and nature is felt in *haiku* poetry and is seen in such a volume as *Wind in My Hand: The Story of Issa, Japanese Haiku Poet* by Hanako Fukada. Ann Nolan Clark also reminds us that there are other appreciations besides those of beauty. The child and adolescent reader should learn to understand fear and the bravery which is necessary to combat it, and also to face the fact that many persons suffer both joy and sorrow in life as well as in fiction. Such volumes of poetry as the one compiled by Arnold Adoff, *I Am the Darker Brother: An Anthology of Modern Poems by Negro Americans* and *Black Roots, An Anthology,* edited by Jay David and Catherine J. Green, help readers to appreciate better the joys and sorrows, the frustrations and disappointments, and the courage and fear experienced by the Negro trying to find his identity in modern society.

Mexican-American Literature

Mexican-American literature for children should meet the criteria of all other good ethnic literature. In "The Mexican American in Children's Literature," Gloria T. Blatt indicates that many Americans share an inaccurate picture of Mexican-Americans. The author warns critics about the equating of customs of a people with festivals and holidays. Some primary grade stories about Mexican-American children, such as *Nine Days to Christmas* by Marie Hall Ets and Aurora Labastida, tend to emphasize special holiday customs such as the breaking of the piñata, but many books are being written which relate other aspects of the Mexican-American

12. Ann Nolan Clark, *Journey to the People* (New York: The Viking Press, 1969), p. 45.

culture. A new biography for younger children entitled *Caesar Chavez* by Ruth Franchere is somewhat disappointing. The subject is relevant since Chavez frequently appears in newspaper headlines about current Mexican-American figures. Somehow the illustrations by Earl Thollander border on stereotyping in art. Some of the scenes show persons with mouths formed in artificial poses. If more pictures were similar to that one of Chavez appearing on page forty-one, the book would appear to be more sincere and genuine, but such pictures as the one of three Mexican-American laborers on page ten seem to negate some of the honest problems of the migrant worker striving for recognition through the National Farm Workers Association.

A helpful book list on Mexican-American literature appears in *Latin America,* an annotated list of materials for children selected by librarians, teachers and Latin American specialists in cooperation with The Center for Inter-American Relations. Although these reviewers offer little introductory material concerning their selection and rejection of books, some of the annotations on books not recommended are helpful. Under the title "Not Recommended," certain statements appear, such as "Evangelical Church propaganda," "stereotyped and condescending," "too much dialect," "deplorable language faults," "stereotyped situations of boy who wants a burro and American tourists who help him get it," "too much stress on Aztec cruelty," "too superficial, poor transition," "slanted and dated," "too many factual errors," "stereotyped illustrations," "many errors of fact and interpretation," "artificial, exaggerated," "overly didactic, boring," "too slanted by the attitudes of the foreign missionary," "condescending to Mexicans," "sentimental and condescending," "unbelievable plot," and many others. Most of these qualities have been referred to previously. The added warning is against poor language style which results from poor translations of the Spanish or Mexican language. Many of these same criticisms could be applied to literature of other minority groups.

The Information Center on Children's Culture has also published a valuable list entitled *Africa: An Annotated List of Materials Suitable for Children,* but these committee members have failed to give reasons for not recommending certain books about various African countries.

Other criteria for good and poor literature concerning minority people can be developed through studying several issues of the *Bulletin of the Center for Children's Books,* edited by Mrs. Zena Sutherland. This bulletin is published monthly except in August by the University of Chicago Press and uses the symbols of *R* for Recommended, *M* for Marginal and *NR* for Not Recommended, as well as several others. An interested librarian or teacher can select books about ethnic cultures and compare annotations on those which are recommended and those which are not, and some specific criteria can be developed.

Other helpful criteria for evaluating books appear in *We Build To-gether,* edited by Charlemae Rollins, and *Negro Literature for High School Students* by Barbara Dodds.

Some differentiation might be made between excellent children's literature and other literature for children which is merely good. In an illuminating article entitled "A Children's Editor Looks at Excellence in Children's Literature," Jean Karl outlines several criteria for excellent children's literature, but in one part of her article she remarks that no one of us can see anything in the world "uncolored by what he is. I see you, but what I see may not be the self you see." In her estimation an excellent book permits one to experience something worthwhile that one could not experience for oneself. Incidents are rearranged to convey deeper truths as perceived by the author. The author's skill in assisting readers or listeners to walk around in someone else's shoes is similar to that of the royal griot telling his tale. He sees his art as eloquence in speaking words which are pure and free of all untruth. If one listens to the tale of an excellent author, one sometimes learns many truths. Such a perception might come from reading a novel such as *The Shoes from Yang San Valley* by Kim Yong Ik. Little Sang Do is a refugee child living alone in war-torn Korea. He searches through dung heaps for scraps to eat and wear, but he also dreams of the beautifully fashioned, silk-brocaded slippers artistically cre-ated by the father of Soo. The determination and courage of Sang Do who quests beauty in spite of loneliness, hunger, cold,, and other adversi-ties protects this little book from being overly sentimental and keeps an "unquenchable spark of hope" alive.

In an interesting article appearing in the April 1969 issue of *Social Education,* E. F. Gibson warns us that both black and white children in our schools have been indoctrinated with the three D's of "Distortion, De-letion, and Denial." Historians have distorted the image of black people as well as that of the Indian or the Mexican-American person, or they have deleted the contributions of persons of an ethnic group who do not conform to a particular stereotype. In many instances the place of an ethnic char-acter in an historical episode has been ignored. Stereotypes with a general-ized mental pattern, oversimplified opinions, affective attitudes, and un-critical judgment of a person's race should be eliminated since stereotypes are frequently untrue to reality or are dangerously simple. However, the critical reader should be wary of the "remanufactured past" approach in historical novels and biographies. Numerous newer biographies speak of minority American newspaper publishers, inventors, physicians, and artists in a way to indicate that these persons are more numerous and prolific than they are in reality. Critical readers should note whether or not the biography is about a significant member of a minority group.

Discerning readers should also be quite cognizant of racially potent words such as "mammy," "Aunt Jemima," "boy," "you people," "darkies," "pickaninny," "Inkspot," and "nigger." Such expressions as "the fat mammy waddled into the kitchen," or the "cute little pickaninny rolled on the cabin floor," or "the terrified coon rolled the whites of his eyes" should be avoided.

The author of a minority literature book should use the eloquence of the ancient African griot to see that characters act, think, and talk as one reared in the culture being depicted. Persons should be presented in clear authentic characterizations with little quaintness and no sense of benevolence toward an ethnic character. The story should be created in a manner to make the reader feel at home in the cultures and customs of another country, but no more background material should be included than is necessary to present life in a real manner. For instance, in the young adult novel *Zulu Woman* by Rebecca Hourich Reyher, one senses the struggle of Christiana to be a Christian and to reject her native religious ways and the customs of her Zulu people. Certain specific customs including the problems of polygamy with the many wives of a king are presented, but these customs are unfolded gradually, in a natural way, in relation to the Zulu cultural pattern and differences which are not stressed. Children reading about different cultural patterns should understand likenesses and differences between persons living in variant cultures.

A book should be correct in its essential details and descriptions of the life of a culture. This is particularly significant in nonfictional, historical, and biographical materials. A physician or a newspaper publisher who has made a significant contribution to the cultural history of the United States should not be overglamorized or idealized. He should not be nobler than other men unless he is a character who is of heroic proportions.

Authors and publishers should not use literature for children and adolescents as propaganda. Novels for these readers should not become religious or political tracts presenting distorted ideas in a didactic, rabble-rousing manner, devoid of the imaginative fervor and truth of the characters and events.

Individual diversities of persons should be esteemed and honored in our pluralistic democracy. For instance, in a nonfictional book for young adults entitled *American Fever: The Story of American Immigration* the author, Barbara Kaye Greenleaf, divides her story about immigrants between nationalities or regions of origin. She includes descriptions of the British, Irish, German, Scandinavian, Eastern and Southern European, Chinese, Japanese, black and Puerto Rican immigrants. In her discussions of newcomers she points out their contributions to the expanding economy of the United States and stresses the hardships suffered by new settlers struggling against prejudices of older ones. Her book includes appropriate photographs and prints from historical collections.

Summary

In order for literature to be artistic, authors must have a freshness of language and a plot which progresses naturally to a strong characterization of a few characters, with not too many diverse characters and episodes to confuse the immature reader. An author should also use a natural dialogue which does not have artificial dialect, patronizing expressions, or slurs or ignorant nonstandard usage, unless such oral speech belongs in the characterization of a person. The plot should have enough exciting details to hold the interest of the young reader, and the factual content of fictional, imaginative short stories should not be too overloaded even though information has been carefully researched. The reader must feel that the author is immersed and engrossed in the problems of a character. Characterizations

Reactions—Questions and Projects

1. Select a book which is a poor example of ethnic literature. Demonstrate your reasons for considering it a poor book.
2. Study at least three picture books written prior to 1945 with illustrations of Chinese, Japanese, Indian, black-American, or Mexican-American characters. Discuss these pictures as demonstrating negative stereotypes. Compare and contrast these books with three multi-ethnic picture books published after 1965.
3. Study some Mexican-American, black-American, or Oriental books in relation to the dialect or language used. React to the nonstandard and standard dialects. Also notice the use of derogatory terms and the lack of such terms. Does the language seem artificial in relation to the plot and characterization of the author?
4. Do some research on stereotypes in minority literature. You may wish to study the article by David K. Gast entitled "The Dawning of the Age of Aquarius for Multi-ethnic Children's Literature," in *Elementary English,* dated May 1970. Select three books about Mexican-American themes or heroes and discuss the stereotypes or lack of stereotypes.

should emerge naturally and appropriately; the character should seem real to his occupation, economic status, educational level, and social class. In other words, characters in a novel should think, talk, and act as one reared in the culture being depicted. If an author is fully immersed in the lives which he is artistically creating, he is not condescending or patronizing. If the plot is good, the characterization vivid, and over-moralizing is avoided, a reader will enjoy the book, particularly if it has a rousing beginning with incidents leading to a climax and an ending consonant with the story development. The art of an author writing for children and adolescents unites with that of the learned griot, Djela Mamadou Kouyaté, master of the art of eloquence in service of the princes of Mali who jealously guarded secrets many centuries old and who knew that the spoken word was "pure and free of all untruth."

5. Conduct a brief action-research project on children's prejudices and stereotypes which they have gained from previous experiences. For instance, Louisa Caucia worked with some fifth-grade pupils in Hayward, California. She read a book or two from the Peanuts Series by Charles Schulz, such as *Happiness Is A Warm Puppy* (Determined Publications) or *I Need All the Friends I Can Get* (Determined Publications). Children were asked to pretend that they were transforming some of these characters into a picture book for Mexican children. Most pupils drew cartoons of a Mexican with a sombrero, serape, mustache, or a child or man dressed in a revolutionary type of bandit outfit. Then the teacher showed these children a picture of a Mexican family eating dinner. She asked the group what the family was eating. The children listed such foods as enchiladas, tacos, beans, tortillas, and other well-known Mexican food. She then asked the children to look at the way Mexican children really dressed in the urban center of Hayward and also what foods these families ate. Children were quite surprised to discover that much clothing and food was similar to that of any child living in an urban setting.

6. In her book *Journey to the People,* Ann Nolan Clark discusses certain differentiating factors about some of the Indian people, such as a way of reckoning time. T. D. Allen has written some adult books: *Navahos Have Five Fingers* (Norman, Oklahoma, University of Oklahoma Press, 1963) and *Miracle Hill, The Story of a Navaho Boy* by Emerson Blackhorse Mitchell and T. D. Allen (Norman, Oklahoma: University of Oklahoma Press, 1967). Discover some ideas in these books which change your thinking about the Navajo Indian.
7. Make a chart showing differences and similarities which Mexican-Americans have to white Anglo-Saxons lower-class persons such as those living in Appalachia. Do research to find some persons of a Mexican heritage that might be good ones to use as heroes in a biography for intermediate grade children.
8. Read reviews of some multi-ethnic books appearing in the *Bulletin of the Center for Children's Books,* or from the *Booklist* (American Library Association), or in some other periodical which reviews children's books. Select three multi-ethnic fiction and three multi-ethnic nonfiction books which might be purchased for a school library.

BIBLIOGRAPHY

BOOKS FOR PRIMARY GRADE CHILDREN

ETS, MARIE HALL, and LABASTIDA, AURORA. *Nine Days to Christmas.* New York: Viking Press, 1959.

FRANCHERE, RUTH. *Caesar Chavez.* New York: Thomas Y. Crowell Company, 1970.

FUKUDA, HANAKO. *Wind in My Hand: The Story of Issa, Japanese Haiku Poet.* Haiku translated by Hanako Fukado. San Francisco: Golden Gate, 1970.

GREENBERG, POLLY. *O Lord I Wish I Was A Buzzard.* New York: Macmillan Company, 1968.

HADER, BERTA and ELMER. *The Story of Pancho and the Bull with the Crooked Tail.* New York: Macmillan Company, 1942.

IK, KIM YONG. *The Shoes from Yang San Valley.* Garden City, New York: Doubleday and Company, 1970.

LAWRENCE, JACOB. *Harriet and the Promised Land.* New York: Simon and Schuster, Windmill Books, 1968.

MIRSKY, REBA PAEFF. *Nomusa and the New Magic.* Chicago: Follett Publishing Company, 1962.

———. *Thirty-One Brothers and Sisters.* New York: Dell Publishing Co., a Yearling Book, 1969.

———. *Seven Grandmothers.* New York: Dell Publishing Co., a Yearling Book, 1969.

BOOKS FOR INTERMEDIATE GRADE CHILDREN
AND ADOLESCENTS

ADOFF, ARNOLD, ed. *I Am the Darker Brother: An Anthology of Modern Poems by Negro Americans.* New York: Macmillan Company, 1968.

ARMSTRONG, WILLIAM H. *Sounder.* New York: Harper and Row Publishers, 1969.

CREDLE, ELLIS. *Across the Cotton Patch.* Camden, New Jersey: Thomas Nelson and Sons, 1935.

DAVID, JAY, and GREEN, CATHERINE J., eds. *Black Roots: An Anthology.* New York: Lothrop, Lee & Shepard Co., 1971.

GREENLEAF, BARBARA KAYE. *American Fever: The Story of American Immigration.* New York: Four Winds Press, 1970.

HOLLAND, RUTH. *Mill Child: The Story of Child Labor in America.* New York: Crowell-Collier and Macmillan, 1970.

JENNESS, AYLETTE. *Dwellers of the Tundra: Life in an Alaskan Eskimo Village.* New York: Crowell-Collier and Macmillan, 1970.

JORDAN, JUNE. *Who Look at Me.* New York: Thomas Y. Crowell Company, 1970.

KRUMGOLD, JOSEPH. *And Now Miguel.* New York: Thomas Y. Crowell Company, Apollo Edition, 1970.

NIANE, D. T. *Sundiata: An Epic of Old Mali.* Translated by G. T. Pickett. London and Harlow, England: Longmans, Green and Co., 1969.

SWEARINGTON, ESTELLE MARGARET. *Pickaninny.* New York: Duffield and Company, 1925. (For comparative, critical study purposes only.)

WALKER, MARGARET. *Jubilee.* New York: Bantam Books, 1969.

PROFESSIONAL AND ADULT BOOKS

ACHEBE, CHINUA. *Things Fall Apart.* New York: Astor-Honor, 1959.

————. *Arrow of God.* Garden City, New York: Doubleday and Company, Anchor Books, 1969.

ASSOCIATION ON AMERICAN INDIAN AFFAIRS. *Preliminary Bibliography of Selected Children's Books About American Indians.* 432 Park Avenue, South, New York, New York 10016, 1969.

CLARK, ANN NOLAN. *Journey to the People.* New York: Viking Press, 1969.

DODDS, BARBARA. *Negro Literature for High School Students.* Champaign, Illinois: National Council of Teachers of English, 1968.

EDMAN, MARION. "Literature for 'Children Without' " in *A Critical Approach to Children's Literature.* Thirty-first Annual Conference of the Graduate Library School, August 13, 1966. Sara Innis Fenwick ed. Chicago and London: The University of Chicago Press, 1967.

GIBSON, E. F. "Three D's: Distortion, Deletion, Denial." *Social Education* 33. (April 1969): 405-409.

INFORMATION CENTER ON CHILDREN'S CULTURES, United States Committee for UNICEF *Latin America: An Annotated List of Materials for Children* selected by a Committee of librarians, teachers and Latin American specialists in cooperation with the Center for Inter-American Relations, 331

East 38th Street, New York, New York 10016, Information Center on Children's Cultures, United States Committee for UNICEF, 1969.

JOINT COMMITTEE OF THE AMERICAN LIBRARY ASSOCIATION CHILDREN'S SERVICES DIVISION AND THE AFRICAN-AMERICAN INSTITUTE. *Africa: An Annotated List of Printed Materials Suitable for Children,* 331 East 38th Street, New York, New York 10016, Information Center on Children's Culture, United States Committee for UNICEF, 1968.

KARL, JEAN. "A Children's Editor Looks at Excellence in Children's Literature." *The Hornbook Magazine* 43. (February 1967): 31-41.

MILLENDER, DHARATHULA H. "Through a Glass Darkly." *School Library Journal* (December 1967) 13: 29-34.

NEWMAN, JERRY. "Indian Association Attacks Lies in Children's Literature." In *Interracial Books for Children* 2, no. 3 (Summer 1969): 2, 8.

REYHER, REBECCA HOURWICH. *Zulu Woman.* New York: New American Library, Signet Books, 1970.

RICHARD, ETHEL. "Book Review." In *Interracial Books for Children* 2, no. 3 (Summer 1969): 8.

ROLLINS, CHARLEMAE. *We Build Together: A Reader's Guide to Negro Life and Literature for Elementary and High School Use.* Champaign, Illinois: National Council of Teachers of English, 1967.

SUTHERLAND, ZENA, ed. *Bulletin of the Center for Children's Books,* Graduate Library School, University of Chicago, The University of Chicago Press.

CHAPTER THREE

Walking Around in Someone Else's Moccasins: Some Teaching Ideas to Help Readers to Better Understand Ethnic Literature

The reading of selections of multicultural literature can frequently help youngsters to identify with the problems of others. If one can imaginatively walk around in somebody else's shoes, one can feel compassion for the outnumbered ones who frequently suffer difficulties in adjusting to the mainstream of a white Anglo-Saxon society. Various ways of developing a sensitivity toward others are going to be discussed in this chapter. One concept which needs to be developed in the minds of children and adolescents is that most newcomers usually have a period of loneliness and isolation before they become good neighbors in a new neighborhood.

Understanding Problems of the Outnumbered Ones

A story "The Shimeradas" by Willa Cather, appearing in *The Outnumbered: Stories, Essays, and Poems about Minority Groups by America's Leading Writers,* edited by Charlotte Brooks, suggests this sense of loneli-

ness of a Bohemian family. Often these newcomers are called the "uproot-
ed ones." They have their accustomed cultural patterns, their ways of
earning a living, and their friends. With this combination, they try to
establish themselves in a new land with different customs. The father in
"The Shimeradas" was an old frail weaver who was a skilled workman in
tapestry and upholstery materials in the old country, but he knew nothing
about farming. He brought his fiddle along from the old country to keep
alive his best-loved tunes and songs.

An example of a book about some white "hillbillies" who had considerable difficulty in adjusting to urban Chicago is *Up From Appalachia*
by Charles Raymond. Lathe Cantrell and his family are forced to leave
Appalachia because the coal mines are worked out, and they suffer the
direst form of poverty. Bart, the older son who has a good job as a truck
driver, determines to establish his family in Chicago where he hopes they
can get employment and better schooling, but Lathe and his family suffer
many pangs of loneliness, discouragement, and several hardships before
they become accepted members in an urban Chicago neighborhood. When
the gang shuts out Lathe from their activities and calls him a "briarhopper"
and a "hillbilly," he wonders, "Do they shut out all newcomers?" Did he
have to prove himself in some way? Maybe they didn't like Kentuckians.[1]
The Cantrell family members are poor white Appalachian hillbillies, but
they have pride. Ma will not go job hunting until Pa finds a job as she
fears it might hurt Pa's dignity.

Two other books about Appalachia may be used to develop more
background to supplement this novel. One is a nonfiction book by Bruce
and Nancy Roberts, *Where Time Stood Still: A Portrait of Appalachia,*
with photographs and a bibliography. This is an unsentimental straight-
forward account of poverty, suffering, ignorance and stubbornness which
are contrasted with beauty, loyalty and hope. Peg Shull has also done
another photography essay entitled *Children of Appalachia.* A more sensitive and literary book designed for younger children is *Hoagie's Rifle-Gun*
by Miska Miles. This little book shows how hunting with a gun in Appalachia is not a sport but a part of survival. Hoagie does not waste his
bullets, but when he tries to shoot a wildcat, Old Bob, he misses because
he cannot shoot an animal with a name; it is too close to his inner feelings.

A book which also focuses upon a father's pride as well as poverty is
No Promises in the Wind by Irene Hunt, which has been mentioned previously. This is principally the story of Josh Grondowski, an adolescent
Polish child, who suffers in the United States depression of 1932. Dad has
been out of work for eight months and resents the boy's piano playing. As
times grow harder, the proud Polish father resents Josh more and more.

---

1. Charles Raymond, *Up From Appalachia* (Chicago: Follett Publishing Company,
1966), p. 69.

Formerly the father had bragged about pulling himself up by his own boot straps; now he can not face the depression years with courage. The climax of quarreling comes when Josh asks for more potatoes at the supper table since he is ravenously hungry. Dad shouts, "Do you think your paltry little job gives you special privileges to eat when everyone else at the table is hungry too? Do you realize that your mother ironed all day to buy the food set before us, that she never asks for second helpings."[2]

The teacher or librarian should help readers of these novels to understand people's problems. They should be able to climb into the shoes of characters who are suffering from pride, humiliation, poverty, and disappointments. Questions can be asked, such as: How does it feel to be hungry? Can you think about someone who has been out of a job for a long time? What might be your feeling if you could not find a job and your wife and children were hungry and afraid? Why do you think Dad in *No Promises in the Wind* resents Josh so much? What reasons can you give for the resentment which Josh felt about Dad in the story? After two or three children have read a novel like *No Promises in the Wind* or *Up From Appalachia,* time should be given for a class discussion in a small circle or in a panel discussion group. In this way children may develop a more positive feeling for newcomers and jobless persons.

A Comparison of Biographies About the Same Person

One approach to the study of multi-ethnic literature is to compare and contrast several novels or stories about the same subject. For instance, several biographies have been written about Harriet Tubman and George Washington Carver. Pupils can read various versions of the Tubman or Carver story. Some books written at different grade levels are: *Harriet and the Promised Land* by Jacob Lawrence—for younger children, *Harriet Tubman, Conductor on the Underground Railway* by Anne Petry, and *Freedom Train: The Story of Harriet Tubman* by Dorothy Sterling. Some biographies on George Washington Carver are: *A Weed Is A Flower* by Aliki, *Dr. George Washington Carver* by Shirley Graham and George Lipscomb, and *George Washington Carver* by Henry Thomas.

Several versions of the *Amistad* affair have been published by different authors. Mary Dahl has written *Free Souls,* a book which gives insight into human feelings through the eyes of young Antonio. This book includes engravings from various historical collections such as those of the New Haven Colony Historical Society. Two panels in a mural painted by Hale Woodruff, a Negro artist, depict the mutiny aboard the *Amistad*

2. Irene Hunt, *No Promises in the Wind* (Chicago: Follett Publishing Company, 1970), p. 31.

(when Singbe is fighting with a ship's cook and Antonio is climbing a rigging) and the *Amistad* captives on trial in Connecticut. Another book for children written on the same subject is *The Long Black Schooner* by Emma Gelders Sterne. This novel commences with a chapter entitled "The Barracoon." In this incident the governor of Cuba, Nicholas Trist, and two sugar planters, Pedro Montez and Pepe Ruiz, as well as a Yankee sea captain, Ezra Stone, are discussing the transportation of slaves on the *Amistad*. From the governor's palace one can see the walls of the barracoon, or the slave pens, where slaves were kept ready for the market. The hero in this book is Cinque, son of a Mandi* chief, who always keeps dreams of his African homeland and freedom alive. He successfully leads a mutiny aboard the *Amistad* and seizes command of the ship. Another book on the same subject for more mature readers is *The Amistad Affair* by Christopher Martin. This same story appears in "Cinque and the Amistad Mutiny" as one of the tales in *Black Heroes in World History*. This short story opens with a scene in a New England courthouse in Hartford, Connecticut during the year of 1839. A Negro man in a crimson shirt with the neck open and displaying his tribal tattoos raises his right arm with its large hard fist and shouts the few English words he knows, "Give us free!" "Give . . . us . . . free!" This shortened version gives the dramatic story of the *Amistad* and differentiates *ladinos* who came to the New World prior to 1820 and *bozales* who were recently captured from Africa and spoke no English. *Bozales* were illegal cargo. The torture of the slaves who suffer from seasickness and dysentery, known as the "Bloody flux," aboard the Portuguese slaver *Tecora* is vividly depicted. Unfortunately the last two or three paragraphs of this version shatter some ideas of the heroic stature of Cinque. After a dramatic trial in which John Quincy Adams succeeded in winning freedom immediately for the slave mutineers, Cinque and some of his followers were returned to their African homes with funds raised by abolitionists. Cinque married, but later he became a successful slave trader himself which is somewhat disillusioning.

Pupils can learn much more information at depth by reading different versions of many biographies. Various techniques used by individual authors can be compared. For instance, Sterne refers to no basic sources in her book *The Long Black Schooner: The Voyage of the Amistad*. Dahl, on the other hand, in *Free Souls,* a book about the same hero offers a bibliography with specific information about the *Amistad* case, and some facts about the Mende tribe. One book is listed which discusses slavery in Cuba. Sterne speaks of Joseph Cinque; Cinque is called Singbe by Dahl, and is spoken of as the son of a Mandi chief. Dahl speaks of such books as *The Mende of Sierra Leone* published by the International Library of

---

*This word is spelled as both Mandi and Mende in various books.

Sociology, in 1965, and *The Mende Language* by F. W. H. Migeod which was published in London in 1908.

Identification through Creative Drama or Role Playing

Some of the actual trials of the *Amistad* affair are dramatic enough to be enacted as creative dramas. Little rewriting is necessary to recreate portions of the Dahl book in a play with characters of Ruiz and Montez expanded, and those of Cinque, Lewis Tappan, the United States Marshal, Richard Madden, and John Quincy Adams as the principal characters. Older junior high school pupils or adolescents may enjoy projecting themselves into the feelings of characters appearing in the Dahl book or those which are depicted in the short story in *Black Heroes of World History*.

Considering Different Viewpoints

Children may also consider two novels or short stories which take different viewpoints of an episode or incident. For instance, numerous books are available on the mission story of California and many of them are quite laudatory about the beneficial treatment of the Indians by mission fathers and the artisans and soldiers from Spain and Mexico. Many stories for children paint a glorified picture of the Spanish conquistadors who arrived in the western shores of the United States. *Pasquala of Santa Ynez Mission* by Florence Rowland describes little Pasquala, one of the Tulare Indians who loves mission life. She and her parents have left their village and people, the Tulare Indians. Now they are living peacefully at the mission and enjoying its church festivals, as well as trips to the mountains to gather piñon nuts. On the other hand, the novel *The Wrath of Coyote* by Jean Montgomery, records the resentment of Miwok warriors toward Spanish soldiers, missionaries, and artisans who built a mission on their land. The cruel punishment of Indians who wanted to desert the mission is vividly described. Teams of pupils can be assigned to read different novels, and then can discuss the feelings which were favorable and those which were hostile to the encroachment of newcomers to Indian lands. Pupils should probe for reasons for hostile feelings, such as misunderstandings of language, fear of loss of land or possessions, newer or strange customs and ways, resentments over a new religion, the decimation of tribes by disease, newer economic possibilities for mission Indians, and others.

Numerous Indian novels feature the character of an Indian chief of a tribe. Pupils may enjoy reading different novels depicting various Indian chiefs, and then they can compare and contrast characteristics and achievements of such men. For instance, Marin, chief of the Tomales, is the chief in *The Wrath of Coyote*. Marion Lawson has written a biography entitled *Proud Warrior: The Story of Black Hawk*. This great Sauk chief was a foe of settlers encroaching on his land. The Sauk were tricked into signing treaties which they did not understand and suffered many hardships and murders at the hands of the white man.

In Search of Meaning through Religious Expression

Another approach toward novels is a consideration of different religious customs and ceremonies and a pursuit of the idea that each group of persons has wanted some type of a religious experience, although symbols, rituals, and customs vary. For instance, older pupils may enjoy reading *Black Elk Speaks: Being the Life Story of a Holy Man of the Oglala Sioux*. Another committee of pupils may pursue Jewish religious ceremonies and customs through such a book as *A Day of Pleasure: Stories of a Boy Growing Up in Warsaw* by Isaac Bashevis Singer. Younger pupils or persons who are more immature readers may enjoy learning about Jewish customs and rituals in *All-of-a-Kind-Family* and *More-All-of-a-Kind-Family* by Sydney Taylor.

A story for very young pupils is *Purim* by Mollie Cone. Helen Borten has beautifully illustrated this book about the Spring Jewish holiday which mentions some of the adventures of Queen Esther. Another Jewish holiday, the Hanukkah, or festival of lights, is described in a book entitled *Hanukkah,* written by Norma Simon and illustrated by Symeon Shimin.

Although numerous books about the Jewish people tend to overemphasize Jewish holidays, children may enjoy *Jewish Holidays: Facts, Activities, and Crafts* by Susan Gold Purdy, which describes many traditional ways of celebration. After a description, directions are given for creating something related to a holiday, such as puppets and costumes, a toy, a recipe book, or a greeting card. Another book about Jewish holidays is *Let's Talk about the Jewish Holidays* by Dorothy K. Kripke which is a small book of fifty-two pages written principally for children in grades two through four. This presents a brief nonfictional account of eleven Jewish holidays including Independence Day and Tisha-B'av.

Some readers who are interested in novels about the Jewish people which have less emphasis on Jewish customs but still illuminate ideas about them may enjoy reading *Rifka Bangs the Tea Kettle* by Chaya M. Burstein. Rifka lived with her hard-working parents and her brothers Elli and Velve in 1904. The end of the work week was commemorated with observances of Jewish festivals and holidays, but Rifka wanted to learn to read more than anything else.

A book for high school readers which dramatically depicts Peter and Karl as German Refugees during World War II in Denmark is *Star of*

Danger by Jane Whitbread Levin. This novel is more about brotherhood than religion, but it does give information about the Jewish People.

Another story which describes Czech and Hungarian folk customs is *A Papa Like Everyone Else* by Sydney Taylor. The story is located in Czechoslovakia after the First World War when Mama, Szerena, and Gisella hoped to join Papa. Some of the rituals and patterns of a Jewish community are shown. Teachers and adults may wish to supplement class discussions of the Jewish people and cultural patterns with information learned from *Life Is With People: The Culture of the Shtetl* by Mark Zborowski and Elizabeth Herzog. This is an anthropological study of a culture which does not exist today. Children have been scattered to various countries to be reared as Americans or Israelis or as members of collective farms in Eastern Europe. The opening chapter entitled "Sabbath Eve" gives an idea of the significance of this religious day to the Jews as they live from Sabbath to Sabbath working all week to earn money for religious rites. This is "a day of rest, joy and devotion to God. None must work, none must mourn, none must worry, none must hunger on that day."[3]

Some mature adolescent readers at the ninth grade level may appreciate the biography, *Asoka the Great: Indian Royal Missionary* by Emil Lengyel. Asoka, who was a Third Century B.C. Maharaja of India, was later converted to Buddhism. He had many of his royal sermons inscribed on a stone and urged people to stop their gambling, gossiping, and hypocrisy. Summaries on the teaching of Buddhism and Hinduism appear in this book also. Another novel about the Buddhists is *Orange Robed Boy* by Patricia Wallace Garlan and Maryjane Dunstan. This is about a Burmese boy who leaves his family and gives up his name to live in a monastary in order to learn the teachings of Buddha. When he puts on the orange robe, he enters the entrance ceremony of the Shimbyu and becomes Ariya. Not all intermediate grade and junior high school pupils will enjoy this tale as it has little plot, but the authors do explain some unusual customs. Another youngster interested in finding out more about the Buddhist religion will enjoy *The Prince Who Gave Up the Throne: A Story of the Buddha.* This is the story of Siddhartha Buddha which is partly factual and almost a legend. The black and white illustrations are similar to the frescoes in the Ajanta Cave. The book is highly fanciful and includes much of the miraculous, but it would be helpful in a unit on religion. A few adults might wish to consult a paperback book, *The Ochre Robe* by Agehananda Bharati. Younger primary grade children may possibly enjoy *The Cat Who Went to Heaven* by Elizabeth Coatsworth, which is illustrated by Lynd Ward.

3. Mark Zborowski, and Elizabeth Herzog, *Life Is With People: The Culture of the Shtetl* (New York: Schocken Books, 1969), p. 37.

Another novel for intermediate grade readers about different religious customs is one by Mildred Jordan entitled *Proud to be Amish*. This is a little story about the life of the Amish people living on farms in Pennsylvania and the temptations of children who want to enjoy the radio and other modern ways.

A simple little book for primary grade children about a Quaker child, Obadiah Starbuck, is one entitled *Thy Friend, Obadiah,* written and illustrated by Brinton Turkle. It is a slight little story about a boy and a sea gull, but Obadiah learns that persons can become friendly by helping others.

Older children working on a unit on world religions may enjoy reading a nonfiction book, *The Quakers: the Religious Society of Friends,* written and illustrated by Kathleen Elgin. The work of Quakers before and during the Civil War is shown through the attitudes of Levi Coffin.

A good story about a Japanese family and the father who was priest in the village of Kyoto is *In-Between Miya* by Yoshuko Uchida. Miya Okamoto is an "in between child," one who is not fully appreciated because she is in the middle. Miya is given heavy responsibilities in working for relatives in Tokyo. Her brave attitude toward her difficulties shows the struggle of a child to earn self-esteem in a family which has conflicting goals.

A nonfiction book about the Mormons is *The Mormons: The Church of Jesus Christ of Latter Day Saints,* which is written and illustrated by Kathleen Elgin. The author discusses the Mormon migration westward in the first section. In the second section a biography of Charles Coulson Rich is given which offers interesting information from the diaries of some of his wives. A short history of the Morman religion is included, and the persecution of members of this religious group is described.

Teachers who are launching a unit on the world religions may wish to read *In Search of Meaning: Living Religions of the World* by Carl Hermann Voss. This discusses the origin of such religions as Buddhism, Christianity, Confucianism, Taoism, Hinduism, Islam, Jainism, Judaism, and Shintoism. Junior high school readers can read this nonfictional book independently, and it will illuminate portions of novels about various religious rites and symbols. The books mentioned in this chapter concerning various modes of worship are not a complete list of novels and nonfiction books on religious customs. It is a list of a few suggested titles only, and there are many gaps. Hundreds of other juvenile books about persons of various religious beliefs might have been mentioned.

Persons who wish to know about publications on other ethnic groups, books on such topics as "Neighbors Abroad," "Races and Nations," and "Holidays and Holy Days," as well as listings on several subjects may consult *Books for Friendship: A List of Recommended Books for Children,* published by the American Friends Service Committee and Anti-Defamation League of B'Nai B'rith.

Raising the Aspiration Level of Readers or Listeners

Many books about minority heroes might be used in a way to inspire juvenile readers to try harder to attain their goals, as well as to raise their aspiration level. For instance, *Annuzza, A Girl of Romania* by Hertha Seuberlich, which has been mentioned previously, is about a peasant child living in a Carpathian Mountain village who overcomes many obstacles to attain an education. Roosevelt, the little Negro sharecropper in *Roosevelt Grady* by Louisa Shotwell, also longs for more education and wants to find out about "putting into" arithmetic. The book *The Way of the Wind* by Polly Mark, reveals some of the problems of a girl getting an education in Borneo.

Docudrama Develops Sensitivity

During the last few years a different type of literature for a pluralistic society seems to be emerging. Publishers are beginning to publish documentary books. Most of these little volumes might technically be considered as nonfiction since little story line, plot, or characterization emerges. In many instances, photographs are used and children in ghetto or urban areas dictate their thoughts on tapes which are later carefully edited. Such a book is *It's Wings that Make the Birds Fly: The Story of a Boy* by Weiner, which has been mentioned previously. Another type of book consists of the actual words dictated by slaves concerning slavery, such as *To Be A Slave* by Julius Lester, or *Steal Away: Stories of the Runaway Slaves* by Abraham Chapman. Such books are good ones to use in creating a docudrama. This newer type of drama, similar to Readers Theater, seems to be emerging. Chairs or tall stools are arranged in a stage position and a few props are used. In docudrama, narrators usually select excerpts from various documents and add additional background information which is interspersed with music played on the piano, guitar, harmonica, recordings, or on tapes. Music and poetry supplement the documentary material.

Numerous aids can be used to vitalize and embellish docudramas. The cast can use tape recordings of voices of important persons in history, such as those of Presidents or leaders of social protest. Reproductions of photographs or facsimiles of early newspaper pictures can be projected on the wall with opaque projectors or transparencies, and overhead projectors can be used. Short excerpts on film loops of an appropriate movie can be projected, or film strips and slides can be used. Large posters can be made to serve as a backdrop to set the mood for a drama.

Writing Original Folktales or Poems

In addition to docudramas based on nonfictional material, students can create original folktales in the style of a particular ethnic group. If possible, teachers should give children a short unit on folklore and techniques of gathering oral versions of tales told by grandmothers or other adults. Although pure versions of folklore are rapidly disappearing, alert adults can discover an individual from an ethnic cultural group who can sing folk songs and tell folk tales. Children can gain more respect for the Punjabi culture when they learn that particular songs are sung and proverbs told as a bridal headdress is being woven. The teacher can help the child to see the use of proverbs by the Ibo storyteller in Nigeria, by the Punjabi Indian from India, and by numerous cultural groups of the world.

Teachers can help pupils to understand the particular structural patterns of myths, legends, and folk tales. Children can listen to recordings by such talented storytellers as Harold Courlander; and later, young authors can write original folktales in the style of people representing a particular country, people, or religion. Folktales can be written as part of a unit being studied about a certain country. For instance, Marilyn Miller and Harriet D. Merritt have described a project on Japanese folktales in an article entitled "A Fourth Grade Composes a Japanese Folktale," which appears in the February 1969 issue of *Childhood Education*.

One third-grade class in the Del Rey School of San Lornezo, California studied numerous African folk tales as part of a unit on the Zulus of Africa. Pupils listened to professional recordings of folktales, and then committees were formed. Each group wrote a different "How and Why Tale" about animals. Then children voted on the best tale according to predetermined established criteria for a good African folk tale, and the winners composed an original play. Later, head and shoulder masks were made of papier mâché using balloons as a base. Children then presented the play and wore the masks while narrations and sound effects were given through the use of a tape recorder.

Music and the Arts

Sometimes students can empathize more with customs of an ethnic group if they can experience the art, music, creative movement or some of the dances of a culture. For instance, Franco Monti has published a book entitled *African Masks*. This volume is an inexpensive one which shows colored illustrations of masks, such as a fetish mask of wood berries, mirrors and cowry shells worn in Mali, and a doubleheaded dance mask of the Ekoi, constructed of wood, animal skins and hair. The significance of the mask in the traditions of a tribal people of an African country should be presented along with the picture. For instance, the author states that the African mask is not worn merely as a means of escaping from the realities of everyday life, but it is also used as a means of participating in various aspects of life in the universe. Man can represent the spirits of good and evil through his mask; and he can also symbolize animals and man, or communication between a divinity and man. Other people, such as the Aztecs of Mexico, valued their masks highly as well as did the people of many world countries. The Hopi Indians used *kachina* dolls and masked dancers recreated numerous symbolic rites in almost the same way.

Pupils who are reading African folk tales may project themselves better into the cultural customs of a particular African tribe through doing some of the projects outlined in *African Crafts for You to Make* by Janet and Alex D'Amato. Girls might enjoy making an Ashanti doll or Akua-ba and learning that women of the Ashanti tribe carried a doll tucked in their waist bands because they believed it would make their unborn children healthy and beautiful. Boys might like to make a bird headdress similar to ones carved by the Senufe tribe. This group believed that this sacred mythological bird was one of the first five creatures of the earth.

Adolescent pupils may enjoy some experiences in reproducing some of the work created by African artists. *Getting Started in African Crafts* by Jeremy Comins, offers some simple directions and pictures of such crafts as mask art, wood and cardboard sculpture, slotted animals, wood relief, slate engraving, Afro-Combs, beads, containers, and other objects, such as the Dashiki and tote bag.

Several paperback books are available on world folk songs which can be used in correlation with folktales. Some of these are *Folk Songs of the World* by Charles Haywood; *A New Treasury of Folk Songs,* compiled and arranged by Tom Glazer; and *Round the World Folk Sing,* edited by Herbert Haufrecht. In many instances, these folksongs can be dramatized through the use of a few pupils. For instance, if one were reading a book about a Czechoslovakian child, he might enjoy dramatizing and singing "Aněcka, Dušička" [Annie, My Darling] from the book edited by Herbert Haufrecht, as the song is a question and answer one between a boy and a girl. Another book for persons more talented in music is *Folk and Traditional Music of the Western Continents* by Bruno Nettl. In addition to other information, this book has chapters entitled "African Music South of the Sahara," "Negro Folk Music in the New World," and "The American Indians." The chapter, "Western and Western-Descended Folk Music in the Americas," includes a discussion of South American folk music as well as a brief mention of music of other ethnic minorities of the United States such as the Amish and German folk cultures. A valuable aspect of the book is the bibliography and discography which comes at the end of each chapter.

An informative book on African music and the similarity and differences of such music to music in the United States is *The Music of Africa,* with an introduction by Dr. Fred Warren with Lee Warren. This book underscores the place of music in traditional African life where music is a part of the process of living. Special music celebrates the birth of a baby, as well as the appearance of the first tooth. Instruments such as the drums of Northern Nigeria, an African harp of covered wood of the Azanda people in the northeast Congo, the Kissar lyre of Central Africa, the carved ivory trumpet of the Mangbetu tribe of Central Africa, a xylophone with gourd resonators, and the Mbira thumb piano, as well as other instruments are illustrated. Africans have modified the modern version of pop and soul music which is known as "highlife." A valuable contribution of this book is its bibliography and discography. The list of records includes a large number of recordings, such as the music of the Mende of Sierra Leone by Folkways; and Folk Music of Africa, produced by the African-American Institute; and Atumpan, The Talking Drums by the U.C.L.A. Institute of Ethno-musicology. In addition to music recorded in the United States, some records which are part of "The Music of Africa Series" consists of authentic folk music recordings made in Central and Southern Africa which can be obtained from the International Library of African Music, P. O. Box 138, Roodepoort, Transvaal, South Africa. An interesting book on African musical instruments is *Musical Instruments of Africa: Their Nature, Use, and Place in the Life of a Deeply Musical People* by Betty Warner Dietz and Michael Babatunde Olatunji. This book gives some specific things for pupils to do. For example, in the section on "Body Percussion," directions are given for doing a stamping dance of the Masai herders of South Africa. A picture of the *Sakara* drum is shown in another section, and pupils are told how to make the instrument with a clay circle covered with hide.

In some instances, a literature book can be enlivened and made more meaningful through the addition of music. For example, a recent biography is *Somebody's Angel Child: The Story of Bessie Smith* by Carmen Moore. At the conclusion of this volume a listing is given of a selected discography which includes the date of its issue. A young adolescent reading about Bessie Smith will enjoy listening to some of these Columbia recordings made by the great Negro blues singer.

Junior and senior adolescent readers will understand the Negro experience in white America more through reading such a volume as *Blues People: Negro Music in White America* by LeRoi Jones.

Most adolescents will be interested in reading portions of the volume *The Story of Rock* by Carl Belz. In this book Belz considers rock-and-roll as a part of the folk art of the United States, and the volume includes contributions of certain recognized rock musicians such as Fats Domino, Wilson Pickett, and James Brown, as well as the Beatles and the Kingston Trio. Adolescents can understand *Jazz Country* by Nat Hentoff better if they read some nonfiction books about jazz, such as *The Story of Rock,* along with the book. Langston Hughes has written *The First Book of Rhythms* and *The First Book of Jazz* which are helpful to pupils experiencing a little novel such as *The Jazz Man* by Mary Hays Weik.

Surrounded by Books about Ethnic Groups

Readers can become aware of multi-cultural influences which abound in almost any rural or urban area of the United States. Several approaches can be made to develop an awareness of the wealth of literature of ethnic peoples composing the social structure of the United States. A teacher can incorporate novels, biographies, and short stories as part of a literature or social studies unit being conducted in the classroom. For instance, a teacher in a third grade can develop a unit such as "Folktales or Folk Songs of the World." Pupils can use a large map, read numerous folk tales, and then locate countries where the tales originated. Children can study a folk tale from the Philippines, one from Cambodia, and one from Cuba or Mexico, as well as some Jack tales of the United States or some Grimm tales of Europe. In some instances, such a large covering of folk tales may be valuable from a cognitive standpoint, but a Mexican-American, Chinese, black-American, or an Indian child may not feel that he has any identity with peoples in other countries.

Telling a story to Chicano students with a puppet.

A second approach is to concentrate on some specific literature and creative arts units focusing upon the literature of one particular ethnic group, such as the Irish, the Italians, the Indians, Mexican-Americans, or black-Americans. In this approach, a child might study several examples of literature about one group of people. For instance, a teacher could develop a rich unit on African folk tales and trace many of them from Africa to the Caribbean, to certain Southern states, and up to Michigan or Illinois. In a unit such as this one, differences should not be overplayed. Readers should understand that all people have certain needs, aspirations, problems, and beliefs.

A third approach is an individualized one in which a census is made of all the outnumbered or minority peoples in a particular classroom. The teacher might then help the child of each ethnic group to discover books about his own people. Under this plan many white Anglo-Saxon middle-class children representing the majority group of a certain suburban or urban area may gain an appreciation of the rich contributions which diverse people make to the growth of this country.

A Way of Human Understanding

Numerous school districts are currently issuing curriculum guides which offer assistance to teachers and librarians who are approaching studies of ethnic literature for the first time. One such publication is *Intergroup Education—A Guide for Human Understanding,* which was developed and produced by the Hayward Unified School District for classes ranging from kindergarten through the sixth-grade level. This Guide offers basic goals, such as those of knowledge and understandings, attitudes and feelings, and skills. A helpful list of literature books and audio-visual materials is included.

Insights into a "Life of Feeling"

A book which is written to help teachers understand human feelings and the black experience in America is *A Gift of the Spirit: Readings in Black Literature for Teachers* by Karel Rose. The author hopes that the book will help both Negro and white middle-class teachers to understand persons of deprived backgrounds. The book hopes to be a "sensitizing catalyst" to make the reader aware of the black man's feelings about his experiences which have alienated and intimidated him.[4] The author indicates that "Soul" expresses a "growing reaction of Negroes against op-

4. Karel Rose, *A Gift of the Spirit: Readings in Black Literature for Teachers* (New York: Holt, Rinehart & Winston, 1971), p. vii.

Stuffed scarecrow for oral storytelling to primary grade children.

pression and rejection on one hand and against assimiliation and absorption on the other."[5] Much literature written by black artists causes readers to reexamine their beliefs and values. Some of the stereotypes of black people are disappearing from current literature, but David White in his critical book *Black on White: A Critical Survey of Writing by American Negroes* warns sophisticated white and European readers not to rush to "adopt each Negro novelist's new agonized hate-filled hero as the norm."[6] The readings collected in this volume commence with *The Life of Olaudah Equiano* by Gustavus Vasa, an autobiography written in 1791 to Chapter Two, "Mascot," from *The Autobiography of Malcolm X*.

5. *Ibid.*, p. 23.
6. *Ibid.*, p. 25.

Changing Cultures—Some Curriculum Products

Most societies are undergoing cultural changes. A look at ways different customs impinging on persons living in one culture inflict "cultural shock" provides an interesting focus on the study of ethnic literature. Leon E. Clark has edited a series of books under the general title Through African Eyes: Cultures in Change. The first volume, entitled *Coming of Age in Africa: Continuity and Change,* includes a selection "Growing up in Acholi" which was written in 1966 by Anna Apoko. She described her Acholi tribe which is a first-hand account of life in a tribe of 250,000 members living in Northern Uganda in East Africa. A second literary selection entitled "Song of Lawino: A Lament" by Okot p'Bitek, vividly depicts a traditionally oriented Acholi wife, Lawino, complaining about her husband Ocol who wants her to "use the primus stove," "dance the balloon dance," and "do my hair as white women do." The third literary selection entitled "African Child" includes excerpts from *Dark Child* by Camara Laye.

Camara Laye was born in 1928 and grew up in Guinea. His father was a representative of the Malinke people, who originally founded the Mali empire in the thirteenth century. The author studied and worked in Paris for six years and wrote his autobiography during this period of time. The complete biography, *The Dark Child* by Camara Laye, with an introduction by Philippe Thoby-Marcellin, is available in paperback form. The introduction tells how the "griots, or troubadours of black Africa," relate the deeds of their ancestors to the Malinkes of the present time.[7] Poems ending the Clark book are: "Ancestral Faces" by Kwesi Brew, who was born at Cape Coast, Ghana; "Pardon Me" by Ismael Hurreh, who was born in Somalia; and "Totem" by Léopold Sédar Senghor, who was formerly President of Senegal and was one of the principal speakers for négritude.

A valuable contribution to this book is an accompanying booklet which contains a list of helpful source materials and twelve lessons which will aid teachers in interpreting ideas of cultural change to ninth-grade readers during a semester study of Africa. Several basic goals are outlined as reasons for this study, but certain values included are: (1) the breaking down of Western stereotypes of Africa; (2) an elimination of ethnocentrism; and (3) a means of helping students to study societies objectively.[8] Some of the teaching strategies suggested in this booklet are interesting and thought provoking.

---

7. Camara Laye, *The Dark Child* (New York: Farrar, Straus and Giroux, 1954), p. 9.
8. Leon E. Clark, ed., *Coming of Age in Africa: Continuity and Change,* Through African Eyes: Cultures in Change, unit 1, lesson plans (New York: Praeger Publishers, 1969), p. vi.

The same format is followed in the second volume of the series, which is entitled *From Tribe to Town: Problem of Adjustment,* Unit II of *Through African Eyes: Cultures in Change.* This volume includes the story of "Kobla" by St. Clair Drake; "Trying to Beat the Odds," by J. A. K. Leslie; "Tell Me Josephine," edited by Barbara Hall; "Marriage Is a Different Matter" by Chinua Achebe; "Men of Two Worlds," from *Drum Magazine* of Lagos, Nigeria; "Returning Home" by Mongo Beti; "Life in the Copperbelt" by John V. Taylor and Dorothea A. Lehman; "Listening to the Radio" by Hortense Powdermaker, an excerpt from an anthropological study; and excerpts from an autobiography, *Tell Freedom* by Peter Abrahams. The episode concerns some experiences in the Bantu Men's Social Center in Johannesburg, South Africa. "Let Me See Your Pass, *Kaffir,*" by Bloke Modisane, is an exceprt from his autobiography *Blame Me on History.* It is a vivid description of the affects of apartheid on Bloke Modisane's life. This volume has an instructive teacher's manual also, with a list of source materials and fourteen lesson plans. The preface to these two volumes states that these products are ones produced by the Educational Materials Project (EMPathy) established in June 1967 for the purpose of developing curricular materials for the study of other cultures.

A Way of Happening

In this chapter several teaching suggestions for assistance in understanding multi-ethnic literature have been suggested. Underneath all literature appreciation lies the fundamental suggestion that a good book sets up an electric charge between the listener or reader and the book. Louise M. Rosenblatt in her excellent article, "A Way of Happening" says:

> This live circuit between the reader and the text is the literary experience. Literature is, first of all, this sensing, feeling, thinking, this ordering and organizing of feeling, image, and idea in relation to the text.[9]

Teachers need to foster this quality of a literary experience which is a personal and perceptive response to the sound, rhythm, and meanings of words in a book.

Whatever the approach decided upon by the teacher and her pupil, one thing is certain. All children should be surrounded by a wealth of excellent books, both fiction and nonfiction, which help the child to gain a compassionate feeling for his fellow man and a sense of "climbing into his skin and walking around in it."

9. Louise M. Rosenblatt, "A Way of Happening," *Educational Record,* Summer 1968, p. 341.

Summary

This chapter is mostly concerned with some of the ways in which teachers might assist their pupils in their encounters with ethnic literature. It suggests ways to help children and adolescents empathize with the fears, hopes, and aspirations of characters who represent an ethnic minority.

One technique of gaining some understanding of the problems of people is the use of open-ended questions and small discussion groups so that pupils can learn to diagnose human relations and needs of persons, such as the Bohemian Shimeradas, the white hillbillies from Appalachia, or the members of the Polish Grondowski family. An older book, *Diagnosing Human Relations Needs,* published as one of the Studies in Intergroup Relations by the American Council on Education, suggests numerous values of open questions which cause children and adults to examine values and feelings rather than facts and ideas.

Some readers can enhance the depth of literature appreciation through studying different biographies about the same person, such as several biographies on Harriet Tubman or George Washington Carver. Also, pupils can study different interpretations of novels based on true historical events such as the seizure of the *Amistad* by a group of slaves. Pupils can critically examine various novels and contrast ways that authors handled the material relating to the same historical incidents.

Reaction—Questions and Projects

1. Decide upon an ethnic group or a representative of a minority cluster in your community which has not been discussed much in this chapter. Conduct research in your neighborhood or college library or in a well-stocked book store. Discover books which are available and prepare an annotated list of a few of them. Develop some open-ended questions which might help children to grasp problems in the book more accurately.

2. Imagine that you are going to be an author of children's books. Decide upon a minority group which needs more novels or biographies about it. Create a plot outline of a proposed book which might be submitted to a publisher.

3. Little has been said about the teaching of poetry of various ethnic peoples. Select some examples of poems written by Indian, Spanish-American, Oriental, or Mexican-American poets. Suggest some

Creative play making, sociodrama, role playing, and docudramas are some of the dramatic techniques which can be used to help pupils identify with characters in a novel, biography, or short story.

Readers can consider attitudes of ethnic characters from different viewpoints. The mission story of California can be examined from the viewpoint of a beneficent padre or from an explanation made by a Californian Indian boy who was bound to the mission against his will.

Pupils and teachers can do a comparative study of various religious beliefs and learn differences and similarities between Jewish, Amish, Catholic, Buddhist, and Mormon beliefs, rites, and symbols.

Certain biographies and novels can be presented in a way to help poorly motivated readers to raise their aspiration levels.

Pupils can also study both the structure and content of certain tales as a model for initiating original folktales in the style of a folklorist in a particular foreign country.

Music, art, dance, and creative movement, as well as dramatic experiences, help readers to identify with cultural characteristics of a people.

Numerous activities can be used to initiate enthusiasm and interest in various ethnic books, but rich resources of books, recordings, film strips, movies, realia, and other multimedia can do much to make literature the "way of happening" which completes the live circuit between the reader and the text.

activities which you might use to make poetry more meaningful to children in your class or library group.

4. Collect documents about an historical period in the history of your state and include documents about minority groups which played a part in an historical epoch. For instance, Chinese laborers played an important role in building the transcontinental railroad to the West Coast and were also significant businessmen in early gold mining operations in California. After collecting documentary material from early newspapers, historical quarterlies, or diaries, sketch out a docudrama which might be used by children in schools.

5. Study the criteria of a good biography about an ethnic hero which is not mentioned in this chapter. Read the biography and analyze it critically in relation to your specified criteria.

6. Investigate some other creative media such as creative stitchery shadowgraph plays, folk dances, or special fabric designs. The volume *Literature for Children: Enrichment Ideas* by Ruth Kearney

Carlson (Dubuque, Iowa: William C. Brown Company Publishers, 1970) has a large number of creative ideas. Use one of the creative arts of an ethnic group in a way to develop the sensitivity of your pupils in appreciating the culture of this group.

7. Survey some instructional materials which could embellish the teaching of multi-ethnic literature. For instance, Joanna Foster has written "Audio-Visual Materials for Teaching Children's Literature," in the October 1968 volume of the *Wilson Library Journal,* pages 154-159. This supplies lists of several films and suppliers which will be helpful.

8. Margaret M. Heaton has written a book entitled *Feelings Are Facts* (New York: National Conference of Christians and Jews, 1957). The March 1969 issue of *Childhood Education* focuses upon the theme, "Feelings as Related to Learning." Study this issue, but read "Classifying Feelings through Peer Interaction" by Hugh V. Perkins, and "Literature for Young Children" by Claudia Lewis. Report on these articles to your committee or class.

9. The January 1970 issue of *Childhood Education* includes an article by Gertrude M. Lewis entitled "I Am—I Want—I Need: Preadolescents Look at Themselves and Their Values" pages 186-194. This is a survey of health interests, concerns, and problems of 5,000 Connecticut students in selected schools from kindergarten through grade twelve. Some aspects surveyed included the general categories of "Understanding Others" and "Social Concern." Read this article and select some of the questions which these children asked. Tell how you might help to answer some of them through involvement with more multi-cultural literature.

10. Study some teaching suggestions offered by Jean Dresden Grambs in *Intergroup Education Methods and Materials* (Englewood Cliffs, New Jersey: Prentice Hall, 1968). Follow some of her suggestions and plan how you might do them. For instance, page 49 suggests the use of cameras by children in taking documentary pictures. This was done by Harlem youth and explained in the book by Charlotte S. Mayerson, *Two Blocks Apart* (New York: Holt, Rinehart and Winston, 1965).

11. Study a source like *The Music of Africa—An Introduction* by Dr. Fred Warren, with Lee Warren, art by Penelope Naylor (Englewood Cliffs, New Jersey: Prentice-Hall, 1970). See if you can obtain some recordings of African music and compare them with modern Soul or Pop music of the United States.

BIBLIOGRAPHY
BOOKS FOR PRIMARY CHILDREN

ALIKI. *A Weed is a Flower: The Life of George Washington Carver.* Englewood, Cliffs, New Jersey: Prentice-Hall, 1965.

CONE, MOLLIE. *Purim.* New York: Thomas Y. Crowell Company, 1967.

LAWRENCE, JACOB. *Harriet and the Promised Land.* New York: Simon & Schuster, Windmill Books, 1968.

WEIK, MARY HAYS. *The Jazz Man.* New York: Atheneum Publishers, 1966.

BOOKS FOR INTERMEDIATE CHILDREN

BURSTEIN, CHAYA M. *Rifka Bangs the Teakettle.* New York: Harcourt, Brace and World, 1970.

CHAPMAN, ABRAHAM, ed. *Steal Away: Stories of the Runaway Slaves.* New York: Praeger Publishers, 1971.

COATSWORTH, ELIZABETH. *The Cat Who Went to Heaven.* New York: Macmillan Company, 1931.

DIETZ, BETTY WARNER, and OLATUNJI, MICHAEL BABATUNDE. *Musical Instruments of Africa: Their Nature, Use, and Place in the Life of a Deeply Musical People.* New York: John Day Company, 1965.

HUGHES, LANGSTON. *The First Book of Rhythms.* New York: Franklin Watts, 1954.

———. *The First Book of Jazz.* New York: Franklin Watts, 1954.

JORDAN, JUNE. *Who Look at Me.* New York: Thomas Y. Crowell Company, 1969.

JORDAN, MILDRED. *Proud to be Amish.* New York: Crown Publishers, 1968.

KRIPKE, DOROTHY K. *Let's Talk About the Jewish Holidays.* New York: Jonathan David, 1970.

LAWSON, MARION. *Proud Warrior: The Story of Black Hawk.* New York: Hawthorn Books, 1968.

LESTER, JULIUS. *To Be a Slave.* New York: The Dial Press, 1968.

LEVIN, JEAN WHITBREAD. *Star of Danger.* New York: Harcourt, Brace & World, 1966.

MARK, POLLY. *The Way of the Wind.* New York: David McKay Company, 1965.

MILES, MISKA. *Hoagie's Rifle-Gun.* Boston: Atlantic Monthly Press; Little, Brown and Company, 1970.

MONTGOMERY, JEAN. *The Wrath of Coyote.* New York: William Morrow and Company, 1968.

PURDY, SUSAN GOLD. *Jewish Holidays: Facts, Activities and Crafts.* Philadelphia: J. P. Lippincott Co., 1969.

RAYMOND, CHARLES. *Up From Appalachia.* Chicago: Follett Publishing Company, 1966.

ROWLAND, FLORENCE WIGHTMAN. *Pasquala of Santa Ynes Mission.* New York: Henry Z. Walck, 1961.

SHOTWELL, LOUISA. *Roosevelt Grady.* New York: World Publishing Company, 1963.

SIMON, NORMA. *Hanukkah*. New York: Thomas Y. Crowell Company, 1967.

STERLING, DOROTHY. *Freedom Train: The Story of Harriet Tubman*. Garden City, New York: Doubleday & Company, 1954.

STERNE, EMMA GELDERS. *The Long Black Schooner: The Voyage of the Amistad*. Chicago: Follett Publishing Company, 1968.

TAYLOR, SYDNEY. *All-of-a-Kind-Family*. New York: Dell Publishing Company, a Yearling Book, 1966.

————. *More All-of-a-Kind-Family*. New York: Dell Publishing Company, a Yearling Book, 1966.

————. *A Papa Like Everyone Else*. Chicago: Follett Publishing Company, 1966.

TURKLE, BRINTON. *Thy Friend Obadiah*. New York: Viking Press, 1969.

UCHIDA, YOSHIKO. *In-Between Miya*. New York: Charles Scribner's Sons, 1967.

WEINER, SANDRA. *It's Wings That Make Birds Fly: The Story of a Boy*. New York: Random House, Pantheon Books, 1968.

WINDERS, GERTRUDE H. *Harriet Tubman: Freedom Girl*. Indianapolis: Bobbs-Merrill Co., 1969.

BOOKS FOR ADOLESCENTS

BELZ, CARL. *The Story of Rock*. New York: Oxford University Press, 1969.

BHARATI, AGEHANANDA. *The Ochre Robe*. New York: Doubleday & Company, 1969.

CATHER, WILLA. "The Shimeradas." In *The Outnumbered: Stories, Essays, and Poems about Minority Groups by America's Leading Writers*, edited by Charlotte Brooks. New York: Delacorte Press, 1967.

CHAMBERS, BRADFORD, comp. and ed. *Chronicles of Negro Protest: A Background Book for Young People Documenting the History of Black Power*. New York: Parents Magazine Press, 1968.

CLARK, LEON E., ed. *Coming of Age in Africa: Continuity and Change*. Through African Eyes: Cultures in Change, unit 1 and Lesson Plans. New York: Praeger Publishers, 1969.

————. *From Tribe to Town: Problems of Adjustment*. Through African Eyes: Cultures in Change, unit 2 and Lesson Plans. New York: Praeger Publishers, 1969.

COMINS, JEREMY. *Getting Started in African Crafts*. New York: Bruce Publishing Company, 1971.

DAHL, MARY B. *Free Souls*. Boston: Houghton Mifflin Company, 1969.

ELGIN, KATHLEEN. *The Quakers, The Religious Society of Friends*. New York: David McKay Co., 1969.

————. *The Mormons: The Church of Jesus Christ of Latter-Day Saints*. New York: David McKay Co., 1969.

GARLAN, PATRICIA WALLACE, and DUNSTAN, MARYJANE. *Orange-Robed Boy*. New York: Viking Press, 1967.

GLASS, PAUL. *Singing Soldiers: A History of the Civil War in Song*. Rev. ed. New York: Grosset and Dunlap, 1968.

GRAHAM, SHIRLEY, and LIPSCOMB, GEORGE D. *Dr. George Washington Carver, Scientist*. New York: Julian Messner, 1944. Also available in paperback, New York: Washington Square Press, 1969.

HENTOFF, NAT. *Jazz Country*. New York: Harper and Row, Publishers, 1965.

HUNT, IRENE. *No Promises in the Wind*. Chicago: Follett Publishing Company, 1970.

JONES, LEROI. *Blues People: Negro Music in White America*. New York: William Morrow and Company, 1968.

JORDAN, JUNE. *Who Look at Me*. New York: Thomas Y. Crowell Company, 1969.

KAYIRA, LEGSON. *I Will Try*. New York: Doubleday & Company, 1965.

LAWSON, MARION. *Proud Warrior: The Story of Black Hawk*. New York: Hawthorn Books, 1968.

LAYE, CAMARA. *The Dark Child*. New York: Farrar, Straus & Giroux, 1954.

LENGYEL, EMIL. *Asoka the Great: Indian's Royal Missionary*. New York: Franklin Watts, 1969.

LESTER, JULIUS. *To Be A Slave*. New York: The Dial Press, 1968.

LEVIN, JEAN WHITBREAD. *Star of Danger*. New York: Harcourt, Brace & World, 1966.

MELTZER, MILTON, ed. *In Their Own Words: A History of the American Negro, 1916-1966*. New York: Thomas Y. Crowell Co., 1967.

————. *Bread and Roses: The Struggle of American Labor, 1865-1915*. New York: Alfred A. Knopf, 1967.

MONTGOMERY, JEAN. *The Wrath of Coyote*. New York: William Morrow and Company, 1968.

MOORE, CARMEN. *Somebody's Angel Child: The Story of Bessie Smith*. New York: Thomas Y. Crowell Company, 1969.

MCPHERSON, JAMES M. *Marching Toward Freedom: The Negro in the Civil War, 1861-1865*. New York: Alfred A. Knopf, 1968.

NEIHARDT, JOHN G. [Flaming Rainbow]. *Black Elk Speaks: Being the Life Story of a Holy Man of the Oglala Sioux*. Lincoln, Nebraska: University of Nebraska Press, 1961.

PETRY, ANNE. *Harriet Tubman, Conductor of the Underground Railway*. New York: Thomas Y. Crowell Company, 1955.

ROBERTS, BRUCE and NANCY. *Where Time Stood Still: A Portrait of Appalachia*. New York: Crowell-Collier and Macmillan, 1970.

ROSE, KAREL. *A Gift of the Spirit: Readings in Black Literature for Teachers*. New York: Holt, Rinehart & Winston, 1971.

SANDERLIN, GEORGE. *Across the Ocean Sea: A Journal of Columbus's Voyages*. New York: Harper and Row, Publishers, 1966.

SERAGE, NANCY. *The Prince Who Gave Up the Throne: A Story of the Buddha*. New York: Thomas Y. Crowell Company, 1966.

SEUBERLICH, HERTHA. *Annuzza, A Girl of Romania*. Chicago: Rand McNally and Company, 1962.

SHULL, PEG. *Children of Appalachia*. New York: Julian Messner, 1969.

SINGER, ISAAC BASHEVIS. *A Day of Pleasure: Stories of a Boy Growing Up in Warsaw*. New York: Farrar, Straus and Giroux, 1969.

STERNE, EMMA GELDERS. *The Long Black Schooner: The Voyage of the Amistad*. Chicago: Follett Publishing Co., 1968.

SULLY, FRANCOIS. *Age of the Guerrilla: The New Warfare*. New York: Parents Magazine Press, 1968.

TAYLOR, SYDNEY. *A Papa Like Everyone Else*. Chicago: Follett Publishing Company, 1966.

THOMAS, HENRY. *George Washington Carver*. New York: G. P. Putnam's Sons, 1958.

TRIPP, ELEANOR. *To America*. New York: Harcourt, Brace & World, 1969.

TUESDAY MAGAZINE. *Black Heroes in World History*. New York: Bantam Books, Bantam Pathfinder Editions, 1969.

VIERICK, PHILLIP, comp. and ed. *The New Land: Discovery, Exploration, and Early Settlement of Northeastern United States, from Earliest Voyages to 1621*. New York: The John Day Company, 1967.

VOSS, CARL HERMANN. *In Search of Meaning: Living Religions of the World*. New York: World Publishing Company, 1968.

WARREN, FRED, and WARREN, LEE. *The Music of Africa: An Introduction*. Englewood Cliffs, New Jersey: Prentice-Hall, 1970.

PROFESSIONAL BOOKS AND BOOKS FOR ADULTS

AMERICAN FRIENDS SERVICE COMMISSION (QUAKERS) and ANTI-DEFAMATION LEAGUE OF B'NAI B'RITH. *Books for Friendship*, a List of Books Recommended for Children, Fourth edition, "Books are Bridges," American Friends Service Committee, 160 North 15th Street, Philadelphia, Pennsylvania 19102; Anti-Defamation League of B'nai B'rith, 315 Lexington Avenue, New York, New York 10016.

D'AMATO, JANET and ALEX. *African Crafts for You to Make*. New York: Julian Messner, a division of Simon and Schuster, 1969, p. 8.

FAUST, HELEN F. "Books As An Aid in Preventing Dropouts." *Elementary English* 46 (February 1969): 191-198.

GLAZER, TOM. *A New Treasury of Folk Songs*. New York: Bantam Books, 1964.

HAUFRECHT, HERBERT, ed. *Round the World Folk Sing*. New York: Berkeley Publishing Corporation, Berkeley Medallian Books, 1968.

HAYWARD UNIFIED SCHOOL DISTRICT. *Intergroup Education—A Guide for Human Understanding*. Kindergarten-Sixth Grade Level. 25377 Huntwood Avenue, Hayward, California 94544. Rapid Printing Lithographers, 1969.

HAYWOOD, CHARLES. *Folk Songs of the New World*. New York: Bantam Books, a subsidiary of Grosset & Dunlap, 1968. Gathered from more than one hundred countries, selected and edited, with commentary on their musical cultures and descriptive notes on each song; in the original languages with English translations, with chord suggestions for instrumental accompaniment.

MARTIN, CHRISTOPHER. *The Amistad Affair*. New York: Abelard-Schuman, 1970.

MELTZER, MILTON, ed. *In Their Own Words: A History of the American Negro, 1916-1966*. New York: Thomas Y. Crowell Company, 1967.

MILLER, MARILYN, and MERRITT, HARRIET D. "A Fourth Grade Compares a Japanese Folktale." *Childhood Education* 45 (February 1969): 329-332.

MONTI, FRANCO. *African Masks*. London, England: Paul Hamlyn, 1968.

NETTL, BRUNO. *Folk and Traditional Music of the Western Continents*. Englewood Cliffs, New Jersey, 1965.

ROSE, KAREL. *A Gift of the Spirit: Readings in Black Literature for Teachers*. New York: Holt, Rinehart & Winston, 1971.

TABA, HILDA; BRADY, ELIZABETH HALL; ROBINSON, JOHN T.; and VICKERY, WILLIAM E. *Diagnosing Human Relations Needs*. Washington, D.C.: American Council on Education, 1958.

ZBOROWSKI, MARK, and HERZOG, ELIZABETH. *Life Is With People: The Culture of the Shtetl*. New York: Schocken Books, 1969.

PART TWO

Toward
More
Humane
Persons

CHAPTER FOUR

The
African Link
of Literary
Experience:
Some Ways to
Develop
Cultural
Understanding

Introduction

Much Afro-American literature has strands stretching back to various countries of Africa which lead toward the present experiences of black people living in the pluralistic society of the United States. Sometimes, parts of African cultural traditions and literary ideas migrate to the Caribbean Islands, South America, and the United States and take new patterns in a different setting. Frequently, Afro-American novels, short stories, and poems have settings in Africa as well as in certain states in the United States. In many instances, a study of African literature offers an edge of awareness to the interpretation of the problems, experiences, and visions of black persons living in ghetto regions such as Watts or Harlem, on the rural farms of a Southern state, or in urban areas where black people are struggling to find their identity in the mechanized, technological, urban cities of the United States.

Afro-American literature being discussed in this chapter will include the African folk tales, novels, short stories, nonfiction books about African

73

music, art, and dance, books about the current political and geographical African scene, and poetry by African poets.

The African Folktale

Black folktales seem to have four streams or tributaries. Some African folktales are indigenous to various countries of the African continent. Other African stories are transported to one of the Caribbean Islands and are altered somewhat in their new setting. A third type of folk tale is more original to the plantation areas of the United States and shows little resemblance to the content or style of a typical African story. A fourth type of black folktale is one related by raconteurs in urban ghettos such as those in Harlem or the South Side of Chicago.

The African folk tale is the source of much African literature being written currently. These African folktales are a part of the heritage of Afro-Americans living in the United States who look across the waters to an African country as the source of their culture. Feldman has said that nearly a quarter of a million stories have circulated in countries of the African continent south of the Sahara; by 1938 about five thousand of these different tales had been recorded. Numerous African tales feature a highly humanized animal trickster, such as the spider in *Anansi the Spider*[1], who is often the principal hero under various names in West African folk tales told in gatherings on the Gold Coast, Ivory Coast, Sierra Leone, Liberia, Togoland, Dahomey, Hausa, Yoruba, Warry Fiort, Cameroons, Congo, and Angola.[2] Hare is also a well-known culture hero in East Africa among the Jukun and Angan of Nigeria. The tortoise is an example of another popular animal figure in tales of the Yoruba, the Edo, and the Ibo of Nigeria.[3]

Some of these African folktales with trickster figures have been transported to the islands of the Caribbean and then have later been dispersed to the plantations of the United States where the hare becomes Brer Rabbit in such collections as those made by Joel Chandler Harris.

Other black folk tales seem to be indigenous to the former plantation locales of the southern states of the United States. Here imaginative raconteurs originated Old Marster stories on the plantations which were later retold in Northern cities and farms as Negroes travelled northward for freedom and better employment opportunities. Most of these tales were ones about Old Marster, talking parrots, preachers, and colored folk who

1. Susan Feldman, ed., *African Myths and Tales* (New York: Dell Publishing, 1963).
2. *Ibid.*, p. 14.
3. *Ibid.*

were slyly innocent.[4] Currently, many tales of this type are appearing in collections published by such folklorists as J. Mason Brewer and Richard M. Dorson.

A fourth stream of oral folktale is one created by dwellers in urban ghettos. These include sophisticated elements of social protest and jests about race relations. Roger D. Abrahams in his narrative folklore from South Philadelphia entitled *Deep Down in the Jungle* records this type of story. Here appear obscene jokes, rhymed toasts, and dialects heard in poolrooms, dives, and slum buildings. According to Dorson, Brer Rabbit has been transformed into a "fast-talking, sporty hipster" in such ghettos as Harlem, Watts, the South Side of Chicago and other similar metropolitan ghettos.[5]

African Folktales and Myths

In her introduction to *African Myths and Tales,* Feldman indicates that cunning is the principal virtue of an African hero and that the trickster episodes appear in myths, fairy tales, and realistic stories, as well as in animal tales. These tales provide more than entertainment for a village child. They include sacred myths and stories as well as moral and explanatory tales. Feldman states that Bush Negroes told Spider stories to the dead during the seven days in which the body lay in the village death house prior to burial. In some Yoruba tales, the god Eshu was similar to the trickster tortoise. In these stories animals were transformed into men and gods, and vice versa. Sometimes the animal trickster was a god or man who usually had control of a situation and could manipulate events to his own advantage. The victim of the trickster was always larger and stronger, but he was usually slower-witted. Sometimes a trickster hero showed great cunning. In a Kru tale, when Noyomo was ordered by the king to weave a mat of rice grains, he asked for a mat of the same type for a pattern. When Turtle was asked to carry water in a basket, he asked for a carrying strap of smoke. Feldman points out that a fairy tale hero usually accomplished an impossible task with supernatural aid, but an African trickster hero operated in a real world where he substituted his clever cheating for magic.

Perhaps one of the most prominent humanized animal tricksters is Anansi, a character who frequently overcomes force with cunning. This quality of cleverness gives a young child a respect for the abilities of his

---

4. Richard M. Dorson, comp., *American Negro Folktales* (Greenwich, Connecticut: Fawcett Publishing Co., a Fawcett Premier Book, 1967), p. 18.
5. *Ibid.*

ancestors and a feeling that a Negro can succeed by using his wits as well as his muscles. Anansi the Spider is the trickster character. He is the principal figure in many West African folktales and is known by different names in the folklore of the Gold Coast, and in many other sections of West Africa.

Several of the Anansi tales have been recorded as oral and literary folk tales for children. *The Hat Shaking Dance and Other Tales from the Gold Coast* by Harold Courlander, with Albert Kofi Prempeh, has a title story referring to a wild dance which Anansi* performed when he wanted to disguise his greediness by hiding a pot of hot beans under his hat; this is one of the reasons that all spiders are bald. It is thought that many Anansi tales came from the Ashanti people of the Gold Coast of Africa.

Another version of these Ashanti tales is *Ananse the Spider: Tales from An Ashanti Village* by Peggy Appiah. Peggy Appiah, while living in Kumasi, the capital of Ashanti, originally asked her husband to tell these tales so that they could be enjoyed by their four children. The artist, Peggy Wilson, derived her drawings of birds, beasts, insects and humans from some of the brass weights designed and cast by the Ashanti for the weighing of gold dust. This volume has a different version about the baldness of the spider which is explained in "How Kwaku Ananse Became Bald." The spider is caught plundering the crops belonging to his neighbors; so he is forced to pour boiling palm oil over his head, and all of his hairs come out.

A single tale, *A Story A Story,* is about Kwaku Ananse, or Spider Man, and has been retold and beautifully illustrated by Gail E. Haley. This is another version of a popular tale showing how Ananse the Spider Man succeeded in buying all of the Sky God's stories from Nyame, the Sky God. In this version of the tale, the price of the stories was the capture of Osabo, the leopard-of-the-terrible-teeth; Momboro, the hornet who stings like fire; and Mmoatia, the fairy whom-men-never-see. A good version of these spider stories is *The Adventures of Spider* by Joyce Cooper Arkhurst, which includes variants of many of the spider tales previously mentioned.

Other animal characters which are favorite ones in African oral folk tales are ones of the hare and tortoise. According to Feldman the hare is better known among the Jukun and Angan of Nigeria, and the tortoise is a favorite character related in tales of the Yoruba, Edo and Ibo of Nigeria, and in other places in East Africa.

Some of these stories about Hare as well as ones about other East African animals appear in *Jambo Sungura: Tales from East Africa* by Eleanor B. Heady. In the eastern part of Africa, Sungura the Hare is

*This word is spelled as Anansi and Ananse in different books of African folk tales.

similar to Brer Rabbit, since stories about Sungura are frequently related there. The Hare is also a trickster character who steals some honey from the elephant, uses trickery to get fish from the otter and badger, and out-wits Simba, the lion. In "The Scarecrow" one sees one version of Brer Rabbit and Tar Baby. The author, Eleanor B. Heady, has also written another collection of East African tales entitled *When the Stones Were Soft: East African Fireside Tales.* This volume includes some stories fre-quently told in such portions of East Africa as Kenya, Uganda, and Tanzania.

Another variant of the favorite Tar Baby stories appears in *The Dancing Palm Tree and Other Nigerian Folk Tales,* as retold by Barbara Walker. These tales were related to the author by a Nigerian student, Olawale Idewu. The title story of this volume, "The Dancing Palm Tree," is principally about Tortoise, who finds an easy way of gathering food from the villagers by frightening them with a dancing palm tree and magic words. Finally, the king calls an old wise man who fashions a *sigidi,* a seated image of a man from clay, and paints it with a sticky substance known as *amo.* Tortoise becomes curious about this silent creature and slaps it so hard that his hands and feet are stuck.

Another volume of folk tales featuring stories about rabbits, ant-bears, tortoises, shrews, leopards, spiders, jackals, and water buffalos is entitled *Where the Leopard Passes: A Book of African Folktales* by Geraldine Elliott. One of the popular characters in this collection of tales is Kalulu the Rabbit, who bears some resemblance to Brer Rabbit. In the first tale the Rabbit's wife and the Leopardess have a dispute about their husbands and Kalulu's wife brags that Kalulu is brave, clever, and hand-some. Here again the trickster rabbit and his wife use red earth and white clay with turaco feathers to frighten Nyalugwe, the leopard. An-other collection by the same author is *The Long Grass Whispers: A Book of African Folktales.* Here one meets the African Brer Rabbit, Kalulu, again in such stories as "The Iguana who was always Right,". Children are introduced also to another trickster character, Kamba the Tortoise, in such stories as "The Tortoise and the Hyena," and "The Well." The Tortoise is almost as cunning and unpredictable as Kalulu the Rabbit.

Other tales from Nigeria appear in *Olode the Hunter and Other Tales from Nigeria* by Harold Courlander, with Ezekiel A. Eshugbayi. This col-lection of stories comes from the Yoruba people of Nigeria, as well as from the Ibo and Hausa. Some counterparts of these same tales appear in Asian, American, and European literature. Ijapa the Tortoise, is some-times a hero and at other times a villain. He frequently appears in Ameri-can Negro folklore as Brother Terrapin.

Another collection of traditional African stories is *Tales of Temba* by Kathleen Arnott, who has adapted many traditional stories of the Bantu-speaking persons. These tales have been retold by using the name of Temba for the hero in each case and by arranging them in a sequential order from boyhood to manhood. In the story "The Yam Child" one learns about the almost Herculean tasks which Temba has to perform before he arrives at the palace of Puwa. Some other stories from the area, formerly known as the Belgian Congo but now known as the Republic of the Congo, appear in *Congo Fireside Tales* by Phyllis Savory. Additional tales from Central Africa appear in *The Magic Drum: Tales from Central Africa* by W. F. P. Burton. Fables in this collection are animal characters usually endowed with human characteristics; so there is Gulungu, a trustworthy bushbuck; Nge, a crafty leopard; Penge, a kindly warthog; and Kalulu, a sly, trickster rabbit who appears in numerous other folktales. In a preface to this volume, the author says that Congo native parents prepared children for adult life by teaching them stories around campfires. Here children learned about their responsibilities to their community and gained an accurate knowledge of trees, animals, and insects of the forest. The tribal young ones also learned some of the elements of geography, tribal history, medicine, handicrafts, and other areas of knowledge through these tales.

In Luban villages the *balute,* or "men of memory," were the historians of the village who often related two or three hundred years of Luban history telling about wars, certain tribal customs, tribal boundaries, migrations of the people, and changes. Some of the wise men used proverbs effectively. In law cases, an orator sometimes gave the first part of a proverb and listeners supplied the answers. The significance of proverbs in African tribal life is seen in *African Proverbs* compiled by Charlotte and Wolf Leslau. In this colorful little volume are used such proverbs as the Ashanti ones, "The poor man and the rich man do not play together;"[6] one from Somalia, "A Coward is full of precaution"[7]; and one from Uganda, on page 59 of this book is "A roaring lion kills no game."

Burton states that a Luban child of twelve is able to distinguish between two hundred different trees, and can give the uses of their leaves, bark, fruit, woods, and roots. He can also recognize most of the birds both by sight and song. He can depict accurately the habits of most common animals in his environment and can also take care of different diseases through the use of native remedies. Of course he also learns the proper time for sowing and harvesting of the various crops grown by his people. His contact with learning incorporated in fireside stories helps to prepare him for his life activities.

Verna Aardema has published a few African folktales in *Tales for the Third Ear from Equatorial Africa*. The Hausa storyteller asks his audience

6. Charlotte and Walf Leslau, *African Proverbs* (Mount Vernon, New York: Peter Pauper Press, 1962), p. 7.
7. *Ibid.,* p. 13.

to add a third ear and listen to what he has to tell. Trickster spider Ananse appears here again in the story "Ananse and the King's Cow." Verna Aardema also published *Tales from the Story Hat,* a popular book of folk-tales for young listeners.

Edythe Rance Haskett has collected and edited *Grains of Pepper: Folktales from Liberia,* and has illustrated her own book in beautiful paintings under the name of Musu Miatta, a name given her by Liberian school girls when she was teaching in West Africa in an Episcopal High School in Robertsport, Liberia. *Grains of Pepper* includes animal tales, or fables, in which animals are given the faults and virtues of humans; riddle tales which give a chance for audience participation; tales of "frisky" spirits; and ones of warriors, kings, and hunters who lived in the village at earlier times. Another similar book by the same author is *Some Gold, a Little Ivory: Country Tales from Ghana and the Ivory Coast.*

A recent book of West African tales is *Animals Mourn for Da Leopard, and other West African Tales,* retold by Peter G. Dorliae, Paramount Chief of the Yarwin-Mehnsonoh, Chieftain of Lower Nimba County, Liberia. Old Man Spider in these tales is a scoundrel also.

An earlier collection of tales by Harold Courlander and Wolf Leslau is "The Fire on the Mountain and Other Ethiopian Stories." Ethiopian tales include cultural ideas from the Middle East, Africa, and the West. Some of these have similar types in Moslem-Africa, Arabia, and India; others are similar to stories told in central and western Europe. Most of these stories are told around campfires but are transported by cattle herders, traders, and camel caravans. Here again principal characters may be animals or men, and many stories are like fables revealing the vanities and weaknesses of human beings. The hare, the jackal, and the monkey often cleverly defend themselves against the power of the lions and ele-phants. The story "The Fire on the Mountain" tells how a wise man helps Arha to win his bet against Haptom Hasei, who bets that Arha could not stand naked all night without food, drink, blankets, or clothing.

African Village Folktales by Edna Mason Kaula is a book which is organized differently from many other collections. Twenty tales collected from the Bushmen of the Kalahari Desert, the Hausa of West Africa, the Amhara of Ethiopia, the Zulas of South Africa, and others are included. Many stories similar to Aesop's fables or Brer Rabbit offer morals. These tales are told in the style of a fable, but African animals are used, such a Lion and Honey Badger, Warthog and Hornbill, Kalulu the Hare, and others. Kaula supplies an introduction to each tale by giv-ing a description of the people from whom she heard the story and some-thing about their village and customs.

Three volumes of tales for older pupils are René Guillot's *African Folktales, Tales Told Near a Crocodile* by Humphrey Harmon, and

African Folktales by Jessie Alford Nunn. Guillot collected the folk tales in his book during the twenty years that he lived in West Africa. The shorter tales are similar to ones in other collections telling how one man outwits the others. These story fables also include such characters as the clever hare, the unintelligent hyena, or the trickster spider. Some of the longer tales are almost legends in that man faces problems larger than himself. "Aziza" is an African story of creation telling how Aziza descends from the heavens and uses his hands as a potter to fashion a new animal each day, such as a crawling worm, a dragonfly, a porcupine, a lizard, and a frog. "The Caravan that Was Crushed" is a beautifully written story about Nila, Nita, and Nika and the dwarves who fashion gold for their master, the Devil.

The book *Tales Told Near a Crocodile: Stories from Lake Nyanza* consists of stories told by people of six African tribes living near Lake Victoria, which is a coastline for Kenya, Uganda, and Tanzania. Hundreds of islands dot this lake and are populated with snakes, fish, birds, and crocodiles.

The book *African Folk Tales* by Nunn offers a list of Swahili words such as *baraza* for "a lengthy discussion," *manyatta* for "a homestead consisting of huts and animal pens," and *ngoma* for "a festival or celebration." She speaks of the Mzees, or tellers of tales, who created stories for children so that they could learn many things.

Single Folktales

Several folktales for young children are being issued as a single tale. For instance *Crocodile and Hen* is a tale from Bokongo, Africa retold by Joan M. Lexau, with pictures by Joan Sandin. Another story with this format is *Beeswax Catches a Thief,* from a Congo folktale, which has been written and illustrated by Ann Kirn. This is a story of a trickster jackal that outwits other animals of this type at the water hole but is caught by beeswax on the shell of a turtle. A third tale which is wonderful for group participation is *The Clever Turtle,* adapted and illustrated by A. K. Roche. In this story the turtle has crushed the corn, and people decide different punishments for it, but the turtle keeps begging, "please do not throw me in the river," and this is exactly what the turtle wants. This tale could easily be dramatized spontaneously as creative drama, or it could be a puppet play using stick puppets.

Terry Berger has adapted her *Black Fairy Tales* from *Fairy Tales from South Africa* by E. J. Bourhill and J. B. Drake. These stories differ somewhat from others as they are mostly about princes and princesses and kings and queens who live in the open kraals and dress in animal skins and colored beads. Most of the stories are about people who lived in the South Africa of long ago and the different black peoples discussed are the Swazi, Shangoni, and Msuto.

The Chain of Folktales

Some African folktales are original, and have been related around the camp fires or in the dense forests of Africa. As black persons were seized as indentured workers and slaves, they brought their tales with them to Haiti, Jamaica, and other islands of the Caribbean, and then such stories came to Louisiana, Georgia, and other Southern states as black people moved as a labor force to different geographical and cultural areas. Harold Courlander has collected twenty-six island tales in *The Piece of Fire and Other Haitian Tales.* Most of the Haitian folklore consists of tales, legends, and *cantes fables,* the latter being a narrative form interspersed with songs. These tales are hybrids of European, African, and Haitian creations. Some of the stories can be traced to Nigeria, Dahomey, and other West African sites, but they were altered considerably in a new locale. In these stories, Ti Malice inherited the canny ways of Ananse, and Bouki was the one who was boastful, greedy, hungry, foolish, and often ineffective. In some locales a story chief is called a *maitconte;* in other places he is a *samba.* The narrator dramatizes his story. He impersonates characters, mimicks actions, and moves around with gestures. Frequently a teller of tales says "crick!" Listeners say "crack," and the story begins. A formula ending might often be, "Wire Bend" and all who listen reply "Story end."[8]

Sir Philip Sherlock has created *The Iguana's Tail: Crick Crack Stories from the Caribbean.* Most of these tales are animal stories which are partially fables in which animals speak and act like human beings. Some of these stories come from West Africa; others were created in the islands of the Caribbean, and a few of them are versions of European tales, such as ones about Cinderella or Bluebeard. "Chimpanzee's Story" has many of the qualities of Turtle or Tortoise stories told in Cambodia, Laos, and Vietnam. In this story, as well as in many other versions, Tortoise once had a highly polished back which was admired by the other animals and birds, but he wanted desperately to fly and spent his time storing cast-off feathers in his cupboard. Finally, one day when Chicken Hawk gave his party, Tortoise flew off with the flying birds to the party. Tortoise was an impolite guest; so the birds took back their feathers and Chicken Hawk pushed Tortoise to the bottom of the mountain where his beautiful

8. Sir Philip Sherlock. *The Iguana's Tail: Crick Crack Stories from the Caribbean* (New York: Thomas Y. Crowell Co., 1969), p. 3.

mirror-like shell was scratched. A book of stories from Haiti which includes "The Singing Turtle," another tale about this wily animal, is *The Singing Turtle and Other Tales from Haiti* by Philippe Thoby Marcelin and Pierre Marcelin.

Richard M. Dorson feels that many black folktales are original ones created by Negroes in the United States and do not necessarily come from Africa. Most oral narratives of Negroes were created in Southern plantations during slavery days and travelled to the North by migrating story tellers. In 1880 some of these oral tales became available through the publications of Joel Chandler Harris in *Uncle Remus: His Songs and His Sayings.* In early days Uncle Remus was an elderly plantation slave who entertained the white boy of the house with his Brer Rabbit stories. Dorson discusses some of the scholarly work of two Negro folklore collectors. Zora Neale Hurston collected tales in Middle Georgia, and J. Mason Brewer gathered stories mostly in North and South Carolina and on the Brazos bottoms of East Texas. Dorson concludes that a repertoire of Negro tales comes through two main streams. One points toward Africa, the Atlantic and the Caribbean Islands, and northeastern South America; the other one points to Europe and the Anglo-Americas. These consist mostly of stories told in the plantation states of the South. All of these stories, however, come from many sources.

J. Mason Brewer has published a large volume, *American Negro Folklore,* which includes tales, sermons, and prayers about the Negro's religion, his songs (including spirituals, folk blues, and slave, secular, and work songs), stories of personal experiences, and other items of folklore such as superstitions, proverbs, rhymes, riddles, and games. Another similar book, edited by Langston Hughes and Arna Bontemps, is *The Book of Negro Folklore.* These authors indicate that over three hundred versions of the "Tar Baby" story have been traced to different sources. Brer Rabbit was lacking in physical power, but according to Hughes and Bontemps he was a "practical joker, a braggart, a wit, a glutton, a lady's man, and a trickster."

Two poetic versions of the Brer Rabbit story by Ennis Rees are *Brer Rabbit and His Tricks* and *More of Brer Rabbit's Tricks.* Both of these books are cleverly illustrated by Edward Gorey. These little books are planned for young children, but the rhyme is so humorous and clever that most adults enjoy them also.

Mythology for More Mature Readers

Some myths of Africa should probably be related to the mythology of other countries, such as the stories created about man and the universe by the Greeks, Romans, and Scandinavians. Almost all people of the world have wondered about their origins, the beginning of the earth, and the origins of life and death. Ulli Beier has edited an anthology *The Origin of Life and Death: African Creation Myths.* Some of the myths in this collection, such as "Why the Sky Is Far Away," are simple enough to be told or read by young children. This Bini story of Nigeria tells about a world when the sky lived close to the earth and man merely snipped off a bit of the sky and ate it when he was hungry. Then man became too wasteful, cut off more than he could eat, and left big heaps of rubbish. The sky grew angry and warned man that he would move far away as he kept on being so greedy. A selfish woman did not heed the warning. She cut off a huge piece of sky and wasted a lot of it. Then the sky moved way above the earth and man had to work hard tilling the ground for food, all because he was too greedy.

Some of the stories, such as "The Woman Who Tried to Change Her Fate" and "How Moon Fathered the World," are too complicated and mature for younger children and should probably be read by sophisticated secondary pupils who are comparing the myths of various peoples of the world.

A second collection of African mythological tales is *African Mythology* by Geoffrey Parrinder. This includes numerous myths and legends of various African countries with photographs of sculpted and carved figures which were created to depict the tales. For instance, a picture is shown of the unique double antelope headdresses of the Bambara of Mali who performed rites reenacting the myths of the birth of Agriculture. A carved wooden dance mask of the Senufo people of the Ivory Coast shows a cameleon and a hornbill on a head. The cameleon is a creature which is often featured in African myths.

African Folktales and Sculptures, one of the Bollingen Series, includes a large collection of folktales selected and edited by Paul Radin. These include such tales as "How Spider Obtained the Sky-God's Stories," an Ashanti myth; "How the Stars Came" by the Ekoi, and "Why There are Cracks in Tortoise's Shell" by the Baila. This is a wonderful collection of myths categorized under The Universe and Its Beginnings, The Animal and His World, The Realm of Man, and Man and His Fate. African sculpted pieces illustrate the volume. A separate collection of these myths and folktales also appears under separate cover.

Poems of Africa

From ancient times primitive man has sung his songs of life about the significance of the world which was close to him. In Volume 1 of his scholarly study of primitive poetry entitled *The Unwritten Song: Poetry of the Primitive and Traditional Peoples of the World,* Willard R. Trask includes many oral poems of Africa. Most of the traditional poetry of these early poets was sung as a poet created his words. Often gestures, pantomimes, physical movements, or dance correlated with poetic rhymes and rhythms; in Madagascar in 1686 everyone, even children, composed their own songs. Sometimes songs or poems were created as herdsmen tended their cattle. Youths praised their kinsmen's sweethearts and cattle, and sang a poem of happiness and beauty.

Several African songs and poems can be expressed in choral speech. For instance, the Masai of Kenya have some verses, "Women's Song for Fighting Men Delayed on a Raid," in which a solo voice shouts the word "Tear out" one or two times in different stanzas and the chorus replies, "The brand-marks of the people!"[9] The expression "tear out the brand marks" refers to the power of an enemy.

3000 Years of Black Poetry, edited by Alan Lomax and Raoul Abdul, is a noteworthy anthology which places black poetry of the United States within the setting of world-wide black poetry. This volume also puts such poetry in the cultural context of world history. The authors delineate Negroes who have played a significant part in the cultural and political history of the world: Terence (Terentius Africanus), who was an African slave in Rome, was an innovator of polite comedy; Alexander Pushkin, the mulatto poet and playwright of Russia who influenced the works of Moliere, spoke bravely for liberty and justice at a time of Russian autocracy and tyranny; Alexander Dumas, the son of the black Haitian general, was creator of the duelist figure D'Artagnan modelled after his brave father. Dumas was one of the most prolific writers of all time. It is estimated that he wrote over twelve hundred books and plays, and many more articles for newspapers.[10]

This anthology *3000 Years of Black Poetry* commences with the primitive song of the Gabon Pigmy. Any one of a Pigmy band could commence a song and each person contributed a part; hence pigmy songs were improvised and had a complex counterpoint. Pygmies* mastered both song and dance and entertained the pharaohs of Egypt. "Song for the Sun that Disappeared Behind the Rainclouds" was created by a Hottentot and translated by Ulli Beier. The Susu in "The Sweetest Thing" spoke of the sweetness of sleep. A Twi song, "Prelude to Akwasidae," is written in

9. "Women's Song for Fighting Men Delayed on a Raid," by the Masai of Kenya from *The Unwritten Song: Poetry of the Primitive and Traditional Peoples of the World,* vol. 1. Compiled by Willard R. Trask (New York: The Macmillan Company, 1966), p. 95.
10. Alan Lomax and Raoul Abdul, eds., *3000 Years of Black Poetry* (New York: Dodd, Mead & Company, 1970), p. 64.

*These authors spell this as Pigmy and also as Pygmies; p. 1.

the newer style of concrete poetry, a style in which the visual arrangement of phrases enhances the aural rhythms of the words. This prelude of Akwasidae speaks of the drummer and drum at the festival which pays homage to a chief and pours libations for the gods.

An introduction to this volume tells about the origin of *mutima,* or heart, and the sense that every person has a heart that "longs for and searches after God." Man longs for a oneness with the universe. The African tradition of poetry is a praise song. Each of the early African hymns lists the powers and deeds of a diety which "controls the natural order of things." The poet recites its names and characteristics, and summons it to life. In black Africa some of the ancient poetry becomes a unification of poetry, magic, and religion as poets entreat their gods to come to the dancing floor. Many poems created by African poets frequently allude to myths. Such allusions usually illuminate the significance of the poetic lines.

These authors point out that African religion humanizes death. Ancestors watch over the African and return to join him in feasting and dance. Poetry is in praise of things around the poet, and the ebb and flow of life—that is, the realities of birth and death, of planting and harvest, and of the male and female—is a vital part of life and poetry.

Lomax and Abdul state that "hot rhythm or polymeter means that two or more contrastive meters, two directions, two moods—one male, one female" are working together in the same musical framework, pulling against one another in combination and in conflict.[11] One of the books which clarifies some of the myths of the Yoruba people and includes a few poetic passages is *Orisha: The Gods of Yorubaland* by Judith Gleason. Much black poetry has a "sexually freighted rhythmic style" characterizing African music and poetry, and shaping the African tradition from the verse of the black Arab Antar to the poetry of LeRoi Jones.

This anthology by Lomax and Abdul offers contributions of black authors ranging from Antar of the Arab world, who created *The Romance of Antar* and stated that the worthy man should make love and verse, to Valinte Goenha Malangatana, whose poems appeared in *Black Orpheus.* His poem, "Woman," is included in this anthology, translated by Dorothy Guedes and Philippa Rumsey. The latter part of the volume is entitled "U.S.A." It traces poetry in the United States from the oral traditional, such as "I Vision God" (A Folk Sermon) from *Jonah's Gourd Vine* by Z. N. Hurston, to a concluding poem by Victor Hernandez Cruz, a Puerto Rican who grew up in New York City. He wrote "Today Is a Great Day of Joy," a poem which shouts for the power of poetry, a poetry which will "choke politicians" and knock down many walls.

11. Lomax and Abdul, *op. cit.,* p. xxiv.

Poems from Black Africa, an anthology edited by Langston Hughes, includes a selection of poetry from a large number of African poets. Hughes states in the foreword to this book that the best black poets who are writing today in English or French in Africa south of the Sahara are not so much propagandists for African nationalism as they are speaking for various aspects of *négritude.* This is a word coined by French speaking writers to express "a pride and love of the African heritage physically, spiritually and culturally."[12] Hughes points up differences between English and French poets of African countries as explained by Ezekiel Mphahlele. The Nigerian poet sings about things which affect him personally and in the immediacy of his experience. He is not attempting to protest or vindicate his blackness. The French-speaking poet of Africa, on the other hand, if he is of the *négritude* school, uses broad symbols which extend beyond the "immediacy of individual experiences."[13] He utilizes symbols of blackness and of African traits which are expected to be a unifying force for Africans and for the whole Negro world.

Many poems of Africa are a vital part of tribal life, where some Africans still know the names of the non-Christian gods, or *orisha,* and sing mass chants at village festivals. Oral poetry is still significant in much tribal life as it is chanted, sung and danced as part of the sacred rituals of a particular tribe. For instance the myth "Ogus" tells the story of Ogus who was the father of Urn as well as a warrior and a hunter. It includes a praise song as Ogus forges implements of war such as swords, knives, cutlasses and the iron tips of arrows. The poem depicts him as a being with powerful shoulders and one with "flaming eyeballs" and a "bloodshot countenance."[14]

The book, edited by Hughes, commences with oral traditionals and the poem "Three Friends" created by the Yoruba of Nigeria and translated by Ulli Beier. An interesting poem is "Pass Office Song," which was created in Johannesburg, South Africa and transcribed by Peggy Rutherford. This sings about the pass office where male Africans must go and wait in queues for hours or days to obtain the necessary pass.

Poetry by English-speaking poets of Sierra Leone, Nyasaland, Liberia, Kenya, Nigeria, South Africa, and Ghana is included in this small anthology. Abioseh Nicol of Sierra Leone speaks of an Africa with its red roads and its scarlet hibiscus blooms and mauve passion-colored bougainvillia flower twining through the palm trees fronds. He grows tired of "white ghostlike faces" and returns to the Guinea Coast to find the more sophisticated cities of Accra, Lagos, Liberia, and Freetown, and discovers

12. Langston Hughes, *Poems from Black Africa* (Bloomington and London: Indiana University Press, 1963), p. 11.
13. *Ibid.,* p. 13.
14. Gleason, *op. cit.,* p. 49.

that "freedom is really in the mind." He goes up-country to the bush to find the real Africa. Finally he discovers that the happiness and contentment found in his Africa is "a small bird singing on a Mango tree."[15]

The latter part of this anthology includes translations of a Portuguese-speaking poet of Mozambique and of French-speaking poets of Madagascar, the Congo, and Senegal. David Diop, in the poem "Those who Lost Everything," translated by Langston Hughes, speaks of a beautiful people gliding on the river and wrestling death from the crocodiles, and also of the primitive rhythm of the tom-toms. Then conquerors come and bring slavery and misery to the people.

A Book of African Verse has been edited by John Reed and Clive Wake. This anthology also includes poetry written by Africans in English, as well as translations of poems written by Africans in French. Some poets, such as James Jolobe, have written in their native language as well as in English. He wrote *Thuthula* in his Xhosa language and also created an English version of the same poem. Much of the imagery of African poets is fresh and unhackneyed. The Nigerian poet and playwright, John Pepper Clark, wrote the poem "Ibadan" which has the terseness and imagery of a Japanese *haiku* poem. The city is a splash of rust and gold scattered about seven hills. The poem "Thuthula" by James J. R. Jolobe appears in the narrative blank verse style of Alfred Lord Tennyson. It speaks of the days of tribal custom with herds of cattle and cows yielding milk for the gourd, but it is principally the tale of Thuthula's flight from Gaxa's home and those who righted the wrong against the Ndlombe tribe.[16]

African Poems and Love Songs has been compiled by Charlotte and Wolf Leslau. A preface to this little volume reiterates that poetic literature in one of participation, a part of religious rites, and a vital part of the African culture. Most of these poems are ones concerning a struggle for survival and a desire for freedom, as well as ones concerning desolation and despair. This collection does include a few poems of satire and humor. The "Mocking Song" from the Sudan is a question and answer type of poem, one in which the wife is asked about the dancing agility of her husband and she replies that since she married him he likes to sit and eat and no longer moves around.[17]

Several excellent poems are included in *African Heritage: An Anthology of Black African Personality and Culture,* selected by Jacob

15. Abioseh Nicol, "The Meaning of Africa," in *Poems from Black Africa,* edited by Langston Hughes (Bloomington, Indiana: Indiana University Press, 1963), p. 43.
16. James J. R. Jolube, "Thuthula," an abridged version, in *A Book of African Verse,* edited by J. Reed and C. Wake (New York: The Humanities Press, 1967). pp. 83-102.
17. "Mocking Song," in *African Poems and Love Songs,* compiled by Charlotte and Wolf Leslau (Mount Vernon, New York: Peter Pauper Press, 1970), p. 10.

Drachler. This collection includes a critical analysis of Dahomean Poetry in an essay entitled "Creative Impulses in Dahomean Poetry" by Melville and Frances Herskovits. This essay discusses the significance of poetry in almost every aspect of their life in Dahomey. The country has professional verse-makers who sing songs of praise honoring ancestors of important families or the exploits of men of importance such as the chiefs. These verse-makers are known as *nolodoto,* or "good-memory say person," and *ayisumo,* or "heart-much-understand."[18] Singers wove old proverbs and phrases into their songs.

Numerous poems were created by the Dahomeans for various occasions. Special songs were sung to the deities of the Earth pantheon, Sagbata. According to Herskovits, songs were created in two distinct styles. Poems of improvisation were used in the worship of gods and a set formula song, the *gbo,* was needed to perform magical rites.[19]

Another form of song committed to memory a sequence of events such as the important events in the history of Dahomey. The king's "remembrancer" offered the genealogy of the ruler by a chant which he sang at daybreak. This is the way in which records of wars were kept.[20]

Other songs were created at naming ceremonies, such as the ones in which husbands gave new names to their wives.

Sometimes people living in different quarters of a city sang satiric songs, making fun of each other at a dance called the *avogan,* and greatest honors went to the singer who could expose the shortcomings of his rivals.

Songs were also created for numerous events of daily life. One wife protested about another in a song while she pounded her pestle, and co-operative work groups of men, *dokpwe,* sang songs about the good or poor hospitality of their hosts. When kings ruled Dahomey, subjects were encouraged to create parables and songs mocking the king at rites held annually. These songs were therapeutic in nature since people could shout their grievances and make the kingdom strong again.[21] Poetry was also frequently used in this same manner when Eskimos of the Arctic coast sang their *nith* songs which were songs of contention when a Greenlander considered himself injured by another person.

Another type of song was created at the annual meeting of the hunters where the men chose their *degā* as chief of the hunt for the next year. The rite was held under a sacred tree where millet beer was drunk and exploits

---

18. Jacob Drachler, ed., *African Heritage: An Anthology of Black African Personality and Culture.* (New York: Crowell-Collier Publishing Company, 1969), p. 250.
19. Melville and Frances Herskovits, "Creative Impulses in Dahomean Poetry," *African Heritage,* ed. Drachler, pp. 250-251.
20. *Ibid.,* p. 251.
21. *Ibid.,* p. 253.

of brave hunters were recounted. Brave deeds with the help of the *aziza,* against the giants or fire-eating monsters, and the *yehive,* or other dangerous creatures, were recited.[22]

Numerous poems and songs are included in the anthology compiled by Jacob Drachler. A Sudanese mother's song entitled "Song of a Mother to Her First-Born," which has been translated by Jack Driberg, describes her joy at the birth of a son, as well as the belief that the child is an "incarnation of a dead ancestor."[23]

Six songs from Dahomey are somber ones which are mostly laments or prayers begging for relief from burdens. In "To the Sun-God," the singers beg the god not to "ravish the world" with the ram which paws "the earth with hooves of flame."[24]

B. W. Vilakazi, in his poem "In the Gold Mines," expresses the horrors of life where men worked with "screaming, fire-breathing machines" in the mines of South Africa. Here one senses the suffering of black workers enduring the close suffocating heat.[25]

Two poems by David Diop which are translated from the French by Anne Atik are "Africa," and "He Who Has Lost All." In "Africa" the poet speaks of an African who will spring up "patiently" and "obstinately" and whose fruits will ripen with the "bitter flavor of freedom."[26]

Many other poems by African poets appear in this splendid anthology.

Another recent volume of African poetry is *Yoruba Poetry: An Anthology of Traditional Poems* compiled and edited by Ulli Beier. The section entitled "Children" includes many poems which are appropriate for younger boys and girls.

Poems from Black Africa for Younger Readers

African songs were frequently interspersed with melodic poetry which often consisted of a refrain, recitation, or chorus. Some poems from Africa can be appreciated and enjoyed by the elementary school reader. *A Crocodile Has Me By the Leg,* edited by Leonard W. Doob, has numerous poems which can be understood by a primary grade child. This little volume has lullabies and songs, such as "Blessings upon an Infant," and one by a mother who asks her child to hush while the busy-body is gossiping. A little poem about an inconsequential subject is "Ditty for a Child Losing His First Tooth."

22. *Ibid.,* p. 253-254.
23. Jack H. Dreiberg, "Song of a Mother to Her First-Born," *African Heritage,* ed. Drachler, pp. 50-52.
24. Drachler, ed., *African Heritage,* pp. 60-63.
25. B. W. Vilakazi, "In the Gold Mines," *African Heritage,* ed. Drachler, pp. 81-83.
26. David Diop, "Africa," *African Heritage,* ed. Drachler, pp. 106-107.

Ulli Beier has compiled and edited *African Poetry: An Anthology of Traditional African Poems.* Those categorized under such general headings as religious songs, death, sorrow, praise songs, war, love, people, animals and children's songs. Children can understand much of this traditional poetry, and many of these poems are sophisticated enough to be enjoyed by adolescents also. In African society, praise singers, drummers, priests, hunters, and masqueraders recite and invent poetry. Festivals are often the occasion for the recitation of poems. Girls and boys create poems and songs about daily life events.

Novels from Africa

Several small books for younger children have been published recently which have a plot featuring events in one of the countries of Africa.

Books About Africa for the Young Child

During the past few years several books about Africa have been published for children in the intermediate grades and high school. Most African stories for younger readers have consisted of fables, folk stories, legends, and fairy stories. A few nonfiction books for young readers offer some background of this great continent.

One delightful story for younger readers is *Zamani Goes to Market,* which has been written by Muriel L. Feelings and illustrated by her artist-husband, Tom Feelings. The story opens as Zamani gathers clay pots from the front of the hut and moves them to a group of trees at the edge of the compound. When Father promises Zamani that he can take the brown calf to market, the boy is quite excited. He is fond of his market experience and ponders about many possible gifts for his mother. Great was his surprise to discover that a new *kanzu* with orange braid had been placed on his mat. The story is a short one, but one gets a feeling for the African market which Muriel Feelings knows since she spent two years in East Africa where she stayed with a family in a little village of Western Kenya.

Another picture of African village life for older children in grades four to six is in *Bola and the Oba's Drummers,* which is written by Letta Schatz and is also illustrated by Tom Feelings. This is a story of West Africa and has good family relationships in it. Bola is engrossed in watching the ruler and his Royal Drummers because he wants to become a famous drummer. At first his father does not approve of this vocation until Bola learns to play wonderfully. With the help of a young drummer, Bola's father learns that the skill of a Royal Drummer is highly valued. Some teachers may wish to enhance this story with more details about the significance of drums in an African culture. Dr. Joseph H. Howard has written a scholarly volume, *Drums in the Americas,* which includes much information about African drums. He discusses the use of drums in a drinking party, a beer-drinking gathering, a legal hearing, a social occasion or as a phase of cult worship. In some tribal areas, the natives state that drums are "fed" so that they will not lose their power. Feeding consists of blood, palm oil, honey, or purified water. Such treatment of drums probably keep them in a good condition.

A little novel which includes much information about the Masai is *African Herdboy: A Story of the Masai* by Jean Bothwell. Batian is a herdsboy being reared by the nomadic people of East Africa. He tends a little heifer and loves it so dearly that his father gives him the animal even though tribal traditions allow only young warriors to have their own herd. As the young heifer is threatened by an attack of a half-grown lion, Batian bravely throws his spear to kill the animal. Much appears in this volume concerning tribal taboos and new ways of life.

A Few Books about Africa for Secondary Pupils

Numerous fictional books for more mature readers are currently being published on the African scene and about people who have contributed to Africa's past and current affairs. One of these is *African Heroes* by Naomi Mitchison. This consists of eleven tales of famous Africans gathered from the oral tales of the people. Sites of the tales are shown on maps. This same author, Naomi Mitchison, has written *Friends and Enemies,* which is illustrated by Caroline Sassoon. An older brother of Petrus is arrested for political reasons; so Petrus is sent away to live with relatives. Here the boy struggles to adapt to new ways with his own people when he is freed from the domination of the whites.

Esma Rideout Booth has written a two hundred and eighty-two page novel entitled *The Village, The City, and The World.* This story involves characters in the Congo at the time of the independence movement and of conflict in Katanga.

Novels of Africa Concerning Education for Intermediate and Junior High-School Readers

Several novels about Africa depict the tremendous struggle which African children have had in getting an education: These are: *Okolo of Nigeria* by Peter Buckley; *The Narrow Path, An African Childhood* by Francis Selormey; *Zulu Boy* by Fay Goldie; *Daba's Travels from Ouadda to Bangui* by Bamboté; *A Wind of Change* by Gregory Allen Barnes; *Weep Not Child* by James Ngugi; and *I Will Try* by Legson Kayira.

The story of Okolo is more one of nonfiction than fiction since the book includes information about the Ibo of Nigeria as well as a brief mention of the Hausa, Yorubas, the Fulani or nomads, Nupes, Benis, and Efiks. Through the eyes of Okolo, readers learn about many aspects of the Ibo culture, such as the custom of buying titles. A title is what Edeogu wants more than anything else. In this case Okolo's uncle was spending three thousand dollars for his title. In order to buy a title the uncle had to provide banquets, drinks, and dances for most of his acquaintances. Many Ibo customs discussed in *Okolo of Nigeria,* such as the one of buying new titles, are also described in a novel for mature high school readers entitled *Arrow of God* by Chinua Achebe. In *Arrow of God,* one sees the traditional use of the kola nuts to welcome the guest, and the clever use of proverbs, such as, "The offspring of a hawk cannot fail to devour chicks."[27]

Zulu Boy opens with a description of a great drought in the veld resulting from a lack of rain for three months. Sezula fears that his family will starve; so he sends his son, Umfaan to the dorp to earn money by serving Baas Ferriera, the cattle inspector. The boy finds newer ways in the city but meets Old Lembe, the mattress maker, who agrees to teach Umfaan to read and write in order to prepare him for life in a changing African society. The customs of the Zulu tribe, with such values as a fair payment for work and a deep respect for the dignity and wisdom of the elders are shown.

Kofi in *The Narrow Path: An African Childhood,* is not as poverty-stricken as Umfaan and Okolo, but he is extremely lonely and suffers from harshness and misunderstanding from his educated father. His father is stubborn and punishes Kofi cruelly in order to keep him on "the narrow path" of correct behavior. The country is vacillating between the ways of Christianity which are accepted on the surface and the old ways of gods and spirits which are called upon in times of stress. Some of this same struggle between the old and new ways of worship is seen in the books by Reba Paeff Mirsky, particularly the one entitled *Nomusa, and the New Magic.*

Adult readers who wish to learn more about the cultures of Africa may wish to consult a nonfiction book, *Peoples of Africa.*

A Wind of Change, by Gregory Allen Barnes, is also about education, but much of the plot is about civil unrest. Joseph Konda and a gang of classmates destroy the African government school. Later Joseph feels many pangs of conscience as he is pressured to tell on his classmates. However, since he has taken the society oath, he must remain quiet even though he disagrees with the violent, destructive actions of the school militants.

---

27. Chinua Achebe, *Arrow of God* (Garden City, New York: Doubleday & Company, Anchor Books, 1969), p. 144.

Daba's Travels from Ouadda to Bangui, by Bamboté, who was born in Ouadda, a Central African Republic, has been translated from the French by John Buchanan-Brown. It is the story of Daba, who was born in Ouadda. His mother told him about terrible dry seasons when panthers stalked the bush capturing sheep near the village. Daba's parents wanted him to be educated; so he spent many years at the boarding school in Bambari. This novel is also about other experiences which Daba had in the tangled bush, plains, and muddy rivers of Africa where he and his classmates encountered lions, crocodiles, and elephants.

A novel for adolescents is *Weep Not Child* by James Ngugi. This novel is more than a novel about education. It takes place in Kenya where the repression and brutality of the country's white rulers forced Africans to choose between the violent ways of the Mau Mau with promises of freedom and the ways of white settlers with their arrogant despotism. Njoroge wants to walk the middle road, but he suffers great anguish during the Mau Mau holocaust. In chapter two "The Waning Light" one feels how proud Nyokabi is to have a son in school. She loves to ask him to do his sums or read his books. Education is expensive, but it is worth many sacrifices.

A second autobiographical novel for adolescents which is mostly concerned with the problems of getting an education is *I Will Try* by Legson Kayira. He tells how his parents worked to sell enough groundnuts to pay a school fee of six pennies per year to the church of Scotland officials so he could have a little reading, writing, and arithmetic. There was no paper; so work was done on the ground. It is a book of sacrifice by Kayiras' parents so that he could get an education and the difficulties involved in going to the Wenya school. Later Kayira hitchhikes from his home in Karmpale, Nyasaland to Skagit Valley College in Washington or about half way around the world where he succeeded in getting his college education after many difficulties had been surmounted.

Other African Novels

A novel with the locale set in the dense rain forest of Angola is *Time of Fearful Night* by Alice Wellman. In this novel Baule needs to prove his manhood to his chieftain father. He makes friends with Tom and his father who are stationed at a medical station. He has to struggle against his heritage of frightening superstitions and the learning of similarities and differences between the white man's culture and his own. This is a novel in which the hero appreciates some of the values of civilized life but retains many of his tribal ways.

My Friend in Africa by Frederick Franck is a novel which doesn't have as much excitement as the others. It deals primarily with the longing of Bolo to become a doctor so that he can learn the difference between the

African evil spirits and the white man's germs. The setting is Dr. Schweitzer's hospital at Lambarene.

As Tall as a Spear

Another novel for intermediate grade pupils about the Nuer tribe of the African Sudan is *As Tall as A Spear* which has been written and illustrated by Leona Bond. The raiding of the Dinkas, a neighboring tribe, and the friendship between Jany and Pan, the Dinka boy, is a major part of the plot. The place of cattle in tribal life as well as in rites and marriage ceremonies is depicted. The climax of the novel comes with the ravaging of crops and destruction of parts of the village by a plague of durra birds.

A small book about the Beduoins of Tunisia is *Ali* by Mary O'Neill. This novel again shows the clash between the old and new ways and things which the villagers at Matmata had never seen, such as jeeps, airplanes, and equipment. Ali's greatest triumph was not his new learning experience but his capture and freeing of a gazelle.

A novel about the section of Africa along the River Gambia is *Dark Venture* by Audrey White Beyer. Part of the story takes place in Africa where the twelve-year-old boy Demba suffers capture by alien tribesmen, and enslavement. Aboard the slave ship, *Orion,* he meets Adam Waite, a doctor from Bristol, Rhode Island who has joined the crew as the ship's surgeon. Later Bemba goes to New England. The earlier part of this novel gives a clear description of the agonies suffered by slaves as they are being herded to the coast to board ships. The sale of the proud Demba for the price of a handful of beads and the sufferings of human beings on the coffle are clearly portrayed.

Three Novels About the Zulus at Variant Reading Levels

Jenny Seed has written two recent novels about the Zulus. A short novel for primary grade children is *Kulumi the Brave: A Zulu Tale.* This is a Zulu story which is based on historical oral traditions. It is the story of Lokololo of Zululand who ruled over many *kraals* and was afraid that a son would usurp his power and gain his wealth. When Kulumi is born, the mother casts a claw of a lion into the fire and holds the child to the smoke so that he will be as brave as a lion. The boy is given many tests of courage and undergoes several magical experiences, including clashes with an ogress.

A second novel for older pupils by Jenny Seed is *Vengeance of the Zulu King.* This is the story of the powerful King Shako and his warriors, and of dreadful vengeance. His warriors creep into kraals to murder herdsmen and seize slaves. Bongiseni is captured also by the king's aide but flees and meets Mbuyaza, the white man, or the Prince of the Bay of Port Natal, on the coast of southeastern Africa. This novel mostly relates how the unusual white man, Henry Fynn, or Mbuyaza weTheku, Prince of the Bay, wins the admiration and protection of Shaka, the cruel and violent king.

A third, more sophisticated novel for young adults which has been mentioned previously is *Zulu Woman* by Rebecca Hourwich Reyher. This is the story of Christina, a Zulu queen who fights against the polygamous beliefs which Zulu kings have had for centuries. Many of the customs of King Solomon and the problems which he had to settle between his many wives are outlined in the story plot. Nomipasi and Intoyintoy refuse to aid Christina when she is extremely ill at the end of her pregnancy. They also refuse to prepare the king's food in the kitchen. Many quarrels arise among the wives as some of them feel that the king loves some more than others. The author uses similes and images freshly. As she is describing the new wife, Ethel, she says that "all her thoughts jumped about like bull frogs in the night and frightened her."[28] Since her marriage to the king she awoke to days which seemed gray and dark and it was as if "insects buzzed about in her head."[29]

An African Drama

James Ngugi, author of *Weep Not Child* and *The River Between,* has created a powerful play entitled *The Black Hermit.* It is principally the story of Remi who is an educated political leader of his tribe and who persuades his people to join the Africanist Party. He loves Thoni, but his brother marries her first. Then, when his brother is accidently killed, he must marry his brother's widow according to African tribal custom. He marries her but flees to the city where he drowns out his emotions by haunting the night clubs. Remi wants to lead his people politically and crush the shackles of custom and tribalism, but he is blinded to the devotion of Thoni, and the play ends tragically.

Biographies on African People

Many good biographies about African figures are designed for young adolescents from grades seven to twelve. Few biographies with an interesting, clear-cut style have been written for younger readers. Four recent

28. Rebecca Hourwich Reyher, *Zulu Woman* (New York: New American Library, 1970), p. 121.
29. *Ibid.*

biographies are: *Lumumba: A Biography* by Robin McKown; *I Momolu* by Lorenz Graham; *Stanley, African Explorer* by Fredrika Shumway Smith; and *The Lion of Judah: A Life of Haile Selassie I, Emperor of Ethiopia* by Charles Gorham. The biography of Lumumba is somewhat adulatory. His earlier life was one of moderation, and he recognized the accomplishments of the Belgians in the Congo. Later, he became more militant and was finally assassinated after Mobutu's coup. *I, Momolu* depicts both rural and urban patterns in modern Liberia when many natives could not understand military and colonial customs. When soldiers visit Momolu's family and the boy tries on a soldier's uniform, the father becomes enraged as he feels that his son is forgetting his native cultural ways. This book depicts some of the arrogance of colonial rulers toward the native Africans.

John Rowlands spent his early life in a workhouse where he was treated cruelly. Later, he took the name of Henry Stanley from his foster father in New Orleans. This biography by Fredrika Shumway Smith, *Stanley, African Explorer,* describes Stanley's explorations in Africa as both an explorer and journalist. A much more interesting biographical novel for adolescents which gives many additional details about the life and adventures of Henry Stanley in his perilous quest for David Livingstone is *Stanley, Invincible Explorer* by Laura Benet.

The Lion of Judah: A Life of Haile Selassie I, Emperor of Ethiopia offers a history of palace intrigue in Ethiopia and describes the Emperor's struggles to resist the fascist invasion of his country in 1935. Later, the years of exile of the Emperor are described.

An African Epic on Sundiata

One of the most fascinating books for intermediate grade children published recently is *Sundiata: The Epic of the Lion King.* This book is even more interesting if the teacher provides additional background from *Sundiata: An Epic of Old Mali* by D. T. Niane. This is the story of a king who commenced with humble beginnings and managed to form a great kingdom connecting the trading routes joining North Africa and Black Africa. The Arabs were astounded at the cultural and intellectual wealth of Mali when the emperor made a pilgrimage to Mecca with several thousand men, one hundred camels, and nearly ten million dollars in gold. This is the tale of a mute and ugly crippled child whose coming was prophesized and who later grew up strong enough to lead his people against Sumanguru and to found the empire of Mali.

Numerous other books about Africa are listed in *Africa: An Annotated List of Printed Materials Suitable for Children* which has been selected and annotated by a Joint Committee of the American Library Association, Children's Services Division, and the African-American Institute.

African Kingdoms

Unfortunately, much literature published for children and adolescents focuses upon the tribal governments of African regions. Little is known about the highly civilized kingdoms and empires of Africa. Approximately three maps of the United States can be superimposed on the map of Africa; so there is much to learn about this huge and fascinating continent.

Basil Davidson and editors of Time-Life Books have written *African Kingdoms,* a book which discusses hidden cities, civilizations of the Nile, merchant empires, and other aspects of little-known cultural phases of Africa. From splendid tales by travellers one learns of the fabulous Timbuktu which was formerly the intellectual capital of the Western Sudan. It was a city of ornate mosques and windowless huts, and was the site of a university with learned scholars. This book also depicts the Kingdom of Mali, which includes Timbuktu. In the fourteenth century it was a magnificent kingdom in the Western Sudan. Here the sultan ruled from an ebony throne flanked with elephant tusks. Another book for adolescents and adults is *Ancient African Kingdoms* by Margaret Shinnie which depicts kingdoms and empires, such as Kush, Ghana, Mali, Songhai, and Kanem-Bornu, the forest states, the Lands of Zanj, and the Stone Citadel of Zimbabwe.

African Books and Stories for Adolescents

One unforgettable novel for older adolescents is *The African* by Harold Courlander. This is a novel of slavery whose scenes range from Dahomey, Africa to Georgia, in the United States. It includes episodes of an African king who sells his own people to white drivers and of events in the South where black slave drivers forced their own fellows to submission. It also includes an episode where Indians shield runaway slaves from pursuing owners. This novel is an epic one and links life in Africa with that of the southern areas of the United States.

An excellent collection of contemporary prose by Africans in English which includes excerpts from novels and short stories is *Modern African Prose,* an anthology compiled and edited by Richard Rive. This includes eight selections from South Africa, eight from West Africa (four from Nigeria, two from Sierra Leone, and one each from Ghana and Guinea), and three from East Africa (two from Kenya and one from Mozambique).

A newer book of readings by African authors is *Palaver: Modern African Writings,* which is edited by Wilfred Cartey. A palaver is a meeting of African people who come together to confer concerning African problems; most of the wisdom of the conference is imparted orally.[30] This

30. Wilfred Cartey, ed., *Palaver: Modern African Writings* (New York: Thomas Nelson, 1970).

collection includes writings of twentieth century African poets, novelists, and dramatists who are African in spirit even though some of them have been recognized internationally. Diversities of approach are offered, but both the old and the new are brought together through folk myths still existing in African oral traditions. The editor teaches African literature at Columbia University and travels frequently to Africa.

Lightness and Darkness—An Interpretation of Modern African Literature

Some African literature written for adolescents and adults is difficult to comprehend unless one understands African cultural traditions as well as the symbolism used by the authors. Wilfred Cartey, in *Whispers from a Continent: The Literature of Contemporary Black Africa,* gives a penetrating analysis of several novels by African writers. The first section of this book, entitled "Autobiography—Mother and Child," discusses selections from both *The Dark Child* by Camara Laye, and portions of *Weep Not Child* by James Ngugi, as well as a few other autobiographical novels.

The Dark Child by Laye is an autobiography of an African child who was born at Kowroussa in French Guiana, a country rich in traditions of ancient ritualistic society of the Malinke.

Weep Not Child by James Ngugi has been reviewed in this book previously. It is a story of conflict between the white rulers of Kenya and the Africans who need to choose between the dreaded Mau Mau organization offering promises of freedom and the bigotry and oppression of white persons in a position of authority. Njoroge tries to walk a middle path and feels that education will save himself and his people. This novel presents the cruelty and horror of the brutality of the Mau Mau reign of terror.

Cartey interprets the autobiography of Laye as a "movement away from Mother Africa to a growth in awareness." He sees the child in *Weep Not Child* "wrenched away from the world of beauty and lightness where he wrestles with forces of evil."[31]

A good survey of modern African writing appears in an anthology, *African Writing Today,* edited by Ezekiel Mphahlele. This anthology is a collection of poetry, short stories, and excerpts from longer novels. An extract from *Arrow of God* by Chinua Achebe, a noted Nigerian author, commences the collection. This is principally the tale of Ezeulu, the Chief Priest of Ulu and god of the villages, who struggles between the white man's way of education and such ancient traditions as the New Yam Festival and the sacred Python. A story by another Nigerian author, Cyprian Ekwensi, entitled "Night of Freedom," clearly depicts some of the struggles between

31. Wilfred Cartey, *Whispers from a Continent: The Literature of Contemporary Black Africa* (New York: Random House, Vintage Books, 1969), p. 4.

a colonial and an independent Nigerian as well as the problems of love between Francois and Chini.

An extract from *My Life in the Bush of Ghosts* by Amos Tutuola, which appears in the anthology edited by Mphahlele, has much of the strange, ghostly qualities of his well-known novel *The Palm Wine Drinkard*. Tutuola's hero in *My Life in the Bush of Ghosts* commences with a seven-year-old child who knows badness and quarreling in his home. During a slave raid on his village, he escapes into the Bush of Ghosts through a hole in the earth and goes through many transformations. In one episode he marries a ghostess who is described in this excerpt. In *The Palm Wine Drinkard* the reader again enters into a grisly, bewitching world. The boy, who is humored by his father, becomes a palm-wine drunkard—he drinks more than 225 kegs of wine a day. When his chief tapster is killed and buried, the drunkard goes to the Town of the Dead where he has many gruesome experiences.[32]

An interesting anthropological novel is *Return to Laughter* by Eleanore Smith Bowen, the *nom de plume* of Laura Bohannan. This is published in cooperation with the American Museum of Natural History. She is a specialist in anthropology and worked among the Tiv of Northern Nigeria on grants made to her husband and herself. The book delightfully describes the work of a field anthropologist who had many struggles with both African words and customs as well as the natives' belief in witches. She studies many strange beliefs. One day as she returned from a funeral, she sat down to rest on a teak root. Rogo told her that this was dangerous since leaning against a teak tree caused a woman to become barren.[33] One day, when she learned that her namesake was dead, she turned to the mother of the child who said: "My child and your namesake is dead. There is nothing left between us."[34] This book gives deep insight into an indigenous culture of West Africa, a culture where a hopelessly ill child was supposed to be cured by a ceremony in which a goat, five chickens, and a turtle were sacrificed.[35]

A Few Nonfiction Books About Africa—Intermediate Grade Children
Cultural Nonfiction Books on Africa

Two books by Sonia Bleeker which are a part of her series on the tribal cultures in Central and North America and in Africa are *The Ibo of*

---

32. Amos Tutuola, *The Palm-Wine Drinkard and His Dead Palm-Wine Tapster in the Dead's Town* (New York: Grove Press, 1953).
33. *Ibid.*, p. 117.
34. *Ibid.*, p. 125.
35. *Ibid.*, p. 141.

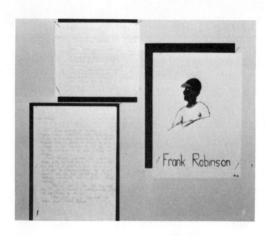

Hall displays by fifth
and sixth grade
children.

Biafra and the *Ashanti of Ghana*. Both volumes are illustrated by the same artist, Edith G. Singer. Mrs. Bleeker uses an anthropological approach describing relationships, mores, and customs, and gives clear descriptions of each society. Details are authentic, and there is a good deal of historical background. The style, however, is not as exciting as that of a fictional book.

Sonia and Tom Gidal have contributed another nonfiction book on Africa for grades four to seven entitled *My Village in Ghana*. In this book a child describes his family life, village crafts, agriculture, mores, and ways of living. The ways of the chiefs and tribal relationships are also explained.

Nonfiction Books for Grades Seven to Ten

Several books of nonfiction about Africa have been written for junior and senior high school readers. In some instances, teachers and librarians may wish to read these juvenile books to gain a background of understanding of the African scene so that the newer African novels and biographies will be better understood.

Barbara Nolan has edited a volume, *Africa Is People: Firsthand Accounts from Contemporary Africa*. The editor has offered an editorial note before each excerpt. Some of the contributions include writing by Jomo Kenyatta, Alan Morehead and Julius Nyerere. Many authors depict the conflict between old and new ways, changing tribal patterns, and changes in the educational and industrial life on the African scene.

Colin M. Turnbull has also discussed changing relationships and patterns of life in Africa through the volume *Tradition and Change in African Tribal Life*. This book includes an anthropological approach to African information and describes the clan, family, lineage, and the tribe. Such concepts or values as loyalty, religion, justice, brotherhood, and initiation rites are described. This is heavy, scientific reading with little humor or narrative relief.

Colin and Margaret Legum have written an informative timely volume entitled *The Bitter Choice: Eight South Africans' Resistance to Tyranny*. Eight chapters discuss Alan Paton, Nelson Mandela, Albert Lutuli, Robert Sobukwe, Beyers Naudé, Nana Sita, Dennis Brutus, and Michael Scott. Such problems as apartheid, guerilla warfare and partition, or international intervention, are considered.

Marc and Evelyne Bernheim have written *From Bush to City: A Look at the New Africa*. This volume has numerous photographs depicting the struggle between old ways and new ones and the fight for recognition of governments in Africa south of the Sahara. Religious, political and educational patterns are considered, as well as economic problems and the activities of foreign countries.

Paul W. Copeland has concentrated upon a different area of Africa in *The Land and People of Libya.* The author discusses the Romans and also some Islamic rituals and pilgrimages.

African Folktales and Sculptures

Students and scholars who wish to further appreciate the cultural heritage of Afro-Americans will greatly appreciate a beautiful volume, *African Folktales and Sculptures.* Here appear many beautiful folktales which were selected and edited by Paul Radin, with the collaboration of Elinore Marvin. Photographs of sculptured art objects were chosen by James Johnson Sweeney. This book has previously been discussed in the part of the chapter concerning African folktales. These folktales include tales and legends of people, as well as those of animals. The pieces of sculpture which are represented here include such objects as a door, an urn, headdresses, spoons, figures, adorned calabashes, necklaces, bracelets, soapstone and terracotta figures, masks, and other magnificent art objects.

The African artist used sculpture as a language which expressed an inner life in which he communicated with an invisible world. Almost each act of his life had a ritual or rite, and a particular image was created to communicate a feeling emotionally. Ladislas Segy explains this use of sculptured figures when he says that a mother prayed to an image for her unborn child, that an image helped her in delivery, and that another one stood outside her hut with a cup for donations to help support her in the days when she could not work. Another image protected the child after birth, and a special piece of sculpture was made if twins were born. Most significant events in a person's life were provided for by different images.

Newer Books About Africa

Judith Gleason has written a somewhat different type of book, *Orisha: The Gods of Yorubaland,* which has been mentioned previously. This is illustrated with pictures of batiks by Aduni Olorisa. This book causes one to understand some of the religious feelings of the Yoruba people. The pictures were modelled after some batik-like cloth created by a Yoruba priestess.

Helmut Nickel has written *Arms and Armor in Africa* which gives evidence of the rich cultural background of African persons who made beautiful weapons and armor. The author is the curator of arms and armor for the Metropolitan Museum of Art.

The African Link of the Literary Experience

In a meeting at Asilomar, California in September 1970, Alex Haley held an audience spellbound for almost two hours with a story of the search for his family heritage. He outlined step by step the story which his slave ancestors passed on from generation to generation through oral tales which were told for about four hundred years. Patiently, Haley struggled to make his ancestral chronicle complete by obtaining each bit of data, from the exact weather conditions for the sailing of the slave ship on which his forebear left the African Coast, to his conversation with his Gambian relatives who provided some important evidence of Haley's ancestral link. Then he knew the greater part of the story of the slave who "disappeared one day while chopping wood." An awareness of the literature of Africa brings a sense of identity and dignity, and makes the Afro-American proud of his forebears. Novels and biographies of tribal peoples give both Negro and white students an awareness of the heritage and traditions of people on the African continent.

Summary

This chapter has extended the strand of Afro-American experience from countries on the African continent to the shores of the United States. Folktales of each African country probably offer part of the quest for identity of some black persons whose ancestors might be traced to a certain African tribe., Some African poetry has been discussed. as well as African sculpture, music, and art. A few African novels for younger children, as well as novels for adolescents and adults have been mentioned and some of these are about a few of the current problems of African peoples. Some nonfiction books about African leaders and their countries have been discussed in order to form a background for a better understanding of the African scene. Some African cultural strands will be discussed in chapter five in relation to the literature by and about black Americans.

Reactions—Questions and Projects

1. Select folktales from other countries of the world such as Burma, Brazil, or Turkey, as well as some from Africa. Make a folklore map and locate the site of each folktale. Discuss similarities and differences of ethnic customs in various countries.

2. Many Afro-American folktales have a moral, or are really animal fables. Read some of Aesop's fables and then tell an Afro-American folk tale in a way which will give the moral at the conclusion of the tale.

3. Certain tribes in Africa are fond of quoting proverbs orally and in their literature. Charlotte and Wolf Leslau have compiled a book entitled *African Proverbs,* with decorations by Jeff Hill (Mount Vernon, New York: Peter Pauper Press, 1969). Select a proverb from some African tribal countries or people such as the Ashanti, Bagurimi, Buganda, Ethiopian, and Ghana. Write an animal fable or a story with a setting in an African country and incorporate the fable in the tale.

4. Practice telling some Afro-American folktales in the style of different African or Caribbean storytellers. Provide for an involvement of the audience in certain refrains.

5. Do a research study on Harold Courlander or some other folklorist. Give brief reviews of his books of folktales on Africa and the Caribbean and arrange a folk tale center.

6. Obtain recordings of some Afro-American primitive music. Work with other people to create choreography, and dance an African folk tale such as "Anansi and the Elephant Go Hunting" from *The Hat Shaking Dance and Other Ashanti Tales from Ghana* by Harold Courlander.

7. Study about trickster figures in Negro folklore and folktales. Give a talk describing various tricksters. I. G. Edmonds has written *Trickster Tales,* which is illustrated by Sean Morrison (Philadelphia: J. P. Lippincott Company, 1966). Some of these trickster stories come from India, Japan, Scotland, Turkey, Germany, Iran, Persia, Greece, and Mexico. After studying characteristics of these tales, high-school pupils may enjoy creating original tales.

8. Sing folk songs from Africa and compare them with folktales in other countries. One source is *Folk Songs of the World,* selected and edited by Charles Haywood (New York: Bantam Books, 1968).

9. Make a survey of some filmstrips and recordings which have African folktales. Criticize them as to their quality, authenticity, and interest to a young audience.

10. Do research on superstitious beliefs and religious ideas of African tribal peoples and discuss how the supernatural spirits are reflected in sculpture and other art forms.

11. Make a survey of nonfiction sources to discover elements of civilization in large cities and kingdoms such as Timbuktu and the Kingdom of Mali. Develop an image of other cultures of Africa besides the tribal village primitive cultural patterns.

12. Select some current books about Afro-American heroes and indicate ways that they can be used to raise the self-concepts of black children and adults.

13. Obtain a copy of *From Tribe to Town: Problems of Adjustment,* edited by Leon E. Clark and its accompanying teacher's guide (New York: Praeger Publishers, Inc., 1970), or *Coming of Age in Africa: Continuity and Change,* edited by Leon E. Clark and its accompanying teacher's guide (New York: Praeger Publishers, 1970). Using some of the teaching strategies shown in one or both teachers manuals, develop a similar curriculum unit using some of the other novels and poetry about Africa.

BIBLIOGRAPHY
BOOKS FOR PRIMARY CHILDREN

AARDEMA, VERNA. *Tales for the Third Ear from Equatorial Africa.* New York: E. P. Dutton & Company, 1969.
————. *Tales from the Story Hat.* New York: Coward-McCann, 1960.
APPIAH, PEGGY. *Ananse the Spider: Tales from an Ashanti Village.* New York: Pantheon Books, division of Random House, 1966.
ARNOTT, KATHLEEN. *Tales of Temba: Traditional African Stories.* New York: Henry Z. Walck, 1967.
ARKHURST, JOYCE COOPER. *The Adventures of Spider: West African Folk Tales.* Boston: Little, Brown and Company, 1964.
BERGER, TERRY. *Black Fairy Tales.* New York: Atheneum Publishers, 1969.
BLEEKER, SONIA. *The Ashanti of Ghana.* New York: William Morrow & Company, 1966.
————. *The Ibo of Biafra.* New York: William Morrow & Company, 1969.
BURTON, W. F. P. *The Magic Drum Tales from Central Africa.* New York: Criterion Books, 1961.
COURLANDER, HAROLD. *The Hat-Shaking Dance and Other Tales from the Gold Coast.* New York: Harcourt, Brace and Company, 1957.
COURLANDER, HAROLD, and ESHUGBAYI, EZEKIEL A. *Olode the Hunter and Other Tales from Nigeria.* New York: Harcourt, Brace and World, 1968.
COURLANDER, HAROLD, and LESLAU, WOLF. *The Fire on the Mountain and Other Ethiopian Stories.* New York: Holt, Rinehart & Winston, 1965.
COURLANDER, HAROLD. *The Piece of Fire and Other Haitian Tales.* New York: Harcourt, Brace and World, 1964.

DOOB, LEONARD W. *A Crocodile Has Me by the Leg.* New York: Walker and Company, 1967.

DORLIAE, PETER G. *Animals Mourn for Da Leopard and Other West African Tales.* Indianapolis, Indiana: The Bobbs-Merrill Company, 1970.

ELLIOT, GERALDINE. *Where the Leopard Passes: A Book of African Folktales.* New York: Schocken Books, 1968.

——. *The Long Grass Whispers.* New York: Schocken Books, 1968.

FEELINGS, MURIEL L. *Zamani Goes to Market.* New York: The Seabury Press, 1970.

HALEY, GAIL E. *A Story, A Story: An African Tale.* New York: Atheneum Publishers, 1970.

HARMON, HUMPHREY. *Tales Told Near a Crocodile: Stories from Nyanza.* New York. Viking Press, 1967.

HASKETT, EDYTHE RANCE, ed. *Grains of Pepper: Folktales from Liberia.* New York: John Day Company, 1967.

——. ed. *Some Gold, a Little Ivory: Country Tales from Ghana and the Ivory Coast.* New York: John Day Company, 1971.

HEADY, ELEANOR B. *Jambo Sungura: Tales from East Africa.* New York: W. W. Norton and Company, 1965.

——. *When the Stones Were Soft: East African Fireside Tales.* New York: Funk & Wagnalls, 1968.

KAULA, EDNA MASON. *African Village Folktales.* New York: World Publishing Company, 1968.

KIRN, ANN. *Beeswax Catches a Thief.* New York: W. W. Norton & Company, 1968.

LEXAU, JOAN M. *Crocodile and Hen.* New York: Harper & Row, Publishers, 1969.

REES, ENNIS. *Brer Rabbit and His Tricks.* New York: Young Scott Books, 1967.

——. *More of Brer Rabbit's Tricks.* New York: Young Scott Books, 1968.

ROCHE, A. K. *The Clever Turtle.* Englewood Cliffs, New Jersey: Prentice-Hall, 1969.

SAVORY, PHYLLIS. *Congo Fireside Tales.* New York: Hastings House, 1962.

SEED, JENNY. *Kulumi the Brave, a Zulu Tale.* New York: The World Publishing Company, 1970.

SHERLOCK, PHILIP M. *Anansi the Spider Man: Jamaican Folktales.* New York: Thomas Y. Crowell Company, 1954.

SHERLOCK, SIR PHILIP K. B. E. *The Iguana's Tail: Crick Crack Stories from the Caribbean.* New York: Thomas Y. Crowell Company, 1969.

WALKER, BARBARA. *The Dancing Palm Tree and Other Nigerian Folktales.* New York: Parents Magazine Press, 1968.

AFRICAN FOLKTALES FOR INTERMEDIATE GRADE READERS

DORSON, RICHARD M., comp. *American Negro Folktales.* Greenwich, Connecticut: Fawcett Publications, a Fawcett Premier Book, 1967.

GUILLOT, RENÉ. *René Guillot's African Folktales.* Edited and translated by Gwen Marsh. New York: Franklin Watts, 1966.

LESLAU, CHARLOTTE and WOLF. *African Proverbs.* Mount Vernon, New York. Peter Pauper Press, 1962.

NUNN, JESSIE ALFORD. *African Folktales*. New York: Funk & Wagnalls, 1969.

RADIN, PAUL, ed. *African Folktales*. New Haven, Connecticut: Princeton University Press, First Princeton Bollingen Paperback Printing, 1970.

THOBY-MARCELIN, PHILLIPE, and MARCELIN, PIERRE. Translated from the French by Eva Thoby-Marcelin. *The Singing Turtle and Other Tales from Haiti*. New York: Farrar, Straus & Giroux, Inc., 1971.

NOVELS AND BOOKS FOR INTERMEDIATE GRADE READERS

BARNES, GREGORY ALLEN. *A Wind of Change*. New York: Lothrop, Lee & Shepard Company, 1968.

BERTOL, ROLAND. *Sundiata, the Epic of the Lion King*. New York: Thomas Y. Crowell Company, 1970.

BEYER, AUDREY WHITE. *Dark Venture*. New York: Alfred A. Knopf, 1968.

BOND, LEONA. *As Tall as A Spear*. Reading, Mass.: Young Scott Books, a division of Addison-Wesley Publishing Co., 1971.

BOTHWELL, JEAN. *African Herdboy, A Story of the Massai*. New York: Harcourt, Brace & World, 1970.

BUCKLEY, PETER. *Okolo of Nigeria*. New York: Simon and Schuster, 1962.

FRANCK, FREDERICK. *My Friend in Africa*. Indianapolis, Indiana: The Bobbs-Merrill Company, 1960.

GOLDIE, FAY. *Zulu Boy*. Toronto, Canada: Macmillan & Company, and New York: St. Martin's Press, 1968.

GORHAM, CHARLES. *The Lion of Judah: A Life of Haile Selassie I, Emperor of Ethiopia*. New York: Ariel, 1966.

MIRSKY, REBA PAEFF. *Nomusa and the New Magic*. Chicago: Follett Publishing Co., 1962.

————. *Thirty-One Brothers and Sisters*. New York: Dell Publishing Company, 1969.

McKOWN, ROBIN. *Lumumba: A Biography*. New York: Doubleday and Company, 1969.

O'NEILL, MARY. *Ali*. New York: Atheneum Publishers, 1968.

SCHATZ, LETTA. *Bola and the Oba's Drummers*. New York: McGraw-Hill Book Company, 1967.

SELORMEY, FRANCES. *The Narrow Path: An African Childhood*. New York: Praeger Publishers, 1968.

BOOKS FOR ADOLESCENT READERS

ACHEBE, CHINUA. *Arrow of God*. Garden City, New York. Doubleday & Company, Anchor Books, 1969.

BAMBOTÉ. *Daba's Travels from Ouadda to Bangui*. Translated from the French by John Buchanan-Brown. New York: Pantheon Books, a division of Random House, 1970.

BEIER, ULLI, ed. *The Origin of Life and Death: African Creation Myths*. London, England: Heinemann Educational Books, 1969.

BENET, LAURA. *Stanley, Invincible Explorer*. New York: Dodd, Mead & Company, 1955

BERNHEIM, MARC and EVELYNE. *From Bush to City: A Look at the New Africa*. New York: Harcourt, Brace & World, 1966.

BOOTH, ESMA RIDEOUT. *The Village, the City, and The World*. New York: David McKay & Company, 1961.

BOWEN, ELENORE SMITH. *Return to Laughter*. Garden City, New York: Doubleday & Company, Natural History Library, Anchor Books, 1964.

CARTEY, WILFRED, ed. *Palaver, Modern African Writings*. New York: Thomas Nelson, 1970.

————. *Whispers from a Continent: The Literature of Contemporary Black Africa*. New York: Random House, Vintage Books, 1969.

COPELAND, PAUL W. *The Land and People of Libya*. Philadelphia: J. P. Lippincott Co., 1967.

COURLANDER, HAROLD. *The African*. New York: Bantam Books, 1969.

DAVIDSON, BASIL. *Africa Kingdoms*. New York: Time Incorporated, 1966.

GIBBS, JAMES L. JR., ed. *Peoples of Africa*. New York: Holt, Rinehart & Winston, 1965.

GLEASON, JUDITH. *Orisha, The Gods of Yorubaland*. New York: Atheneum Publishers, 1971.

GRAHAM, LORENZ. *I, Momolu*. New York: Thomas Y. Crowell Company, 1966.

KAYIRA, LEGSON. *I Will Try*. New York: Bantam Pathfinders Edition, 1967.

LAYE, CAMARA. *The Dark Child*. New York: Farrar, Strauss & Giroux, 1969.

LEGUM, COLIN and MARGARET. *The Bitter Choice: Eight South Africans' Resistance to Tyranny*. New York: World Publishing Company, 1968.

MPHAHLELE, EZEKIEL, ed. *African Writing Today*. Baltimore: Penguin Books, 1967.

MITCHISON, NAOMI. *African Heroes*. New York: Farrar, Straus & Giroux, 1969.

————. *Friends and Enemies*. New York: Doubleday & Company, 1968.

MONTI, FRANCES. *African Masks*. Middlesex, England: Hamlyn House, Center Feltham, 1969.

NGUGI, JAMES. *Weep Not Child*. New York: Macmillan Company, Collier Book Edition, 1969.

————. *The Black Hermit*. New York: Humanities Press, 1968.

NIANE, D. T. *Sundiata: An Epic of Old Mali*. Translated by G. T. Pickett. London and Harlow, England: Longmans, Green and Company, 1969.

NICKEL, HELMUT. *Arms and Armor in Africa*. New York: Atheneum Publishers, 1971.

NOLAN, BARBARA. *Africa Is People: Firsthand Accounts from Contemporary Africa*. New York: E. P. Dutton & Company, 1967.

REYHER, REBECCA HOURWICH. *Zulu Woman*. New York: New American Library, 1970.

RIVE, RICHARD, comp. and ed. *Modern African Prose*. London: Heinemann Educational Books, 1964. Reprinted copies are available from the Humanities Press in New York.

SEED, JENNY. *Vengeance of the Zulu King*. New York: Pantheon Books, a division of Random House, 1970.

SHINNIE, MARGARET. *Ancient African Kingdoms*. New York: New American Library, a Mentor Book, 1965.

SMITH, FREDRIKA SHUMWAY. *Stanley: African Explorer*. Chicago: Rand, McNally & Co., 1968.

TURNBULL, COLIN M. *Tradition and Change in African Tribal Life.* New York: World Publishing Company, 1968.
TUTUOLA, AMOS. *The Palm-Wine Drinkard and His Dead Palm-Wine Tapster in the Dead's Town.* New York: Grove Press, 1953.
WELLMAN, ALICE. *Time of Fearful Night.* New York: G. P. Putnam's Sons, 1970.

POETRY BOOKS FOR ADOLESCENT READERS

AIG IMOUKHUEDE, FRANK. "One Wife for One Man." In *Poems from Black Africa,* edited by Langston Hughes. Bloomington, Indiana: Indiana University Press, 1969.
BEIER, ULLI, comp. *Yoruba Poetry: An Anthology of Traditional Poems.* London: Cambridge University Press, 1970.
———, comp. and ed. *African Poetry: An Anthology of Traditional African Poems.* Cambridge: Cambridge University Press, 1966.
DRACHLER, JACOB, ed. *African Heritage: An Anthology of Black African Personality and Culture.* New York: Crowell-Collier Publishing Company, 1969.
HUGHES, LANGSTON. *Poems from Black Africa.* Bloomington, Indiana: Indiana University Press, 1963.
JOLOBE, JAMES J. R. "Thuthula." Abrid. ver. In *A Book of African Verse,* edited by J. Reed and C. Wake. New York: The Humanities Press, 1967.
LESLAU, CHARLOTTE and WOLF, comp. *African Poems and Love Songs.* Mount Vernon, New York: 1970.
LOMAX, ALAN, and ABDUL, RAOUL, eds. *3000 Years of Black Poetry: An Anthology.* New York: Dodd, Mead and Company, 1970.
NICOL, ABIOSEH. "The Meaning of Africa." In *Poems from Black Africa,* edited by Langston Hughes. Bloomington, Indiana: Indiana University Press, 1963.
REED, JOHN, and WAKE, CLIVE. *A Book of African Verse.* New York: Humanities Press, 1967.

PROFESSIONAL BOOKS

Africa, An Annotated List of Printed Materials Suitable for Children, Selected and annotated by a Joint Committee of the American library Association, Children's Services Division, and the African American Institute, 1968.
BOWRA, C. M. *Primitive Song.* Cleveland and New York: World Publishing Company, 1962.
BREWER, J. MASON. *American Negro Folklore.* Chicago: Quadrangle Books, 1968.
CARTEY, WILFRED. *Whispers from a Continent: The Literature of Contemporary Black Africa.* New York: Random House, Vintage Book, 1969.
FELDMAN, SUSAN, ed. *African Myths and Tales.* New York: Dell Publishing Company, 1963.
HUGHES, LANGSTON, and BONTEMPS, ARNA. *The Book of Negro Folklore.* New York: Dodd, Mead & Company, 1958.

MPHAHLELE, EZEKIEL, ed. *African Writing Today.* Baltimore: Penguin Books, 1967.

PARRINDER, GEOFFREY. *African Mythology.* London: Paul Hamlyn, 1967.

RADIN, PAUL, ed. *African Folktales and Sculpture.* Bollingen Series p. 33. Kingsport, Tennessee: Pantheon Books, Kingsport Press, 1966.

SEGY, LADISLAS. *African Sculpture Speaks.* 3rd ed., enlarged and rev. New York: Hill and Wang, 1969.

TRASK, WILLARD R., ed, and trans. *The Unwritten Song: Poetry of the Primitive and Traditional Peoples of the World.* Volume 1, the Far North, African, Indonesia, Melanesia, and Australia. New York: The Macmillan Company, 1966.

CHAPTER FIVE

Black
Literature
in a
Pluralistic
Society:
Some
Understandings

In recent years hundreds of books about the black experience and the Afro-American heritage have been published in the United States as well as in England and Africa. Readers of such literature should probably examine it with the eyes of Feldman, who reminds us that "certain human conditions, roles, conflicts and questions are universal."[1] Each ethnic group should have its own separate individualities and identities, but all groups should cooperate to form a society where the human experience becomes more humane and universal.

Current black literature can be differentiated into several separate categories which include: (1) black folktales, music, and poetry originating principally in the United States; (2) novels or stories of American history; (3) literature which raises the self-image; (4) literature of social protest; (5) tell-it-like-it-is literature; and (6) imaginative mystical novels with a universal message.

1. Susan Feldman, ed., *African Myths and Tales* (New York: Dell Publishing Company, 1963), p. 10.

Perhaps the largest number of novels about American history concerns episodes of slavery or of the Civil War in which a black person becomes the central character. These are novels for adolescents, such as *North Winds Blow Free* by Elizabeth Howard, and for more mature young adults, a novel such as *Jubilee* by Margaret Walker. Numerous books based on historical source material concern struggles of slaves to escape their bondage. These are such novels as *Voices in the Night* by Rhoda Bacmeister and *By Secret Railway* by Enid L. Meadowcroft. Another beautifully poetic book is *North Star Shining* by Hildegarde Swift. This book has tremendous impact and could be used in choral verse and pageantry to depict the highlights of the Negro's accomplishments in the history of the United States. A few novels, such as *Walk the World's Rim* by Betty Baker, featuring the Negro character, Esteban, place the Negro here in a setting of early Spanish American history in Mexico and the southwestern United States.

A second category of black literature consists of the numerous biographies and autobiographies of Negro persons which are being published. These include biographies of such musicians as Marian Anderson or Bessie Smith, the autobiographies of Frederick Douglass and Malcolm X, and biographies of such figures as Harriet Tubman, Martin Luther King, and George Washington Carver. Many of these biographies are also ones which help to raise the self-image of black persons.

Many books are currently being written with the purpose of improving the self-image of the black reader. Such volumes as *Who Look at Me* by June Jordan and *Black is Beautiful* by Anne McGovern help the Negro child to have an improved self-image. The book by June Jordan includes a collection of paintings of Negroes. Most of the paintings are by some of the finest American artists. The primary-grade reading level book *Black Is Beautiful* helps to counteract some of the negative symbolism of black symbols which have appeared repetitively in literature for both children and adults.

A fourth category of black literature consists of all those books which suggest some of the rich cultural contributions of Africans and Afro-Americans to the culture of the United States. Such books as *The Story of Rock* by Carl Belz; *Somebody's Angel Child, the story of Bessie Smith,* by Carman Moore; and *My Lord, What a Morning,* the autobiography of Marian Anderson, offer contributions of musicians. Books similar to *African Folktales and Sculpture,* Bolingen Series 33, published by Pantheon Books, depict a beautiful collection of African sculpture selected by James Johnson Sweeney. Other similar books, such as *Art in Africa* by Tibor Bodrogi, *African Sculpture Speaks* by Ladislas Segy, and *African and Oceanic Art* by Margaret Trowell and Hans Nevermann, offer examples of the contributions of African artists to American art.

Hall displays by fifth and sixth grade children.

Literature of social protest is a fifth classification of novels, short stories, and biographies which is emerging at the present time. Such literature ranges from such stories as *The Empty Schoolhouse* by Natalie Savage Carlson and *South Town* and *North Town* by Lorenz Graham, to *The Invisible Man* by Ralph Ellison and *Black Like Me* by John Howard Griffin. Such literature usually protests racial discrimination in homes, schools, jobs, and in the community, as well as the gap between the affluent society and people of certain ethnic groups who live at the margin of poverty.

Social protest literature could be classified under the "tell-it-like-it-is" approach, but much literature in the "tell-it-like-it-is" style frequently explicates life in a ghetto environment in a somewhat photographic, panoramic style. Such books are concerned with dope peddling, poverty, rats, race riots, discrimination, muggings, and examples of the seamy side of life. Little of this literature raises the aspiration level of the reader. A few of these books are *Stevie* and *Uptown* by Stephen Steptoe, which are for younger readers; *Manchild in the Promised Land* by Claude Brown; *The Autobiography of Malcolm X,* co-authored by Alex Haley; and *What Manner of Man: A Biography of Martin Luther King, Jr* by Lerone Bennett, Jr., for more mature young adult readers.

Another classification of literature might be called the imaginative, mystical short story or novel. Such writing frequently has symbolism or hidden meaning which does not always come to the surface upon the first reading of the plot by the casual reader. As one studies such a novel more carefully he realizes that the characterization and intricacies of plot cause one to delve beneath the surface to some universal qualities which appear in most good literature. These novels tap the source of something about the black experience, but the emblazoned fervor of a creative mind raises such experience to a universal one shared by persons of any ethnic group. Such literature has been written by the black author, Virginia Hamilton, who has created novels for children and adolescents such as *Zeely, The House of Dies Dreer,* and *The Planet of Junior Brown.* Each novel is an original, creative piece of literature devoid of stereotypes, but with a story which could be applicable to many persons living elsewhere in the United States.

Sources for the Study of Black Literature

During the past few years hundreds of bibliographies and books have been written which give numerous sources of annotated lists and evaluations of black literature. Some of these are:

Association for Childhood Education International. *The World in Children's Picture Books*. Washington, D. C.: Association for Childhood Education International, 1968.

"Bibliography on Afro-American History and Culture." Reprinted from *Social Education* 33, no. 9 (April 1969): 442-461.

Chapman, Abraham. *The Negro in American Literature and A Bibliography of Literature by and about Negro Americans*. Wisconsin State University, Oshkosh, Wisconsin: Wisconsin Teachers of English, 1966.

Crosby, Muriel. *Reading Ladders for Human Relations*. American Council on Education. A large committee under the leadership of Virginia Reid has been working on a current revision of this volume which should be available in early 1972.

Dodds, Barbara. *Negro Literature for High School Students*. Champaign, Illinois: National Council of Teachers of English, 1968.

Glancy, Barbara J. "Black Barbecue: An Essay Review," a reprint. *The Record*—Teachers College, Vol. 70, No. 7, April 1969, pages 661-684.

Jackson, Miles M., Jr., comp. and ed. Assisted by Mary W. Cleaves and Alma L. Gray. *A Bibliography of Negro History and Culture for Young Readers*. Pittsburgh: University of Pittsburgh Press, 1968. (Includes a listing of Audio-Visual materials)

Millender, Dharalhula. "Through a Glass Darkly." *School Library Journal* 13, December 1967.

Miller, Ruth, ed. *Backgrounds to Black American Literature*. Scranton: Chandler Publishing Company, an Intext publisher, 1971.

Rollins, Charlemae, ed. *We Build Together*. Readers Guide to Negro Life and Literature for Elementary and High School Use. Champaign, Illinois: National Council of Teachers of English, 1967.

Sterling, Dorothy. "The Soul of Learning." Reprinted from *The English Journal* 57, February 1968, pp. 166-180.

Thompson, Judith, and Woodard, Gloria. "Black Perspective in Books for Children." *Wilson Library Bulletin* 44, December 1969, pages 416-424.

Turner, Darwin T., and Stanford, Barbara Dodds. *Theory and Practice in the Teaching of Literature by Afro-Americans*. Urbana, Illinois: National Council of Teachers of English, 1972.

Another helpful bibliography entitled "Pages of History: A Bibliography of Great Negro Americans" by Lee Bennett Hopkins and Misha

Arenstein appears in an *Elementary English* article in February 1969. This bibliography is divided into three sections: (1) full length biographies; (2) collections of short biographies; and (3) collected works featuring writings, essays, and documents.

Black Poetry

In recent years much emotional impact is felt in the black poetry and music being read by persons interested in ethnic literature.

American Negro Folktales and Music

Most black folktales which have originated in the United States appear in scholarly volumes compiled by folklorists. Few of these have been adapted by imaginative authors for reading by children and young adolescents. Some of these tales can be integrated in a special unit on folklore which can be directed by a skilled teacher.

Four basic sources of American Negro Folktales are: *American Negro Folklore* by J. Mason Brewer; *American Negro Folktales,* collected by Richard M. Dorson; *The Book of Negro Folklore,* edited by Langston Hughes and Arna Bontemps; and *Mules and Men* by Zora Neale Hurston.

American Negro Folklore by Brewer includes tales, songs, memoirs, superstitions, proverbs, rhythms, riddles and names. Brewer states that African slave immigrants brought much Negro folklore from Africa, and in their minds were carried certain complex musical forms, types of dramatic speech, and imaginative stories. Slaves formed enclaves of African culture wherever they settled. These African forms of culture were later infused with local patterns of speech, story, song, and belief.

A valuable contribution of the Brewer book is a collection of spirituals which were formerly sung by Negroes on plantations and battlefields. Some of these were recorded and published by Charlotte Forten in 1864. She heard them sung by Negroes on St. Helena Island, South Carolina. Thomas Wentforth Higginson also listened to various spirituals sung by Negroes around evening campfires. He collected them and they were published in the *Atlantic Monthly* magazine in 1867. Spirituals were also publicized by the Jubilee Singers from Fisk University in Nashville, Tennessee. These spirituals offered hope and vision to poor plantation slaves who dreamed of a wonderful home in heaven away from the trials and tribulations of this earth. Brewer states that these songs reflected three types of philosophy: dreams of a better world to come, reality-thinking songs which admitted the current condition, and spirituals which included parts of a Bible story. Some familiar Negro spirituals are: "Swing Low,

Sweet Chariot," "Steal Away," "The Old Time Religion," "Lord, I Wish I Had Come," "Nobody Knows the Trouble I See, Lord," and others.

Brewer states that the "blues" offer a major contribution of the Negro to American folk song. They do not offer an escape from reality to a better world but face life as it is with its many heartaches, and losses. Blues have a plaintive quality and are often about love. Some blues bemoan a physical condition such as "The Silicosis Blues" created by the folk singer Josh White. He sings about an incurable disease, silicosis, which he caught on the job in the stone quarries. Some folk blues published by Brewer includes "Lonesome Blues," "Worried Blues," "Careless Love," "Frankie Blues," and others.

The third classification of Negro songs described by Brewer consists of slave seculars and work songs. Some of the slave seculars offer complaints about the status of a slave. Others are work songs sung by persons on chain gangs or in rock quarries. Usually such songs were sung in protest against the condition of Negro workers and prisoners. In these songs the guards and foremen were frequently referred to as "Cap'n." A well known song is "Foller de Drinkin Gou'd," which has adaptations appearing in other collections. A story relates that Peg Leg Jo, a member of the Anti-Slavery Society, took frequent trips southward to persuade young Negroes to escape to the North. He taught the song to the slaves. The "Drinkin' Gou'd" was the Great Dipper. Other songs published in the Brewer collection includes such ones as "Lay Dis Body Down," "I Went to Atlanta," "Workin' on de Railroad," "Levee Moan," "Dis Ole Rock Mine," "Carry Me Back to Old Virginny," and others.

The Negroes created a few ballads of which the most popular is "John Henry," about the tall-tale figure who was the hard driving "steeldriving man." "Frankie and Johnny," "De Ballit of de Boll Weevil," and "De Gray Goose" are also popular.

The Richard M. Dorson collection of Negro folktales consists of oral narratives collected in the field. Some classifications are: animal and bird tales, Old Marster and John, Colored Man and White Man, Hoodoos, and Two-Heads, Spirits and Haunts, Witches and Mermaids, The Lord and the Devil, Wonders, Horrors, Protest Tales, Scare Tales, Fool Tales, Lying Tales, Preachers and Irishmen.

The *Book of Negro Folklore,* edited by Langston Hughes and Arna Bontemps, includes lyrics of songs collected under such categories as Spirituals, Gospel Songs, Pastime Rhymes, Ballads, Blues, Work Songs, Street Cries, Playsongs and Games, the Jazz Folk, Harlem Jive, the Problem, and Songs in the Folk Manner. Music is not included as is done in the volume by J. Mason Brewer. The Collection by Hughes and Bontemps also includes chapters entitled "Poetry in the Folk Manner" and "Prose in the Folk Manner." This collection also includes such chapters as

"Animal Tales," and "Animal Rhymes," "Ghost Stories," and "Black Magic and Chance," as well as many others.

Mules and Men by Zora Neale Hurston consists of a collection of Afro-American folklore which Hurston collected in Florida and Louisiana. The collector recorded stories in an informal situation when she listened to workers in the evenings, on trips, at dances, and during rest periods between jobs. This volume has such stories as "Why the Porpoise Has His Tail on Crossways," and "How the Squinch Owl Came to Be." The appendix to the book includes words and music to such work songs as "John Henry," "East Coast Blues," "Please Don't Drive Me," a convict song, and many others. One interesting song in this collection is "There Stands a Blue Bird," which is a children's game. Some strange superstitions also appear in the appendix, such as Formulae of Hoodoo Doctor's, Paraphernalia of Conjure, and Prescriptions of Root Doctors.

Music as Poetry

Folk songs were frequently sung by African tribal story tellers and by tellers of tales in Negro camp meetings held on plantations in the South of the United States. Many of these camp melodies were quite poetic. Most of the songs sung during slavery times expressed the innermost thoughts of the slaves on religion, slavery, their anxieties about their masters, and a longing for freedom and a "heab'n" that was not necessarily the heaven seen by a pastor. Some books which give these poetic tunes and their background are:

Katz, Bernard, ed. *The Social Implications of Early Negro Music in the United States.* New York: Arno Press and the New York Times, 1969. With over 150 songs. Many of them with their music.

Fisher, Miles Mark. *Slave Songs of the United States.* New York: The Citadel Press, 1953. With a foreword by Ray Allen Billington.

Music and Poetry Book

An unusual book interrelating music and poetry is a projected publication *Black America Sings Out* by Andrew C. Nicholaw. This is an anthology with approximately three hundred and forty selections of poetry and about sixty songs by black Americans. It commences with poems of the nineteenth century and continues until 1969.

Another collection of songs and tales is one by Paul Glass entitled *Songs and Stories of Afro-Americans.* A foreword to this book states that Portuguese explorers of the African continent between 1440 and 1480 discovered established empires with big armies and governments governed capably by chiefs. Such cultural attributes as beautiful palaces, valuable jewelry fashioned from quartz, and figures sculpted from stone, tin, and brass indicate that African tribes were far removed from the condition of being ignorant primitives awaiting the benevolence of white explorers. The Ashanti, Yoruba, and Fon of Dahomey recorded their history and customs in song and stories as well as heroic exploits of their tribal peoples. Some of these native traditions were blended with those of Southern plantations. The Paul Glass collection of songs includes ones sung by the Jubilee Singers of Fisk University, and the blues, such as "The Hooking Cow Blues" and "Mood Indigo;" songs of the Civil Rights Movement and Martin Luther King, Jr., such as "We Shall Not Be Moved," "Hallelujah I'm a Travelin'," and "We Shall Overcome," and the "Song of John Henry." Introductory information provides a framework for many songs.

A recent book for young primary grade children is *Lift Every Voice and Sing,* with words and music by James Weldon Johnson and J. Rosamond Johnson. A valuable collection of music and lyrics, also by James Weldon Johnson and J. Rosamond Johnson, is *The Book of Negro Spirituals,* including *The Book of American Negro Spirituals* and *The Second Book of Negro Spirituals.* This second volume by the Johnsons is one of the most complete collections of Negro spirituals available at an inexpensive price.

Black Folktales for Children

One collection of black folktales for children by Julius Lester is considerably different from most of the African folktales. Most collections of African and Afro-American tales written for children are called folk tales, but the stories are usually literary ones quite far-removed from ones collected by folklorists. Lester indicates that some of these tales come from Africa, that some were probably originated during slavery days in the south, and that some tales have unknown origins.

A tale showing the Negro's closeness to God, "How God Made Butterflies," gives a picture of the Lord who gets tired from making the world and settles back in his old rocking chair to smoke his cigar. He asks the little angels to bring him pruning shears. He trims the trees and tosses the trimmings over the bare ground; thus grass, bushes, and flowers are made. As the Lord settles back, he says, "Making a world ain't no easy thing. Takes a whole lot of thinking to make everything fit in place, particularly if it's something that's never been thought of before."[2] Somehow this story reminds one of the play *Green Pastures* by Marc Connelly. These folk-

2. Julius Lester, *Black Folktales* (New York: Richard W. Baron, 1969), p. 16.

tales have had a mixed reaction from various librarian critics, as is indicated in an illuminating article by Binnie Tate with comments from a committee of Los Angeles children's librarians entitled "In House and Out House: Authenticity and the Black Experience in Children's Books," appearing in the October 1970 issue of the School Library *Journal.*

Two journal articles will greatly assist teachers and librarians in using folklore creatively. These are "Folklore As a Mirror of Culture" by Alan Dundes which appears in *Elementary English* of April 1969 and "American Folklore in the Secondary Schools" by Hector H. Lee which is published in the October 1970 issue of the *English Journal.* Dundes states that folklore helps one to view a culture *from the inside out* instead of *from the outside in* and helps us to eliminate our ethnocentrism by means of which persons view things *we* do as right and natural and things which *others* do as "unnatural" and "wrong." Hector Lee offers many values of folklore in his article and states that "folklore can make the student aware of the values and commonalities in the culture of other people. It also helps a student to develop a 'sense of worth of the common man'."[3]

Black Poetry in the United States

Introduction

During the last decade or so, many people have been amazed to discover that the American Negro poet offers a rich contribution to the poetic wealth of the United States which extends back to the singing of spirituals and work songs on Southern plantations. Few people were familiar with the fact that Sterling Brown wrote *Negro Poetry and Drama and the Negro in American Fiction* as early as 1937. This volume has a chapter entitled "Contemporary Negro Poetry, 1914-1936," which was current at the time of its publication. Robert Bone states that this book was written at a time when Richard Wright was unknown and LeRoi Jones was a child of three. At the same time Ralph Ellison had not published any books and James Baldwin and Lorraine Hansberry were still attending school.[4]

In the chapter "Contemporary Negro Poetry," 1914-1936 Sterling Brown calls attention to the "New Negro Poet" who arose during this period of time. Some of his analyses of their poetry is appropriate today. These poets reacted against "sentimentality, didacticism, optimism, and romantic escape."[5] They worked for a less stilted poetic style and de-

---

3. Hector H. Lee, "American Folklore in the Secondary Schools," *English Journal* 59, October 1970, p. 1000.

4. Robert Bone, "Preface to the Atheneum Edition," *Negro Poetry and Drama and the Negro in American Fiction,* by Sterling Brown (New York: Atheneum Publishers, 1969).

5. Sterling Brown, *Negro Poetry and Drama and the Negro in American Fiction* (New York: Atheneum Publishers, 1969), p. 60.

veloped the use of more original language. Race was not to be either caricatured or neglected. Poets wrote in ordinary speech not in stilted "poetic diction." Brown summarized the five major concerns of these poets: (1) a discovery of Africa as a source of racial pride, (2) the use of Negro heroes and their heroic episodes from American history, (3) the creation of poems of propaganda and protest, (4) an attempt to treat all Negroes with more understanding and in less apologetic terms, and (5) a desire for a frankness and a deeper mode of self-revelation.[6] All of these objectives or concerns are currently being expressed in much black poetry and prose being created in the nineteen seventies. In many instances the word Negro is being replaced by the term black American and black poetry, but basic principles outlined by Brown are still being followed by current black poets. This anthology by Sterling Brown traces the history of American Negro poetry from the time of such pioneers as Jupiter Hammon (1730-1800) and Phyllis Wheatley (1753-1784) to the work of Sterling A. Brown in 1932, and Welborn Victor Jenkins in 1934, as well as that of Frank Marshall Davis who published a panoramic style of poetry in *Black Man's Verse* in 1935. A valuable contribution of this book is the chapter entitled "White Poets on Negro Life (to 1914)" as it discusses some poets who were hostile, short sighted, or condescending about the Negro image, but it also discusses others who honestly tried to record what they saw and experienced.

Afro-American Poems for Younger Children

Some current Afro-American or black-American poems are too sophisticated and harsh for young children and should be left for a later period when pupils have more maturity and understanding.

Lee Bennett Hopkins has selected some of the poetry by Langston Hughes and published it under the title, *"Don't You Turn Back: Poems by Langston Hughes.* Poems are placed in sections entitled "My People," "Prayers and Dreams," "Out to Sea," and "I Am A Negro." Most of the poems in this volume have been selected because they can be understood by younger pupils.

Arnold Adoff has edited *I Am the Darker Brother: An Anthology of Modern Poems by Negro Americans.* These poems are arranged in sectional divisions under the titles of "Like I Am," " Geneology," "Shall be Remembered," "If We Must Die," "I Am the Darker Brother," and "The Hope of Your Unborn." Several poems by such noted poets as Langston Hughes, Robert Hayden, Gwendolyn Brooks, James Weldon Johnson, Arna Bontemps, Richard Wright, Paul Laurence Dunbar, Countee Cullen,

6. *Ibid.,* p. 61.

and others are included. Some notes are appended, which gives incidents forming the background of several poems.

Another book, edited by Arnold Adoff, is *Black Out Loud: An Anthology of Modern Poems by Black Americans*. This anthology is for the purpose of letting black people express how they see themselves, and in some instances the poems illuminate change in the current scene as viewed by black poets. Several of the poems and verses help children to become aware of their heritage and to be proud of black, which should be worn "like a banner" and not "like a shroud."[7]

Another good collection of Negro poetry is *Poetry of the Negro, 1746-1949*, an anthology edited by Langston Hughes and Arna Bontemps. This is a comprehensive collection which is organized under such divisions as Negro Poets of the U. S. A., Tributary Poems by Non-Negroes, and Poems of the Caribbean and Africa.

Arna Bontemps has also edited *American Negro Poetry*, which includes poems by such Negro poets as James Weldon Johnson, Paul Laurence Dunbar, Fenton Johnson, Claude McKay, Jean Toomer, Langston Hughes, Richard Wright, Pauli Murray, Gwendolyn Brooks, LeRoi Jones, and many others.

A good anthology for adolescents is *The Book of American Negro Poetry*, edited by James Weldon Johnson, which is a revised edition including much Negro poetry considered as—"folk stuff" rather than an artificial dialect. The preface to the 1921 edition is quite informative.

The volume *The Panther and the Lash, Poems of Our Times* by Langston Hughes should probably be read by adolescents in the junior high school years rather than by younger children. Most of the poems are simple enough to understand, but many of them are poems of protest, such as the ones classified in "The Bible Belt" and others under "Daybreak in Alabama." Some of the bitterness, irony, and poems of oppression and suffering offer a background for an understanding of the Civil Rights movement. Some teachers may wish to present these poems together with some of the music and songs appearing in *Freedom Is A Constant Struggle: Songs of the Freedom Movement*, compiled and edited by Guy and Candie Carawan. Such a presentation will probably be dependent upon a lack of prejudice and the attitude of parents and children toward civil rights and other sociological problems of the current scene.

Two collections of poetry which depict the Negro spirit and soul are *God's Trombones: Seven Sermons in Verse* by James Weldon Johnson, and *For My People* by Margaret Walker, with a foreword by Stephen Vincent Benet. Both of these volumes should probably be presented to older adoles-

---

7. Langston Hughes, "Color," *Black out Loud: An Anthology of Modern Poems by Black Americans*, Arnold Adoff, ed. (New York: Macmillan Co., 1970), p. 3.

cents. Some scholars may wish to study the history of Negro spirituals and the many collections of Negro lyrics appearing in such books as *Religious Folk Songs of the Negro as Sung at Hampton Institute,* edited by R. Nathaniel Dett, and *Negro Slave Songs in the United States by* Miles Mark Fisher.

Older Adolescents and Adults

More mature readers of poetry will enjoy reading poems in *Soulscript: Afro-American Poetry,* edited by June Jordan; *Today's Negro Voices,* edited by Beatrice M. Murphy; and *American Negro Poetry,* edited with an introduction by Arna Bontemps.

Sounds and Silences of the City

Sometimes, urban children may empathize with persons and scenes portrayed in an urban setting even though the poems are not necessarily of and about black persons. Nancy Larrick selected a group of poems with the help of some city youngsters and made an anthology, *On City Streets.* Arnold Adoff edited a collection, *City In All Directions: An Anthology of Modern Poems.* Richard Peck edited *Sounds and Silences: Poetry for Now.* This latter book places poems in subdivisions entitled "Isolation," "Identity," "Realities," "Illusion," "Dissent," "Communication," "Love," "War," "Pain," and "Recollections," and others. It includes such poems as "The Negro Speaks of Rivers" by Langston Hughes. It is a collection of modern poetry which makes poems live and breathe in the bodies and hearts of many people.

In addition to the enjoyment of poetry, short stories, and novels about Negro children in various locales, some of the more recent modern poems help the black child and younger adolescent to understand himself and others better.

Dark Testament and Other Poems by Pauli Murray includes forty-nine of her other poems in addition to "Dark Testament." The poet has worked as an advocate of civil rights and women's rights, and she is also an attorney and a professor of law. She was a protégé of Stephen Vincent Benet. The poem "Dark Testament" encouraged Morris Milgram to embark upon a career of developing integrated housing since the message in the poem taught him that the ghetto features "black unfreedom." Her poem "Words" is effective and speaks of words which are arrogant, cruel, comradely, and shy.

Four books of recent black poetry for mature adolescents and adults are: *Dices or Black Bones: Black Voices of the Seventies,* edited by Adam

David Miller; *Today's Negro Voices,* edited by Beatrice M. Murphy; *Soulscript: Afro-American Poetry,* edited by June Jordan; and *The New Black Poetry,* edited by Clarence Major.

Dices or Black Bones includes some information about the poets but has no introduction. Most of these poems are social protest ones. Some of them are arranged in interesting visual forms similar to poetry created by modern concrete poets. Adam David Miller has written "Crack in the Wall Holds Flowers," in which he speaks of cataclysms and cracks which presage the growth of lilacs in hidden niches, but there is always an uneasy sense of impending danger. Etheridge Knight states that he died once in Korea from a shrapnel wound, and again from a prison sentence, but poetry brought him back to life.

The anthology collected by Beatrice M. Murray collects poems from Negro authors who are under the age of thirty. The anthology serves as a forum or an audience for youths who claim that no one listens to their voices. The editor states that little is omitted from the original poet's language except words which are not in good taste. A few lines about the poet accompanies the poem. Townsend T. Brewster was twenty years old and a student at the University of Denver when he wrote "Black Is Beautiful;" Bernette Golden was nineteen years and a sophomore at American University in Washington, D. C. when she wrote "Morning" and spoke of a day with an invisible weight of expected events. Austin D. Washington was twenty-seven years old and a native of Durham, North Carolina when he wrote "To Be Black Is to Suffer."

Soulscript: Afro-American Poetry, edited by June Jordan, includes poems by many established Negro poets, such as Langston Hughes, Countee Cullen, Robert Hayden, Gwendolyn Brooks, Jean Toomer, and LeRoi Jones, as well as poetry by many other Negro poets.

In her introduction, June Jordan states that "poetry turns the individual drama of being human into words," and she also speaks of poems as being "voice prints of language," or "soulscript."[8]

The New Black Poetry is edited by Clarence Major, who was thirty-one years old when he edited it. His introduction states that "revolutionary black poets feel the urgency of being in a political vanguard."[9] Many of the authors are also full-time "militant activists." Most of these poets feel strongly about the self-determination of black people and impart a feeling that the destiny of black poets is to reshape the world.

8. June Jordan, ed., *Soulscript: Afro-American Poetry* (Garden City, New York: Doubleday & Company, 1970), xvi and xvii.
9. Clarence Major, ed., *The New Black Poetry* (New York: International Publishers, 1970), p. 15.

A rather unusual, creative book is *Search for the New Land: History as Subjective Experience* by Julius Lester. The book jacket describes the book as a bold and contemporary fugue of three parts: (1) the history of America from Hiroshima to the present; (2) an autobiography which includes letters and a journal; and (3) "found poetry," which was taken from newspaper and magazine articles.[10] It is designed to be read by both black *and* white readers and offers the hope that revolutions can be avoided if Americans will become more human. Some of the words are full of the black hatred of white persons, some of the lines are also about love and courage, but some of the language is harsh and militant so the classroom use of the book should probably be limited to young adults.

Voices of Children and Young People

In recent years considerable funds have been made available for the publication of poems by children in elementary and secondary schools. Most critics would classify these as voices of experience and writing which is promising for the future, but few poems use the craftsmanship of practicing poets who have spent years in perfecting their poetic style. The gifted poet, Ciardi, has stated that poetry represents both Art and Humanity. These young poets are trying to express the humaness and inhumaness of man to man. In many cases these writers will need many more years of experience to perfect their poetic art. In some instances, editors have selected the best poems from a large collection of ones which were submitted.

Some of these anthologies are: *The Voice of the Children,* collected by June Jordan and Terri Bush; *The Me Nobody Knows: Children's Voices from the Ghetto,* edited by Stephen M. Joseph; *The World from My Window* by George Mendoza; and *City Talk,* edited by Lee Bennett Hopkins. *I Heard A Scream in the Street: Poems by Young People in the City,* selected by Nancy Larrick; *Here I Am! An Anthology of Poems Written by Young People in Some of America's Minority Groups,* edited by Virginia Olsen Baron; *Talkin' About Us: Writings by Students in the Upward Bound Program,* edited by Bill Wertheim with the assistance of Irma Gonzalez, are other examples of books which illustrate "experience poems" written by young authors.

Some of the reasons for publishing such volumes appear in *Somebody Turned on a Tap in These Kids: Poetry and Young People Today,* edited by Nancy Larrick. This volume has articles by such poets as Myra Cohn Livingston, Karla Kuskin, June Jordan, and others.

10. Julius Lester, *Search for the New Land: History as Subjective Experience* (New York: The Dial Press, 1969), on the book jacket of the the book.

Understanding the Self and Others

Many recent books for children in the primary grades help boys and girls to understand the problems of both themselves and others. In order to enhance the awareness of primary-age readers, teachers and librarians may sometimes read a story orally and later use it as a basis for discussion of a person's feelings and actions. Certain universal qualities appear in novels about any group of persons. Primary grade books are usually small ones of approximately forty or fifty pages; so authors do not have time to develop an extended story line or characterization. Usually, pictures carry much of the message. Sometimes, inappropriate illustrations may ruin a good plot. Only a few representative books can be discussed in this section.

Evan's Corner by Elizabeth Starr Hill, is childlike and sympathetic towards the problems of a little boy who wants to be lonely in his own way. Evan lives in his two-room home in Harlem with both parents and five sisters and brothers. He longs for his own personal place, and his understanding, perceptive mother helps him gain privacy by giving him a corner of a room for himself. Such touches as crayoned pictures, some Queen Anne's lace in a glass, some furniture constructed from orange crates, and a turtle add to his corner. The artist, Nancy Grossman, depicts Evan's family in warm, sympathetic pictures.

A book by Janice May Udry, *What Mary Jo Wanted,* has a rather ordinary plot, but the subject is universal—the longing of a child for a puppy. The book is only twenty-six pages long, but somehow both the author and artist manage to show a pleasant middle-class Negro family in which children have the same longings and problems as children in other ethnic and Caucasian groups.

Another little picture story for young children is *Benjie on His Own* by Joan M. Lexau. Benjie is a small boy living in Harlem with his grandmother. He struggles to be independent and to go to school alone even though the Harlem streets are dangerous. He shows his courage and some growth of maturity when he is able to help his grandmother in an emergency.

A slight little book of fifty-six pages by May Justus is *A New Home for Billy,* which considers the problem of a Negro family wishing to move to a new neighborhood. Billy is baffled when he learns that some white people won't rent or sell property to blacks, and he grows up a little when his father helps him to understand the meaning of prejudice.

Ezra Jack Keats manages to depict much feeling for childhood, as well as fresh perceptions about life, in each one of his picture books. He has shown a black child in *The Snowy Day, Whistle for Willie,* and *A Letter for Amy.* In *Peter's Chair,* Peter is older and bigger and must understand that he is no longer a pampered only child, since he will have to welcome a new baby sister.

Somehow Keats, through the use of collage, paintings, and other artistic skills, manages to convey a message of understanding in a clear-cut, original manner. In *Goggles* a more serious problem of a gang fight enters the scene, and in *Hi Cat!* a cat manages to upstage a group of children who are planning a play and who are dressed in paper bag costumes.

So many books for young people are being written about Watts and Harlem that it is pleasant to meet Sweet Pea with her family and neighbors. *Sweet Pea* is the story of a black girl growing up in Alabama. Father is separated from the family but he visits the children when he can. Sweet Pea is happy, goes to church faithfully, and looks forward to Christmas and a bicycle. This is a story of hard-working Negro people in a rural area, but the fellowship of religion and a friendliness of family life add to the charm of the characterization.

A small picture story of only twenty-two pages by John Steptoe, entitled *Stevie,* offers a situation with which most young children can identify. A small black boy, Robert, is asked to take care of Stevie. Robert is particuarly disgusted when his friends tease him for his baby-sitting task. But when Stevie's mother later moves away and takes Stevie, Robert finds that he really misses him.

Another lovely picture story about a Negro child which opens the awareness of other children's longing to be recognized is *Sam* by Ann Herbert Scott, with illustrations by Symeon Shimin. Sam is like many other children who are lonely. He wants to play and work with various persons in his family. They ignore him since they are busy with their work and study, and he interrupts their tasks. Because Sam yearns for love and attention, he gets into trouble and feels rejected until, gradually, different family members discover what is wrong with him.

This same feeling of lonesomeness, but at a much deeper level, is portrayed in *The Jazz Man* by Mary Hays Weik. Zeke is left alone, at first only during the day while his parents work. Then his mother leaves, and finally, Zeke's father deserts him. Zeke retreats to his memories of the Jazz Man's music coming from an apartment across the court from Zeke's. The reader is required to decide for himself whether the story has a happy ending, with Zeke and his parents reunited, or whether this is delirium fantasy. *The Jazz Man* is a powerful book.

Some critics have felt that *Song of the Empty Bottles* by Osmond Molarsky, which is illustrated by Tom Feelings, might be somewhat contrived and artificial in plot. Thaddeus seems to get his guitar too easily. However, a group of physically handicapped children in one school loved this book. They collected several empty bottles and played "The Empty

Bottle Song" on them. Then they made a roller movie of the story and taped it with sound effects.

Numerous folk tales and fables have been mentioned previously, but *John Henry: An American Legend* by Ezra Jack Keats is a strong, virile rendering of a traditional legend, or tall tale, about the mighty John Henry who competed with the steam hammer and won the contest but "died with his hammer in his hand." Harold W. Felton has done a different version of this story for older children, entitled *John Henry and His Hammer,* but the story by Keats has more appeal to younger boys and girls. The Felton version of the tall tale gives much more characterization of the hero in a tall-tale style of hyperbole.

How Many Miles to Babylon? by Paula Fox depicts problems of inner city adolescents with honest sympathy. James gets tired of the squabbling of his three aunts, Aunt Grace, Aunt Althea, and Aunt Pearl, and longs to communicate with his ill mother. He runs away from school, and runs headlong into a secret deserted house where Gino, Stick, and Blue involve him in stealing dogs in order to collect a reward for finding them. James finds a ring and dreams of his great-great-great grandfather who might have been a king in Africa. The book is somewhat contrived and has an expected ending, but young readers can empathize with the suffering of ten-year-old James Douglas living in a one-room flat in Brooklyn.

Novels and Biographies about Slavery in the United States

A large number of novels and biographies are currently being published about plantation life, slavery, and the quest for freedom. In many instances such literature consists of biographies of persons who have played a prominent part in the history of slavery.

Afro-American children, as well as all people, seek a world where the dignity of each human person is honored. An interesting collection of stories about prominent Negroes contributing to the future of the Negro in the United States is *Four Took Freedom: The Lives of Harriet Tubman, Frederick Douglass, Robert Smalls, and Blanche K. Bruce.*

One of the clearest discussions of life conditions under slavery is an autobiography *Narrative of the Life of Frederick Douglass, An American Slave.* Another version of the same story is *Narrative of the Life of Frederick Douglass, An American Slave,* an autobiography, edited by Benjamin Quarles. This includes an introduction about the achievements of Frederick Douglass as well as a chronological listing of dates and events in which Douglass was active.

Numerous books have been written about Harriet Tubman who was sometimes known as "Moses." She went down to lead over 300 of her enslaved people to freedom over the underground railroad. She also fought on the side of the Union Army during the Civil War and earned the nickname of "General Harriet." *Freedom Train: The Story of Harriet Tubman* by Dorothy Sterling, includes a comprehensive bibliography including such categories as "Books About Harriet Tubman," "Slavery Days," "Riding the Underground Railroad," "With John Brown," "In the Civil War," "The Last Years," and "Songs." Ann Petry has created another biography entitled *Harriet Tubman, Conductor of the Underground Railroad*.

Milton Meltzer has written a thoughtful biography for adolescent pupils, entitled *Thaddeus Stevens and the Fight for Negro Rights*. Meltzer has also written documentaries: *In Their Own Words, A History of the American Negro, 1619-1865; In Their Own Words, A History of the American Negro, 1865-1916*, and *In Their Own Words, A History of the American Negro, 1916-1966*. All of these have been published in paperback form by the Thomas Y. Crowell Company. These volumes are for older pupils in the secondary school. Thaddeus Stevens led the fight for public education and for the freedom of fugitive slaves, and later for the abolition of slavery. He led in the adoption of the Thirteenth, Fourteenth, and Fifteenth Amendments which hoped to guarantee full citizenship to freed slaves. Stevens was bitterly hated by Southern legislators since he promoted legislation which favored Northern businesses. This book gives a picture of many of the problems of Reconstruction.

Harold W. Felton has created a brief biography about a remarkable woman slave, *Mumbet: The Story of Elizabeth Freeman*. She was born as a slave and worked in the home of Colonel John Ashley near Sheffield, Massachusetts. Later she married John Freeman who died as a soldier in the War of Independence. In 1780 Massachusetts established a new constitution declaring that "all men are born free and equal," so Elizabeth Freeman brought a suit against John Ashley demanding her freedom, and she won her case. During Shay's rebellion Mumbet stood off a band of raiders with a fireplace shovel and saved the Sedgwick property from destruction.

Another biography for adolescents about a person who was dedicated to religious and anti-slavery meetings is one on Sojourner Truth whose biography is *Journey Toward Freedom: The Story of Sojourner Truth* by Jacqueline Bernard. Sojourner was born as a slave with the name of Isabelle, but she changed her name when she commenced to preach. She helped soldiers during the Civil War and later worked to aid the homeless and jobless freedman.

Julius Lester has edited a documentary collection of slave narratives most of which were obtained from a federal writers project and stored at the Library of Congress. These statements were in the words of slaves, and the volume is entitled *To Be A Slave.*

Another book about the condition of the black man in the Colonies at an earlier time is *Forten the Sailmaker: Pioneer Champion of Negro Rights* by Esther M. Douty. James Forten was born as a free Negro in the Colony of Pennsylvania ten years before the American Revolution. He owned a sailmaking shop in Philadelphia and became wealthy, but he spent almost all of his own fortune to help American Negroes gain their freedom. He also gave considerable support to the Abolitionist paper, *The Liberator,* published by William Lloyd Garrison.

A good Civil War novel for intermediate grade children is *Voices in the Night* by Rhoda Bacmeister. Jeanie has to leave her widowed mother and go to live with the Aldens. The child becomes curious, and the Aldens tell her that their house is a station for the underground railroad. Jeannie then becomes involved with the escape of slaves to the north. Teachers may wish to use a few music books which have slave songs in them with novels or biographies about slavery. One particularly good one is *Slave Songs in the United States* by Miles Mark Fisher.

A little book which shows the significance of music in the life of slaves is *The Drinking Gourd* by F. N. Monjo. This story originates from a song formerly sung by slaves escaping from an underground railroad. Tommy is sent home from church as a punishment and discovers a runaway slave, his wife, and two children hidden in the hay of the barn. Tommy's father must tell him about the underground railroad movement to help slaves escape from their masters. The book is only sixty-four pages long, but it can be exciting to young children particularly if they learn the song which is printed in full in the book. The song "Follow the Drinking Gourd," adapted and arranged by Theodore Bikel, appears in the volume, *Folksongs and Footnotes by Theodore Bikel.* Notes to the song explain that slaves were allowed to sing by their overseers, but instructions for the escape of slaves were often hidden in words of the songs. The "drinking gourd" meant the constellation of the Big Dipper which pointed northward. The mention of the first quail was used as a warning that escapees should try to escape before the weather got too severe.

Another story about the underground railroad, written for intermediate grade children, is *Steal Away Home* by Jane Kristof. In this story, Amos, who is twelve years of age, relates the details of his flight from station to station as he goes to Philadelphia to join his father, a free man. A third book which has many references to the underground railroad is *The House of Dies Drear* by Virginia Hamilton.

Another book somewhat similar to the autobiographies of Frederick Douglass is *Venture for Freedom: The True Story of An African Yankee* by Ruby Zagoren. In this book the author has leaned heavily upon an autobiography of Venture, who dictated his life story to Elisha Nibs. She had it published as a twenty-four page book. It includes part of the African life of Venture, who was known formerly as Broteer, and was captured by tribal slave traders in 1736. This book discusses differences between the law concerning slaves in a Connecticut colony and those in some of the southern colonies. Binnie Tate, in her article, "In House and Out House: Authenticity and the Black Experience in Children's Books," appearing in the October 1970 issue of the *School Library Journal,* criticizes this novel as one showing a "common perverted concept of loyalty to the master"[11] which remains intact throughout the novel. She also criticizes *Sophia Scrooby Preserved* because it maintains some stereotypes of the "acquiescent, happy, and grateful slave." Both of these books, however, offer vignettes which round out the slave story.

A novel for older, more mature adolescents is *Jubilee* by Margaret Walker. This is a vital novel of the Civil War and the Reconstruction period of the United States which portrays Vyry as dramatically as Scarlett O'Hara is portrayed in *Gone With the Wind*. The author, who is also a poet, uses music and poetry to set the mood and to offer symbolic interpretations of the story. Schools in Washington, D. C. have used this novel in high school classes, and a study guide has been developed to assist pupils in interpreting some of the significance of the novel.

A nonfiction book which gives an excellent background of slavery in many world countries is *People in Bondage: African Slavery in the Modern Era* by L. H. Ofosu-Appiah. This is illustrated with numerous photographs and illustrations taken from different galleries, archives, and museums. The book discusses the history of African Negro slavery and the southern plantation system, but it also describes different methods of slavery carried out by the Moslems and the Ottoman Turks. The abolitionist movement in both Great Britain and the United States is discussed. Josiah Wedgwood, the noted British potter, helped to publicize the work of the British abolitionists with a medallion or cameo which was purchased by thousands of people.

Raising the Self-Image of the Negro Child

One type of literature being published recently is the type which helps to raise the self-image of the Afro-American child. As he reads about

---

11. Binnie Tate, "In House and Out House: Authenticity and the Black Experience in Children's Books," *School Library Journal* (October 1970): 97.

more and more black persons being successful in life, he can gain a higher self-concept. Numerous biographies are helpful, such as *Mary McLeod Bethune* by Emma Gelders Sterne. Through this biography readers learn that education is a vital force in rising up the ladder of social esteem .

Older pupils interested in jazz will enjoy *Somebody's Angel Child: The Story of Bessie Smith* by Carmen Moore, which gives the life of the "Empress of the Blues," and also includes a bibliography and discography giving sources for her recordings.

Several authors have written about black heroes who were prominent in Westward expansion and explorations to the Arctic, as well as about black sports heroes and soldiers. Harold W. Felton has written *Jim Beckwourth: Negro Mountain Man*, which is illustrated with photographs, prints of the period, and maps. The information has been researched, and interesting information has been obtained, but the style of this biography is as laudatory as some of Felton's other tall tales. This biography makes Beckwourth appear as a mountain man larger than life. In some instances the authenticity of interpretation of data indicates much imaginative license.

Two collections of biographical stories of black heroes are *The Black Frontiersman: Adventures of Negroes Among American Indians, 1528-1918* by J. Norman Heard, and *Black Courage* by A. E. Schraff. The first book is an outgrowth of work done by Mr. Heard as part of his historical research for his Ph.D degree and includes numerous reproduced photos from various archives, historical societies, and the Smithsonian Institute. Much documentary information in included as part of the narrative content. The volume *Black Courage* was also created as the result of college study on black contributions to the building of the American West, but no bibliographical material supporting the stories is listed.

Another book about historical heroes is *Black Heroes in Our Nation's History* by Philip T. Drothing which gives a description of many unsung American Negro heroes. Pictures show Peter Salem as a minuteman at the Battle of Bunker Hill; York, who had a role in the Lewis and Clark expedition to the Northwest in 1804-1806; a reproduction of a print showing the all-black 54th Massachusetts Regiment assaulting Fort Wagner on July 18, 1863; as well as many other pictures of black military heroes, cowboys and immigrants.

Black Roots of Experience

An anthology for young readers entitled *Black Roots: An Anthology* by Jay David and Catherine J. Greene, relates childhood experiences of twenty black Americans. The first story is the collection by Jacob Stroyer entitled "Sand-Hill Days" tells about the transfer of wagonloads of young black children to a summer residence where they were fed by elderly women who cooked large pots of corn flour mush and clabber. Horace R. Clayton wrote about a traumatic scene of his childhood in which his mother moved them to the basement and read the Bible to them in great fear because his father had hit a white man, and she feared dreadful reprisals. Stories by Richard White, Lena Horne, Anne Moody, Roy Campanella, James Baldwin, Eartha Kitt, Floyd Patterson, Claude Brown, Langston Hughes, Malcolm X, Dick Gregory, and others appear in this anthology. Most of the stories are excerpts from longer novels, biographies, and autobiographies.

An Odessey of Courage

One figure who appears in many novels about the Southwest is the black slave who accompanied Spanish explorers in quest of the seven cities of Cibola. Maia Wojciechowska has spoken of him as Estebanico—a slave having "the qualities of a pioneer: defiance, a friendly nature, fearlessness, the curiosity of a cat, the brute strength of a bull, and the disposition of an optimist."[12] In *Walk the World's Rim,* Betty presents Esteban as seen through the eyes of an Indian lad, Chacoh. Esteban dreams that good conduct will win him his freedom from Dorientes. The promises of this Spanish master are as illusory as misty rainbows as Esteban is never granted his freedom. Esteban is also one of the major characters in *The Gentle Conquistadors* by Jeanette Mirsky. In this book, the Spaniards and Esteban are idolized as sacred ones, or children of the Sun, by the Indians who think that the explorers have magic medical skills. At times both the Indians and Esteban become slaves to Indian tribes who demand both labor and magical feats. The deluded conquistadors continue dreaming of the Seven Cities of Cibola in a land of prickly pears and the mesquite bean flower. The historically oriented version of Estevanico is different in "The Odyssey of Estevanico," appearing in *The Black Frontiersman.* In this story, Esteban is a gigantic hero striding in tune to reed flutes, shrill fifes, drums, and tinkling bells, with Indian maidens walking behind him as if he were a noble conqueror. As Esteban drew near to the Zuñi pueblo he sent a ceremonial calabash rattle as an honored gift, not knowing that the rattle was made by the hated enemies of the Zuñi. Readers may disagree concerning the discrepancies of information about the powerful black slave in many different stories and biographies, but he remains a hero in most versions of his life and adventures.

A recent book considering the biography of this early Negro hero is *The Discoveries of Esteban the Black* by Elizabeth Shepherd. An author's

12. Maia Wojciechowska, *Odyssey of Courage: The Story of Alvar Núñez Cabeza de Vaca* (New York: Atheneum Publishers, 1965), p. 76.

note in this volume explains that old manuscripts spell this black explorer's name as Esteban, Estevan, and sometimes the diminutive forms, Estevanico and Estebanillo. Much of the story is based on three reports written during the lifetime of Esteban shortly after his death, and these sources appear in the back of this biography.

Two other biographies about significant black Americans are ones on W. E. B. Du Bois and Martin Luther King. A biography of W. E. B. Du Bois, which is written somewhat in a documentary style, is *Cheer the Lonesome Traveler: The Life of W. E. B. Du Bois* by Leslie Alexander Lacy. This is an outstanding biography of a noted black American leader who prophesized many events in the United States, had a distinguished career, and died in Ghana at the age of ninety-five. Most of this biography is quite objective, including the conversion of Du Bois to Communism at the age of ninety-three.

Another recent biography about a popular Negro author is *Black Troubadour: Langston Hughes* by Charlemae H. Rollins. This biography portrays the life of Hughes in relation to his prolific writing of fiction, history, translation, drama, and poetry. Hughes who was in quest of his own identity focused upon the identity of his own Negro people in a society which was only just gradually emerging from a sense of hatred, distrust, and misunderstanding of the contributions of the blacks to the cultural traditions of the United States. This book is illustrated with many photographs of such noted Negro persons as W. E. B. Du Bois, Countee Cullen, Mary McLeod Bethune, Dr. George Washington Carver, the Arna Bontemps family, Gwendolyn Brooks, Paul Laurence Dunbar, and others.

A short biography of Martin Luther King, Jr. is *Martin Luther King: The Peaceful Warrior* by Edward Clayton. This offers information about his early childhood, college educational experiences, his fight for equal rights for Negroes, and other valuable material. Words and music to "We Shall Overcome" are appended. Numerous adult biographies about King, including one by his wife, have been written. One interesting one is *What Manner of Man: A Biography of Martin Luther King, Jr.* by Lerone Bennet, Jr.

Tell-It-Like-It-Is Novels

In recent years many black literature books are being published with a "tell-it-like-it-is" approach. Such books confront social problems of the current scene honestly and authentically, but many of them fail to offer much hope or vision of a better social world. Many scenes are set in such urban ghetto centers as Watts, Harlem, the South Side of Chicago, or Los Angeles, and readers try to interpret plots filled with violence, drug addiction, muggings, crime, and social protest.

Effie Lee Morris of the San Francisco Public Library published an excellent bibliography, "Blowing in the Wind: Books on Black History and Life in America," in the *School Library Journal* of March 1969. She includes several novels on the contemporary scene under such sections as "Toward Black Dignity," "Tell It Like It Was," "Tell It Like It Is," and many others.

A rather sad book of the "tell-it-like-it-is" category is *Edgar Allan,* a novel by John Neufeld. This is an unusual and unpleasant story showing conflict. The Reverend Robert Fickett and his wife and four children live in a California community. The Ficketts adopt Edgar Allan, a Negro boy. The younger children of the Fickett family, Sally Ann and Stephen, enjoy Edgar, but the oldest daughter finds acceptance of the black child much more difficult due to prejudices and attitudes of her classmates. Many problems, such as a burning cross on the lawn, threats of neighbors, and doubts and confusion, make it necessary to send Edgar Allan back to the adoption agency.

A book which is quite popular with intermediate grade pupils is *The Soul Brothers and Sister Lou* by Kristin Hunter, which has been mentioned previously. Louretta Hawkins gradually learns to have a deep identification and pride in her black life, and she slowly untangles her confused emotions through musical experiences in the "Clubhouse" in spite of the violent death of one of the club-members. Blind Eddie Bell helps Louretta to understand her heritage of Negro music. The book has many tragic, as well as happy, overtones, and the characterization of Lou is well developed.

Claude Brown's autobiography, *Manchild in the Promised Land,* offers much illumination on life in the ghetto. So does a book by Piro entitled *The Black Fiddler.* The first book has been discussed frequently in many sources, such as the article "Literature for Children Without" by Marion Edman.

The portrayal of ghetto life and teaching in *The Black Fiddler* is a gripping one for adults or mature young-adult readers. A dedicated drama teacher successfully produced a Broadway play "The Fiddler on the Tin Roof" using black children to represent the Jewish characters in the play. He had to overcome almost insurmountable odds. Conditions in the New York schools were such that the dramatic talents and training of these gifted black drama students were lost in the deteriorating social system of the school. The project was abandoned a year later, and the drama teacher resigned in despair. Piro uses many four letter words which are considered obscene by many librarians and teachers, but he is an Italian teacher trying desperately to communicate on equal terms with many black children who have not previously had an opportunity to raise their self-images by working up to their innate potentialities under inspired leadership.

Dictionary of Afro-American Slang

Many readers of Afro-American literature are confused by certain terminology which has different denotations and connotations because it has developed from the life experience of the blacks living in both farm regions and in clustered ghetto areas. Clarence Major has compiled a *Dictionary of Afro-American Slang* which can help readers to understand certain special terms and dialogues written by authors depicting much of the black experience in literature. In his introduction, Mr. Major states that "Black slang stems more precisely from a somewhat disseminated rejection of the life styles, social patterns, and thinking in general of the Euro-American sensibility."[13] Much black slang is part of the "underground language" of black America. It gives a sense of unity to blacks who understand the informal language of black musicians and certain prison slang and jargon coming out of the drug and crime scene. Some of this Afro-American slang has been generally accepted by others in the mainstream of American culture. For instance, most teen-agers utilize the term "Cloud 9" to express a feeling of euphoria or happiness. Major explains that the word 'cloud' followed by a number refers to "contentment, the kind of ease associated with the floating lightweightedness of clouds."[14]

Documentary Books of the "Tell-It-Like-It-Is" Approach

A somewhat different style of book is a documentary type of literature which uses photographs and tape recordings of real conversations of people living in contemporary, inner-city society. One example of such a book which has been mentioned previously is *It's Wings that Make Birds Fly: The Story of a Boy* by Sandra Weiner. Otis Bennett is a boy whose time is spent in a gray and ugly world of dark alleys and old store fronts. He has dreams beyond his sordid surroundings and thinks about the beauty, wonder, and freedom of birds spreading their wings.

Another similar type of documentary story is a photographic story, edited by John Holland, entitled *The Way It Is: Fifteen Boys Describe Life in Their Neglected Urban Neighborhood.*

Short Stories and Essays

Much black expression is being written in the short story and essay form. Many short stories illuminate newer insights about the Negro who tries to find himself in the current pluralistic, mechanized society by asking

---

13. Clarence Major, *Dictionary of Afro-American Slang* (New York: International Publishers, 1970), p. 10.
14. *Ibid.,* p. 38.

such questions as Who, what, and, how did I come to be? Other questions which he might ask are: What parts of life surrounding the artist should be accepted or rejected? and How can a creative author confront the inevitable conflict between good and evil? Ralph Ellison has spoken of the artist who fails to gain a vision of life and a resourcefulness of his craft. Frequently various Negro-American artists fail to "leave the uneasy sanctuary of race to take their chances in the world of art."[15] *Shadow and Act* is viewed by some readers as the real autobiography of Ralph Ellison. He considers the fate of the Negro as a human being. He critically reviews such books as *Huckleberry Finn* by Mark Twain and points out that Jim is "not simply a slave, he is a symbol of humanity."[16]

Another collection of essays is *Black Expression, Essays By and About Black Americans in the Creative Arts,* edited by Addison Gale, Jr. Several of the essays on folk culture are by such noted authors as Sterling A. Brown, J. Mason Brewer, Arna Bontemps, and W. E. B. Du Bois. One selection of essays is on poetry and another one on drama. The final collection of essays is on fiction. Leroi Jones, in his essay "The Myth of Negro Literature," takes the position that much of this kind of literature is mediocre.

One collection of short stories is *Afro-American Literature: Fiction* by William Adams, Peter Conn, and Barry Slepian. This anthology has fiction organized under such sections as The Family, Black Soldiers: The War Within, On Being Black and Man Alone. Stories or selections from novels by such authors as Ann Petry, James Baldwin, Ralph Ellison, Gwendolyn Brooks, and W. E. B. Du Bois appear in this collection.

A second anthology is *American Negro Short Stories,* edited by John Henrik Clarke. This includes such stories as "The Lynching of Jube Benson" by Paul Laurence Dunbar, "On Being Crazy" by W. E. B. Du Bois, "The Screamer" by LeRoi Jones, and "The Sky is Gray" by Ernest J. Gaines.

Adolescents and Young Adults

A comprehensive volume which includes a large collection of writings by American Negroes is *The Negro Caravan: Writings by American Negroes,* selected and edited by Sterling A. Brown, Arthur P. Davis and Ulysses Lee. This includes a collection of short stories ranging from "From the Heroic Slaves" by Frederick Douglass to "Bright and Morning Star" by Richard Wright. Several selections from novels range from

15. Ralph Ellison, *Shadow and Act* (New York: New American Library, a Signet Book, 1966), p. xix.
16. *Ibid.,* p. 49.

Speculating in Slaves: Quadroon, Octoroon by William Wells Brown to *Steel Mill Rhythm* by William Attaway. A large collection of Negro poetry is included, with such well known poems as "O Black and Unknown Bards" by James Weldon Johnson, "The Negro Speaks of Rivers" by Langston Hughes, and "For My People" by Margaret Walker. A folk literature section of this anthology includes spirituals, slave seculars, aphroisms, ballads, work and social songs, social protest songs, blues, folk tales, and a folk sermon, "From Jonah's Gourd Vine." Dramas, speeches, pamphlets, letters, autobiographies, biographies, and historical social, cultural, and personal essays are also included.

A Different Tune in a Novel About Blacks

Some novelists sing an individual tune about Negro characters and cause a different perception of the black image. *The Cay* by Theodore Taylor and *Sounder* by William H. Armstrong have originality and mood and present a somewhat different image than is seen in many of the hundreds of other novels recently published.

The Cay is principally the story of the survival of a boy, Phillip, and an old West-Indian Negro who are cast off from an explosion of a ship while Phillip and his mother are leaving Curacao during World War II. Phillip has led a somewhat pampered existence until the day of the fateful ship disaster when he is pulled to a makeship raft by Timothy, the West-Indian. At first the boy resents the old black man, but later he evaluates the man without consideration of race or color, and his opinion changes. Gradually after Phillip loses his eyesight, the patient, understanding, dignified and wise old Negro gives the boy his greatest gift—some survival training. The life of the two shipwrecked ones on a barren little island, or cay, is a continuous struggle to keep alive. Timothy is a character who will not soon be forgotten. This novel is recommended for pupils in grades seven through ten, but younger children will also enjoy the pace and suspense occasioned by disaster and the training which Timothy offers in order to make Phillip into a self-sufficient, mature boy.

Sounder by William Armstrong, which has been mentioned previously in Chapter Three of this book, is a taut, terse novel. It is the unhappy story of a black sharecropper's family and of the poverty and cruelty which push the father of the family toward tragedy as he steals sausage and ham for his starving wife and children. The mother painfully and stubbornly does what she must to get sustenance and bare necessities for her family. Patiently, night after night she picks nut meat from the hulls. This is also a story about the intense devotion of the dog Sounder for his master. *Sounder* is a sad but honest story, a sharp indictment against poverty and cruelty.

A Negro author who presents unique stories with a different plot is Virginia Hamilton, who has written *The House of Dies Drear, The Time-Ago Tales of Jahdu, Zeely,* and *The Planet of Junior Brown. Zeely* seems to pull together traditions of an African heritage with a daydreaming, modern Negro girl who visits Uncle Ross in his country farm. The girl renames herself Geeder, and her brother Toeboy, and builds a dream world around Zeely, a tall, six-and-a-half-foot African girl who tends the hogs for her father, Nat Tayber. Zeely is regally lovely in her long smock and her dark ebony skin. Geeder dreams that Zeely was a Mututsi belonging to the Batutsi tribe of giants; perhaps she was a former queen. Geeder wants to trace her through many generations back to Africa. It is Zeely who manages to help Geeder to see reality, and she becomes Elizabeth again, and stops her imagining daydreaming. Each of the other books by Virginia Hamilton offers a unique contribution to developing an understanding of some of the black experience in an unstereotyped manner. Virginia Hamilton somehow manages to invoke positive symbolic images, a philosophy of life, fantasy and reality, and through her artistry she creates a plausible imaginative story.

The Human Experience

Hundreds of short stories and novels are now being published annually about the black experience, but as readers interpret much of the current black literature, they should remember that most great literature is about man as a human being and the place of man in the stream of human experience. An interesting recent anthology is *Brothers and Sisters: Modern Stories by Black Americans.* The writers in this anthology have created their work as black people, but most of the stories are about young brothers and sisters who were born in rural areas of the South, or in Harlem. In his preface Adoff says, "Their stories are a part of the long time-line, stretching like an infinite rope, back to Africa and the ancient tellers of legends and forward to the 1970's and the '80's to the generations to come."[17]

Novels and biographies of slaves and the institution of slavery bring back the compassionate words of Edna St. Vincent Millay who speaks in "Renascence" of ships colliding on great fog banks and the sounds from a thousand screams as she feels the hurt and death of others as if they were her own and she knows "The compassion that was I."[18]

17. Arnold Adoff, ed., *Brothers and Sisters: Modern Stories by Black Americans* (New York: Macmillan Co., 1970), preface.
18. Edna St. Vincent Millay, "Renascence," in *Collected Lyrics of Edna St. Vincent Millay* (New York: Washington Square Press, 1959), p. 6.

Summary

Black literature in our pluralistic society needs to meet the needs of both black persons and those representing the white middle-class culture. Although black poetry, folk lore, and novels interpret much of the black experience in our pluralistic society in the United States, such literature should interpret human conditions and rules and conflicts which are universal in scope.

Black folk tales created in the United States lean heavily on oral traditions and folklore. Few black folktales created in the South have been written in a suitable form and style for young readers. Although many folktales have been recorded by such scholars as Richard M. Dorson, J. Mason Brewer, and Zora Neale Hurston, few of these have been adapted for young readers.

Black poets have sung their lyrics for over a century-and-a-half, although some readers have not equated black folk music with black poetry. Spirituals, work songs, blues, and rock songs have been developed spontaneously by different Negro poets. Some of these lyrics have been created anonymously. Various collectors have attempted to record Negro folk music as accurately and authentically as possible. Folklore can be presented as a unit of study in both elementary and secondary schools. Alan Dundes indicates that folklore helps us view a culture "from the inside out."

Black poets have created much poetry of literary value and are continuing to create poems of individuality and originality. Some poetry of protest and revolution should probably be presented to those adolescents who have already had some principles of literary criticism as background for the study of various propaganda devices which have been explicated by the Institute of Propaganda Analysis. Many youngsters in both elementary and secondary schools are beginning to sing out their songs of protest.

Reactions—Questions and Projects

1. Study some of the black folktales collected by such scholars as J. Mason Brewer and Richard Dorson. Select a folktale or two and rewrite it in a literary form for children in the primary grades.
2. Use recordings of African music or folk music of the United States as a background for the telling of a black folktale. If recordings are not available, children may wish to make some drums and to make drumming noises to heighten the effect of a folktale.

An historical study of literature in the United States indicates that many Negro authors formerly apologized for their people. Recent literature, particularly the poetry and prose that is written for therapeutic purposes, tends to express pride in the traditions of Afro-Americans and an exultant feeling that "black is beautiful."

Young children in primary grade classes tend to identify with Negro characters in stories, poems, and books of nonfiction. Many little picture books for young pupils are designed to help boys and girls to understand both themselves and others. Some young children react to black folk heroes, such as John Henry.

A large number of novels written for middle-grade readers is concerned with aspects of slavery and episodes of the Civil War. There are also some biographies about persons who have played prominent parts in the Civil Rights Movement. The novel *Jubilee* by Margaret Walker builds a new awareness of the contribution of Negroes to the historical period of the Civil War and Reconstruction.

Sometimes the self-image of black children is raised through a study of autobiographies and biographies of important Negro persons who have contributed to the culture of the United States.

A recent phase in both children's and adolescent fiction about Negroes is usually termed the "tell-it-like-it-is" approach to literature, which means that authors present plantation or ghetto episodes with all their cruelty, crime, and ugliness of life. Some novels, such as the autobiography *Manchild in the Promised Land,* ends with a dream of happiness; others, such as *The Black Fiddler,* end with a tragic feeling that man may not survive a deteriorating social scene.

The finest type of black literature offers readers a "certificate of humanity," a feeling that through the imaginative immersion of the reader in the plights and dreams of others, he will recognize that many characters are symbols of humanity and that it is our destiny to feel compassion for our fellow man.

3. *Marassa and Midnight* by Morna Stuart is a hauntingly poignant tale of the plight of black slaves in Haiti. It is the story of two identical twins and includes much that is voodooistic or mystical in spirit. This is the story of slaves who revolted during the "Night of Flames." Compare this novel with a novel about some of the slave revolts on plantations in the United States.

4. A biography for young adolescents is *Black Patriot and Martyr: Toussaint of Haiti* by Ann Griffiths. This is a mature biography

showing how Toussaint L'Óuverture rose from slavery to lead his people against Colonial armies. It also enacts the struggle between native Creoles and mulattoes who felt that more wealth should be contributed by English or French colonial planters and army officers. Compare and contrast the leadership of Toussaint with such a person as Singbé who revolted and commanded mutineers on the *Long Schooner,* otherwise known as the *Amistad.*

5. *Black Images* by Wilfred G. Cartey (New York: Teachers College, Columbia University) traces the literary evolution of the black image of black men from that of slave to a person of "human distinction." It is a critical review of much black poetry by a Trinidadian born author. He contrasts the work of three Antillean poets: Emilio Ballagas, Luis Palés Matos, and Nicholás Guillén. All of these poets reject stereotypes and derogatory images of black persons. Study this volume as well as one concerned with black poets in the United States today. Trace some of the "black images" which are evident in poetry ranging from slavery songs written on plantations to modern freedom songs.

6. Make a detailed study of one Afro-American poet, including both his biography and his literary contributions.

7. Analyze ten black picture books and note the absence or presence of black stereotypes.

8. Make an historical study of some of the novels concerned with the "underground railroad."

9. Study some books of Negro music, select one song, and create an original story around the history of the song's origin.

10. Encourage pupils in your community or in a school classroom to create original songs and poetry about one black historical figure.

11. Make a biographical study of one black artist who illustrates books for young children.

12. Create an original docudrama by working with two or three other persons. Obtain basic documents, authentic recordings of slave or folk songs, and historical data about the period of Reconstruction in the United States.

13. Select some current books on black literature using the "tell-it-like-it-is approach. Discuss cautions which should be used with this type of literature and the dangers of selecting novels using only the criterion of relevance.

14. Do some close reading of *The Cay* by Theodore Taylor. Write a character sketch of Timothy or Phillip. What positive qualities did Timothy have? Read other novels such as the *Island of the Blue*

Dolphins by Scott O'Dell (Boston: Houghton Mifflin, 1960) and *Treasure Island* by Robert Louis Stevenson (Illustrated by Henry C. Pitz. New York: Doubleday & Co., 1956) and compare and contrast survival methods.

15. *Sounder* by William Armstrong is a taut novel almost like a Greek tragedy. Look for the few instances in which happiness was sought by the characters. Write an episode for *Sounder* which will add another aspect to one of the characters, such as the mother, the boy, or the father. See if your episode keeps to the tone, or the mood, of the story.

16. Role-play the court trial of the *Amistad*—the one in which slaves were tried for a mutiny on the high seas.

BIBLIOGRAPHY

BOOKS FOR PRIMARY CHILDREN

FELTON, HAROLD W. *John Henry and His Hammer*. New York: Alfred A. Knopf, 1950.

HILL, ELIZABETH STARR. *Evan's Corner*. New York: Holt, Rinehart & Winston, 1967.

HOPKINS, LEE BENNETT, comp. *Don't You Turn Back: Poems by Langston Hughes*. New York: Alfred A. Knopf, 1969.

JUSTUS, MAY. *A New Home for Billy*. New York: Hastings House, 1966.

KEATS, EZRA JACK. *John Henry, An American Legend*. New York: Pantheon Books, a division of Random House, 1965.

————. *Peter's Chair*. New York: Harper & Row, Publishers, 1967.

————. *A Letter to Amy*. New York: Harper & Row, Publishers, 1968.

————. *Goggles!* New York: The Macmillan Company, 1969.

————. *Hi Cat!* New York: The Macmillan Company, 1970.

————. *The Snowy Day*. New York: Viking Press, 1962.

————. *Whistle for Willie*. New York: Viking Press, 1964.

KREMENTZ, JILL. *Sweet Pea: A Black Girl Growing Up in the Rural South*. New York: Harcourt, Brace & World, 1969.

LEXAU, JOAN M. *Benjie on His Own*. New York: Dial Press, 1970.

McGOVERN, ANN. *Black is Beautiful*. New York: Four Winds Press, 1969.

REES, ENNIS. *Brer Rabbit and His Tricks*. New York: Young Scott Books, 1967.

————. *More of Brer Rabbit's Tricks*. New York: Young Scott Books, 1968.

SCOTT, ANN HERBERT. *Sam*. New York: McGraw-Hill Book Company, 1967

STEPTOE, JOHN. *Stevie*. New York: Harper & Row, Publishers, 1969.

UDRY, JANICE MAY. *What Mary Jo Wanted*. Albert Whitman & Company, 1968.

WEIK, MARY HAYS. *The Jazz Man*. New York: Atheneum Publishers, 1966.

WEINER, SANDRA. *It's Wings that Make Birds Fly: The Story of a Boy*. New York: Pantheon Books, 1968.

BOOKS FOR INTERMEDIATE CHILDREN

ADOFF, ARNOLD, ed. *I Am the Darker Brother: An Anthology of Modern Poems by Negro Americans.* New York: The Macmillan Company, 1968.

————., ed. *Black Out Loud: An Anthology of Modern Poems by Black Americans.* New York: The Macmillan Company, 1970.

————., ed. *City in All Directions: An Anthology of Modern Poems.* New York: The Macmillan Company, 1969.

ARMSTRONG, WILLIAM H. *Sounder.* New York: Harper & Row, Publishers, 1969.

BACMEISTER, RHODA. *Voices in the Night.* New York: Bobbs-Merrill Co., 1965.

BAKER, BETTY. *Walk the World's Rim.* New York: Harper & Row, Publishers, 1965.

BARON, VIRGINIA OLSEN. *Here I Am!: An Anthology of Poems Written by Young People in Some of America's Minority Groups.* New York: E. P. Dutton & Company, 1969.

BURT, OLIVE W. *Negroes in the Early West.* New York: Julian Messner, a division of Simon & Schuster, 1969.

DOUTY, ESTHER M. *Forten the Sailmaker, Pioneer Champion of the Negro Rights.* Chicago: Rand, McNally and Company, 1968.

FELTON, HAROLD W. *Mumbet: The Story of Elizabeth Freeman.* New York: Dodd, Mead & Company, 1970.

————. *Jim Beckwourth, Negro Mountain Man.* New York: Dodd, Mead & Company, 1966.

FOX, PAULA. *How Many Miles to Babylon?* New York: David White Company, 1967.

GLASS, PAUL. *Songs and Stories of Afro-Americans.* New York: Grosset & Dunlap, 1971.

HAMILTON, VIRGINIA. *The House of Dies Dreer.* New York: The Macmillan Company, 1968.

————. *The Time-Ago-Tales of Jahdu.* New York: The Macmillan Company, 1969.

————. *Zeely.* New York: The Macmillan Company, 1967.

————. *The Planet of Junior Brown.* New York: The Macmillan Company, 1971.

HEARD, J. NORMAN. *The Black Frontiersman: Adventures of Negroes Among American Indians, 1528-1918.* New York: The John Day Company, 1969.

HOLLAND, JOHN, ed. *The Way It Is: Fifteen Boys Describe Life in Their Neglected Urban Neighborhood.* New York: Harcourt, Brace & World, 1969.

HOPKINS, LEE BENNETT, ed. *City Talk.* New York: Alfred A. Knopf, 1970.

JACKSON, FLORENCE, and J. B. *The Black Man in America, 1619-1970.* New York: Franklin Watts, 1970.

JAY, DAVID, and GREENE, CATHERINE J. *Black Roots: An Anthology.* New York: Lothrop, Lee & Shepard Co., 1971.

JORDAN, JUNE, and BUSH, TERRI. *The Voice of the Children.* New York: Holt, Rinehart & Winston, 1970.

JORDAN, JUNE. *Who Look at Me.* New York: Thomas Y. Crowell Co., 1969.

JOSEPH, STEPHEN M., ed. *The Me Nobody Knows; Children's Voices from the Ghetto.* New York: Avon Books, a division of the Hearst Corporation, 1969.

LARRICK, NANCY, comp. *On City Streets, An Anthology of Poetry* .New York: M. Evans and Company, 1968.

LESTER, JULIUS. *To Be a Slave*. New York: The Dial Press, 1968.

————. *Black Folktales*. New York: Richard W. Baron Publishing Company, 1969.

MENDOZA, GEORGE. *The World from my Window*. New York: Hawthorne Books, Inc., Publishers, 1969.

MOLARSKY, OSMOND. *Song of the Empty Bottles*. New York: Henry Z. Walck, 1968.

MONJO, F. N. *The Drinking Gourd*. New York: Harper & Row, Publishers, 1969.

NEUFELD, JOHN. *Edgar Allan*. New York: S. G. Phillips, 1968.

OFOSU-APPIAH. *People in Bondage: African Slavery in the Modern Era*. Minneapolis: Lerner Publications Company, 1971.

PECK, RICHARD, ed. *Sounds and Silences: Poetry for Now*. New York: Dell Publishing Co., 1970.

PETRY, ANN. *Harriet Tubman, Conductor on the Underground Railroad*. New York: Thomas Y. Crowell Company, 1955.

ROLLINS, CHARLEMAE. H. *Black Troubadour: Langston Hughes*. Chicago: Rand McNally & Company, 1970.

SCHRAFF, A. E. *Black Courage*. Philadelphia: Macrae Smith Company, 1969.

SHEPHERD, ELIZABETH. *The Discoveries of Esteban the Black*. New York: Dodd, Mead & Company, 1970.

STEPTOE, JOHN. *Uptown*. New York: Harper & Row, Publishers, 1970.

STERLING, PHILIP, and LOGAN, RAYFORD. *Four Took Freedom: The Lives of Harriet Tubman, Frederick Douglass, Robert Smalls, and Blanche K. Bruce*. Garden City, New York: Doubleday & Company, Zenith Books, 1967.

STERLING, DOROTHY. *Freedom Train: The Story of Harriet Tubman*. New York: Doubleday & Company, 1954.

STERNE, EMMA GELDERS. *Mary McLeod Bethune*. New York: Alfred A. Knopf, 1962.

STUART, MORNA. *Marassa and Midnight*. New York: Dell Publishing Company, 1969.

TAYLOR, THEODORE. *The Cay*. Garden City, New York: Doubleday & Company, 1969.

WEIK, MARY HAYS. *The Jazz Man*. New York: Atheneum Publishers, 1966.

WOJCIECHOWSKA, MAIA. *Odyssey of Courage: The Story of Alvar Núñez Cabeza de Vaca*. New York: Atheneum Publishers, 1965.

ZAGOREN, RUBY. *Venture for Freedom: The True Story of an African Yankee*. Cleveland: World Publishing Company, 1969.

BOOKS FOR ADOLESCENTS

ADAMS, WILLIAM; CONN, PETER; and SLEPIAN, BARRY. *Afro-American Literature: Fiction*. Boston: Houghton Mifflin Company, 1970.

ADOFF, ARNOLD, ed. *Brothers and Sisters: Modern Stories by Black Americans*. New York: The Macmillan Company, 1970.

ANDERSON, MARIAN. *My Lord What A Morning*. New York: The Viking Press, 1956.

BELZ, CARL. *The Story of Rock*. New York: Oxford University Press, 1969.

BENNETT, LERONE, JR. *What Manner of Man: A Biography of Martin Luther King, Jr.* Chicago: Johnson Publishing Company, 1964.

BERNARD, JACQUELINE. *Journey Toward Freedom: The Story of Sojourner Truth.* New York: W. W. Norton & Company, 1967.

BIKEL, THEODORE. *Folksongs and Footnotes by Theodore Bikel: An International Songbook.* New York: Meridian Books, 1960.

BONHAM, FRANK. *Honor Bound.* New York: Thomas Y. Crowell Company, 1965.

―――. *Durango Street.* New York: E. P. Dutton Company, 1965.

―――. *Nitty Gritty.* New York: E. P. Dutton Company, 1968.

BONTEMPS, ARNA, ed. *American Negro Poetry.* New York: Hill and Wang, 1968.

BROWN, CLAUDE. *Manchild in the Promised Land.* New York: New American Library, a Signet Book, 1965.

BROWN, STERLING. *Negro Poetry and Drama* and *The Negro in American Fiction.* New York: Atheneum Publishers, 1969.

CARLSON, NATALIE SAVAGE. *The Empty Schoolhouse.* New York: Harper & Row, Publishers, 1965.

CLARKE, JOHN HENDRIK. *American Negro Short Stories.* New York: Hill and Wang, American Centuries Series, 1966.

CLAYTON, EDWARD T. *Martin Luther King: The Peaceful Warrior.* Englewood Cliffs, New Jersey: Prentice-Hall, 1964.

DOUGLASS, FREDERICK. *Narrative of the Life of Frederick Douglass, An American Slave.* New York: New American Library, Signet Books, 1968.

DROTHING, PHILIP T. *Black Heroes in Our Nation's History: A Tribute to Those who Helped Shape America.* New York: Washington Square Press, 1970.

ELLISON, RALPH. *Shadow and Act.* New York: New American Library, a Signet Book, 1966.

―――. *The Invisible Man.* New York: New American Library, a Signet Book, 1952.

FELDMAN, SUSAN, ed. *African Myths and Tales.* New York: Dell Publishing Company, a Laurel Original, 1963.

GALE, ADDISON, JR., ed. *Black Expression: Essays By and About Black Americans in the Creative Arts.* New York: Weybright and Talley, 1969.

GLASS, PAUL. *Songs and Stories of Afro-American.* New York: Grosset & Dunlap, a National General Company, 1971.

GRAHAM, LORENZ. *South Town:* Chicago: Follett Publishing Company, 1958.

―――. *North Town.* New York: Thomas Y. Crowell Company, 1965.

GRIFFIN, JOHN HOWARD. *Black Like Me.* Boston: Houghton Mifflin Company, 1961.

GRIFFITHS, ANN. *Black Patriot and Martyr: Toussaint of Haiti.* New York: Julian Messner, 1970.

HENTOFF, NAT. *Journey Into Jazz.* New York: Coward-McCann, 1968.

HOWARD, ELIZABETH. *North Winds Blow Free.* New York: William Morrow & Company, 1949.

HUGHES, LANGSTON. *The Panther and The Lash: Poems of Our Times.* New York: Alfred A. Knopf, 1967.

HUNTER, KRISTIN. *The Soul Brothers and Sister Lou.* New York: Charles Scribner's Sons, 1968.

JOHNSON, JAMES WELDON, ed. *The Book of American Negro Poetry.* Rev. ed. New York: Harcourt, Brace & World, Harbrace Paperbound Library, 1959.

――――. *God's Trombones: Seven Negro Sermons in Verse.* New York: The Viking Press, Compass Edition, 1969.

JORDAN, JUNE. *Soulscript Afro-American Poetry.* Garden City, New York: Doubleday & Company, 1970.

LACEY, LESLIE ALEXANDER. *Cheer the Lonesome Traveler: The Life of W. E. B. Du Bois.* New York: Dial Press, 1970.

LARRICK, NANCY, comp. *I Heard A Scream in the Street: Poems by Young People in the City.* New York: M. Evans & Company, distributed in association with J. P. Lippincott Company, 1970.

LESTER, JULIUS. *Search for the New Land: History as Subjective Experience.* New York: Dial Press, 1969.

MAJOR, CLARENCE, ed. *The New Black Poetry.* New York: International Publishers, 1970.

MALCOLM X. *The Autobiography of Malcolm X.* New York: Grove Press, 1966.

MEADOWCROFT, ENID L. *By Secret Railway.* New York: Thomas Y. Crowell Company, 1948.

MELTZER, MILTON. *Thaddeus Stevens and the Fight for Negro Rights.* New York: Thomas Y. Crowell Company, 1967.

――――. *Langston Hughes: A Biography.* New York: Thomas Y. Crowell Company, 1968.

――――. *In Their Own Words: A History of the American Negro.* 3 vols. Vol. 1, 1716-1865. New York: Thomas Y. Crowell Company, 1964.

――――. *In Their Own Words: A History of the American Negro.* 3 vols. Vol. 2, 1865-1916. New York: Thomas Y. Crowell Company, 1965.

――――. *In Their Own Words: A History of the American Negro.* 3 vols. Vol. 3, 1916-1966. New York: Thomas Y. Crowell Company, 1967.

MIRSKY, JEANNETTE. *The Gentle Conquistadors: The Ten Year Odyssey Across the American Southwest of Three Spanish Captains and Esteban, a Black Slave.* New York: Pantheon Books, a division of Random House, Inc., 1969.

MOORE, CARMEN. *Somebody's Angel Child: The Story of Bessie Smith.* New York: Thomas Y. Crowell Company, 1969.

MURPHY, BEATRICE, ed. *Today's Negro Voices: An Anthology of Young Negro Poets.* New York: Julian Messner, 1970.

MURRAY, PAULI. *Dark Testament and Other Poems.* Norwalk, Connecticut: Silvermine Publishers, 1970.

NICHOLAW, ANDY C. *Black America Sings Out.* San Francisco: Intext, proposed publication date, 1972.

QUARLES, BENJAMIN, ed. *Narrative of the Life of Frederick Douglass, An American Slave, Written by Himself.* Cambridge, Massachusetts: The Belknap Press of Harvard University Press, 1969.

SWIFT, HILDEGARDE. *North Star Shining.* New York: William Morrow & Company, 1947.

WALKER, MARGARET. *For My People.* New Haven and London: Yale University Press, 1968.

――――. *Jubilee.* New York: Bantam Books, 1967.

WERTHEIM, BILL, ed. *Talkin' About Us: Writings by Students in the Upward Bound Program.* New York: New Century Educational Division, Meredith Corporation, 1970.

PROFESSIONAL BOOKS AND ARTICLES

ASSOCIATION FOR CHILDHOOD EDUCATIONAL INTERNATIONAL. *The World In Children's Picture Books.* Washington, D.C.: Association for Childhood Educational International, 1968.

"BIBLIOGRAPHY ON AFRO-AMERICAN HISTORY AND CULTURE." Reprinted from *Social Education* 33, no. 4 (April 1969): 447-461.

BREWER, J. MASON. *American Negro Folklore.* Chicago: Quadrangle Books, 1968.

BROWN, STERLING A.; DAVIS, ARTHUR P.; and LEE, ULYSSES. *The Negro Caravan: Writings by American Negroes.* New York: Arno Press and the New York Times, 1970.

BODROGI, TIBOR. *Art in Africa.* New York: McGraw-Hill Book Company, 1968.

BUREAU OF LIBRARIES, NEW YORK CITY SCHOOLS. "Books By and About the American Negro." *School Library Journal,* January 1970, pp. 35-44.

CARAWAN, GUY and CANDIE, comps. and eds. *Freedom is A Constant Struggle: Songs of the Freedom Movement.* New York: Oak Publications, 1968.

CHAPMAN, ABRAHAM. *The Negro in American Literature* and *A Bibliography of Literature By and About Negro Americans.* Special Publication No. 15, Wisconsin Teachers of English. Oshkosh, Wisconsin: Wisconsin State University, 1966.

CROSBY, MURIEL. *Reading Ladders for Human Relations.* Washington, D. C.: American Council on Education, 1963. (Currently being revised.)

DETT, R. NATHANIEL. *Religious Folk Songs of the Negro, as Sung at Hampton Institute.* Hampton, Virginia: Hampton Institute Press, 1927.

DODDS, BARBARA. *Negro Literature for High School Students.* Champaign, Illinois: National Council of Teachers of English, 1968.

DORSON, RICHARD W., comp. *American Negro Folktales.* Greenwich, Connecticut: Fawcett Publications, a Fawcett Premier Book, 1967.

DUNDES, ALAN. "Folklore as a Mirror of Culture." *Elementary English* 46 (April 1969): 471-482.

EDMAN, MARION. "Literature for Children Without." *A Critical Approach to Children's Literature,* edited by Sara Innis Fenwick. Chicago and London: The University of Chicago Press, 1967, pp. 32-45.

FISHER, MILES MARK. *Slave Songs of the United States.* New York: The Citadel Press, 1953.

GLANCY, BARBARA J. "Black Barbecue: An Essay Review. A reprint *The Record* —Teachers College 70, no. 7 (April 1969): 661-684.

HOPKINS, LEE BENNETT, and ARENSTEIN, MISHA. "Pages of History: A Bibliography of Great Negro Americans." In *Elementary English* 46 (February 1969) 204-206.

HOWARD, DR. JOSEPH H. *Drums in the Americas.* New York: Oak Publications, 1967.

HUGHES, LANGSTON, and BONTEMPS, ARNA. *The Book of Negro Folklore.* New York: Dodd, Mead and Company, 1958.

————. *The Poetry of the Negro, 1746-1949*. Garden City, New York: Doubleday & Company, 1949.

HURSTON, NORA NEALE. *Mules and Men*. New York: Harper & Row, Publishers, Perennial Library, Torchbook Edition, 1970.

JACKSON, MILES M., JR., comp. and ed. *A Bibliography of Negro History and Culture for Young Readers*. Pittsburgh: University of Pittsburgh Press, published for Atlanta University, 1968 (Includes a listing of Audio-Visual materials).

JOHNSON, JAMES WELDON, ed. *The Book of American Negro Poetry*. Rev. ed. New York: Harcourt, Brace & World, Harbrace Paperbound Library, 1959.

JOHNSON, JAMES WELDON, and JOHNSON, J. ROSAMOND. *The Book of American Negro Spirituals*. New York: The Viking Press, Viking Compass Edition, 1969.

————. *Lift Every Voice and Sing: Words and Music*. New York: Hawthorne Books, 1970.

KATZ, BERNARD, ed. *The Social Implications of Early Negro Music in the United States*. New York: Arno Press and the New York Times, 1969.

KRISTOF, JANE. *Steal Away Home*. Indianapolis, Indiana: Bobbs-Merrill, 1969.

LARRICK, NANCY, ed. *Somebody Turned on a Tap in These Kids: Poetry and Young People Today*. New York: Delacorte Press, 1971.

LEE, HECTOR H. "American Folklore in the Secondary Schools." *English Journal* 59 (October 1970): 994-1004.

MAJOR, CLARENCE. *Dictionary of Afro-American Slang*. New York: International Publishers, 1971.

MILLENDER, DHARALHULA. "Through a Glass Darkly." *School Library Journal* 13 December 1967.

MILLER, ADAM DAVID, ed. *Dices or Black Bones*. Boston: Houghton Mifflin Company, 1970.

MILLER, RUTH, ed. *Backgrounds to Blackamerican Literature*. Scranton: Chandler Publishing Company, an Intext publisher, 1971.

MORRIS, EFFIE L. "Blowing in the Wind Books on Black History and Life in America." *School Library Journal,* March 1969.

PIRO, R. *The Black Fiddler*. New York: William Morrow & Company, 1971.

RADIN, PAUL, comp. and ed. "Native African Folktales." In *African Folktales and Sculpture*. Bollingen Series 32. Bollingen Foundation, distributed by Pantheon Books, a division of Random House, Inc., 1966.

————, comp. and ed. *African Folktales*. Bollingen Series. Princeton, New Jersey: Princeton University Press, Bollingen Paperback printing, 1970.

ROLLINS, CHARLEMAE, ed. *We Build Together: Readers Guide to Negro Life and Literature for Elementary and High School Use*. Champaign, Illinois: National Council of Teachers of English, 1967.

SEGY, LADISLAS. *African Sculpture Speaks*. 3rd ed., rev. New York: Hill and Wang, 1969.

STERLING, DOROTHY. "The Soul of Learning." *The English Journal,* February 1968, pp. 166-180.

SWEENEY, JAMES JOHNSON, comp. "African Negro Sculpture." *African Folktales and Sculpture*. Bollingen Series 32. Published by Bollingen Foundation, distributed by Pantheon Books, a division of Random House, 1966.

TATE, BINNIE. "In House and Out House: Authenticity and the Black Experiences in Children's Books." *School Library Journal* 17 (October 1970): p. 97.

THOMPSON, JUDITH, and WOODARD, GLORIA. "Black Perspective in Books for Children." *Wilson Library Bulletin* 44 (December 1969): pp. 416-424.

TROWELL, MARGARET, and NEVERMAN, HANS. *African and Oceanic Art.* New York: Harry N. Abrams, 1968.

TURNER, DARWIN T., and STANFORD, BARBARA DODDS. *Theory and Practice in the Teaching of Literature by Afro-Americans.* Urbana, Illinois: National Council of Teachers of English, 1972.

CHAPTER SIX

The Path of
Beauty:
Literature
of the
American Indian

In recent years many American Indians as well as others in our pluralistic society are turning back to nature and a closeness to earth as a means of following a more beautiful way of life. In order for one to understand the conflicts which modern Indians have in standing at the edge of two worlds, one needs to familiarize oneself with some of the traditional poetry chanted by tribal people, since poetic song was part of the way of life. In addition to this, various folktales, myths, and legends set the tribal patterns of traditions and beliefs and helped the Indian child and adult to follow the trail of beauty.

Characteristics of American Indian Poetry

Poetic Qualities of the North American Indian Poetry

A brief study of some of the qualities of American Indian poetry impresses one with the beauty and power of the language of the various tribal persons. Almost all poetry consists of songs, chants, and recitatives which are highly significant in the life of the creator. In most cases a poem or a song is created at the time of a deep emotional experience, as was indicated by the tremendous number of songs sung as a part of the Ghost Dance religion.

Almost all Indian poetry expresses a deep reverence for nature. All things are significant to the poet. He may sing of the lowly water bug or of mountainous claps of thunder, but nothing seems too insignificant for a song.

Stylistically, two characteristics are evident in much North American poetry. The first is that the songs are long and repetitive chants going on and on offer a poetic phrase repetitiously. Some song creators have insisted that the phrase be repeated as many times as necessary to review the events of an experience. This kind of repetitive refrain, such as ones appearing in the Navajo poem, "A Prayer of the Night Chant" or in many Navajo myths, makes the rhythmical tune and beauty of a poem. Such phrases as "May it be beautiful" are repeated at least five times in one stanza.

The other style of Indian poetry is the telegraphic style in which poems are written in an abbreviated form similar to the style of Japanese *haiku* verse. The poem is expressed in a terse, clear image of a few words. An example of this type of verse is seen in three songs from the Northwest by the Tlinget Indians, which are quoted in an anthology by Margot Astrov. One of these songs is "Song of Hummingbird" which is only three lines long and expresses a loneliness in which the poet says, "I am crying about myself."[1]

A quality which permeates much Indian poetry is a deep appreciation of beauty which interweaves many of the poems, particularly those of various Indian singers of the Southwest. Some of this beauty is expressed in pictorial symbolism and imagery which can be experienced imaginatively by the reader or listener. An example of such a poem is a Tewa song entitled "Song of the Sky Loom."[2] According to Astrov the Tewa Indians belong to the tribes living in many pueblos of New Mexico, including the Nambé, San Ildefonso, San Juan, Santa Clara, and Tesuque in New Mexico, as well as the Hano in northeastern Arizona.[3] The symbol of the sky loom refers to a light desert rain in which rain showers come from the sky. The warp of the loom is a glittering web which is like soft silver, and

1. Margot Astrov, ed., *American Indian Prose and Poetry: An Anthology* (New York: Capricorn Books, 1962), p. 288.
2. *Ibid.*, p. 221.
3. *Ibid.*

the weft is like amber or rosette rays in the reflection of the late sun. The poet asks that the Mother, the Earth and the Father, the Sky, weave a garment of brightness where the warp is the "white light of morning" and the weft is the "red light of evening."[4] This is in a world where the poet can walk on a land where the grass is green and the birds sing. The poem is a popular one and has been reprinted in many anthologies, including *The Magic World: American Indian Songs and Poems* by William Brandon.

It is difficult to determine various poetic adornments of American Indian poetry unless one is a linguistic master of several dialects or languages. Most translators and scholars have indicated, however, that much Indian poetry uses the repetitive refrain, phrase, or rhyming sounds, such as "a ya ya haa." Also, many Indian poems contain alliterative words and onomatopoetic ones. Additional syllables, such as "Aja, Aja, Aja," sometimes add to the rhythmical beauty of a line, but poems have little rhyming when translated into English. Much use of metrical rhythm is seen through such devices as the repetitive refrain and the repetition of syllables.

Perhaps, the most significant quality of North American Indian poetry is that poetry was created for a purpose. The Indian considered the song or poem important to his being because there was power in the word. The song was often created as part of a ritual used for ceremonial movements, and the significance of the symbolism was often portrayed through dance and marching with certain aids, such as the downy feather of an eagle or the beaded figure of a thunderbird. Many poems were part of a mythical tale and were better known as prose poems reenacting a significant event. A. Grove Day has reviewed numerous characteristics of Indian poetry in his volume entitled *The Sky Clears: Poetry of the American Indians.*

The poetry and song reproduced on recordings and in many scholarly volumes causes one to look anew at the culture of indigenous Indian poets of the past as well as at the original chants and songs created by the modern poet singing songs of relevance in the Red Power movement. It is realized that our pluralistic society must provide space for the individual contributions of a people who have a heritage as rich as the better-known European poets. It is known that much Indian poetry was formerly created in the immediacy of the moment, but a poem like the "Song of Nezahualcoyotl" appearing in *The Sky Clears* by A. Grove Day causes us to respect the philosophical depth of the wisdom of an aboriginal thanatopsis. Here

---

4. "Song of the Sky Loom (Tewa)," in *American Indian: Prose and Poetry* ed. by Margot Astrov, p. 221.

the poet says that "the fleeting pomps of the world" are similar to the transient life quality of green willow trees which suffer from fire, the ax, stormy winds, and age."[5] Poetry and song of long ago give respect to a maligned ethnic group and a hope for a better future.

The Voice that Beautifies the Land

Most Indian poets, and particularly tribal members living in the southwestern United States, sing poems which beautify the land and make the moon, sun, and stars a part of daily worship. Sometimes the poetry of the Indian is a language of the spirit in which an orator helps an ill person; sometimes a chant expresses the day by day living of the people, including an appreciation for the beautiful in life.

Anne Nolan Clark discusses the poetry of a group of Indian children in Phoenix, Arizona. One child writes of herself as a Pima basket made of nature's materials and then goes on to describe herself as being constructed from a willow running in the arrow weeds, a cattail waving in the river with the fishes, a claw on the squash plant, and other things woven into a basket many long years ago.

A valuable collection of Indian poetry appears in *The Sky Clears: Poetry of the American Indians* by A. Grove Day which has been mentioned previously. In this book Day discusses the many uses which the Indians had for poetry. Indians sang poems of praise to the gods to ask for help in living a beautiful, productive life. Sometimes poems were an expression of seasonal celebrations or were used for such purposes as rituals, to work magical cures, or to seek supernatural aid in hunting and fishing. Songs and poems were created to explain the origins of the world, to teach the right rules of conduct, to mourn the dead, or to arouse warlike feelings. Poetry also was sung to ridicule a rival, to praise famous tribesmen, or to show an appreciation for the beauties of nature. Sometimes a song depicted actions in a folktale or lulled a baby to sleep. Rhythmic chants frequently accompanied games and humorous fun activities. A Yaqui tribe of Sonora expressed love for a maiden through a "Tule Love Song" in which girls were compared with flowers in the wind. Indians rarely used rhymes, but gained the effect of rhyming through a repetition of lines as a refrain. These were "rhyming thoughts" similar to those of a Japanese *haiku* verse in which the poem is a "shorthand of ideas."

5. A. Grove Day, *The Sky Clears: Poetry of the American Indians* (Lincoln, Nebraska: University of Nebraska Press, 1951), p. 180.

The Pawnees deified the stars. Many of their myths depicted the gods of the Morning Star and Evening Star; villages were governed by star shrines. Astronomers computed dates for planting and for other calendar events. In an invocation to the Pleides, "Song of the Pleides," the Pawnees spoke of the stars descending and coming to guide their people.

A volume which presents the indigenous background of the poetry of native peoples is volume two of *The Unwritten Song: Poetry of the Primitive and Traditional Peoples of the World* by Willard R. Trask. This volume includes "Song for the Thunder Bird Dance," which is a Kwakiutl poem about the sweeping bird seizing the chiefs in his talons.[6]

Some of the Indians in British Columbia feel that the tribe should face death bravely and yet mournfully, and this is expressed in a "Responsive Song for the Dead Child of a Chief" which is published in the Trask volume. This is a song which is a recitative in which the chief says a line and the chorus replies in a line, "We do not mourn any more."[7] The child will appear again "with his brethren the stars" and his "beloved face" will also be seen in the new moon.

Trask indicates that nothing is too insignificant for a song or poem. The Mandan Indians honor the lowly skunk with a song called "Dancing Song of the Skunk" in which the back and the face is striped.[8] The Mescalero Apache faces the sunrise, holds his arms in a ceremonial pose, and sings "Song at Sunrise on the Last Day of the Gotal Ceremony." Darkness is compared with a black turkey gobbler which spreads its tail and lets the light of dawn whiten the world.[9] "The Little Fly" is a short poem which depicts a small fly buzzing around the sun to take a look at it. This is a poem in *Out of the Earth I Sing: Poetry and Songs of Primitive Peoples of the World,* edited by Richard Lewis. A lovely poem in this volume is "Song of the Sun and Moon," a Navaho poem of North America with the image of the first man holding the sun in his hands in the center of the sky and of the first woman holding the moon in her hands.[10]

Older adolescents may enjoy Indian love songs and incantations, such as the ones appearing in *Walk in Your Soul: Love Incantations of Oklahoma Cherokees* by Jack F. Kilpatrick and Anna G. Kilpatrick. Much of the color symbolism of the Cherokees is present in these poems. For instance, red and the east is symbolic of victory and power; blue and the

---

6. Willard R. Trask, *The Unwritten Song: Poetry of the Primitive and Traditional Peoples of the World,* Vol. 2. (New York: The Macmillan Co., 1967), p. 216.

7. *Ibid.,* p. 220.

8. *Ibid.,* p. 234.

9. *Ibid.,* p. 264.

10. Richard Lewis, *Out of the Earth I Sing: Poetry and Songs of the Primitive Peoples of the World* (New York: W. W. Norton & Co., Inc., 1968), p. 3.

north depict failure, weakness, and spiritual depression; and purple means witchcraft and evil.[11]

Another valuable anthology including both prose and poetry of the American Indian is one edited by Margot Astrov entitled *American Indian Prose and Poetry: An Anthology,* which has already been mentioned. In an essay accompanying this collection of writing, the author states that an idea of "the" Indian is an abstraction. According to her, each Indian is affected by his individual disposition, a group configuration, and a natural environment. Interesting explanatory material accompanies many poems included in this volume. For instance, in talking about "A Warrior's Song of Defiance" from the war ceremony of the Osage, it is explained that this song was sung when warriors were indifferent to taking retaliatory measures against an aggressive enemy.[12] Another song was a Pawnee one, "The Heavens are Speaking." An informant stated that the chief used to walk out into a storm where he heard Tirawa speaking through the clouds, and he knew that the heavens had ruling power and were over all of his people.[13]

The Astrov book also includes the "Improvised Song of Joy" of the Iglulik Eskimo which has been taken from *The Intellectual Culture of the Iglulik Eskimos* by Knud Rasmussen. The explorer and a companion were being served a meal by an old woman, and Rasmussen offered her some tea. She was so happy that she improvised a song in which "all is more beautiful."[14] In "Ulivfak's Song of the Caribou" by the Caribou Eskimo one learns that Ulivfak was old but he sang a song to overcome his grief over his loss of agility.[15] A footnote to "The Dance Song" explains that the "dance song" often served the Copper Eskimo as a daily hometown newspaper; so a composer of a new song was highly valued in the community and sometimes held his rank according to his ability to create good dance songs.[16]

Another volume edited by Willard R. Trask is *The Unwritten Song: Poetry of the Primitive and Traditional Peoples of the World,* Volume One. It includes primitive songs and poems from Greenland, Canada, and Alaska. For instance, in Greenland an Eskimo sings "Taunt Song Against a Clumsy Kayak Paddler" in which the singer envies a paddler for both his paddling skill as well as his art in composing songs. Some of the tasks of the Ammassalik Eskimo of East Greenland are seen in "The Kayak

11. Jack F. Kilpatrick and Anna G. Kilpatrick, *Walk in Your Soul: Love Incantations of Oklahoma Cherokees* (Dallas, Texas: Southern University Press, 1965), p.8.
12. Astrov, *op. cit.,* p.104.
13. Astrov, *op. cit.,* p. 105.
14. Astrov, *op. cit.,* p. 295.
15. Astrov, *op. cit.,* p. 302.
16. Astrov, *op. cit.,* pp. 303-304.

Paddler's Joy at the Weather," and "The Paddler's Song on Bad Hunting Weather" which appear in *The Sky Clears*.[17] These paddlers sing for joy when the weather is good for sealing or hunting. A vivid depiction of the barren grounds and of the Caribou Eskimo is shown in the song "Kibkarjuk Calls to Mind the Times when She Was Her Husband's Favourite Wife and Was Allowed to Hunt Caribou Herself." This includes a chant line which is uttered repetitively: "Iya-ye-ya."[18]

A beautiful volume of Eskimo poems for young children is *Beyond the High Hills: A Book of Eskimo Poems,* collected and translated by Knud Rasmussen, a Danish explorer who visited the Iglulik Eskimos of the Hudson Bay Region and the Musk-Ox people of the copper country. Each Eskimo was considered a poet. In the opening poem of the volume, the Eskimo moves swiftly "as the beat of the raven's wings" to greet the new day as he turns away from the darkness of night to view the new dawn.[19] In a second poem of the book, the poet metaphorically speaks of strength and compares the power of his leg muscles to the shins of a small caribou calf, and the motions of his walking legs to the "sinews of the shins of the little hare."[20] Some poems by the Eskimos of Alaska appear in the 1970 winter number of the *University Review* published by the University of Missouri at Kansas City.

An interesting Eskimo custom explained by Day in *The Sky Clears* is the "nith-song," or "drum song," which is a public poetry contest replacing a law court. If a Greenlander was injured by another person, he composed a satirical song and rehearsed it with his friends; then he challenged his opponent to a duel of song. Songs of wit, wisdom, and satire were sung by the disputants with support from their adversaries, and the audience became a jury to judge the winner of the dispute.[21]

A beautifully illustrated volume of poetry by Natalia Belting is *Calendar Moon,* which consists of poetically created folk sayings of peoples who have wondered about the moon, winds, storms, and rainbows, as well as the stars of the heavens. "January" is about the Klamath Indians of the northwestern United States who hold down the third finger and offer a name of the moon as "This is the moon-of-the-little-finger's partner."[22]

17. Day, *op. cit.,* p. 41.
18. Willard R. Trask, ed., *The Unwritten Song: Poetry of the Primitive and Traditional Peoples of the World,* vol. 1. (New York: The Macmillan Company, 1966), pp. 14-15.
19. Knud Rasmussen, *Beyond the High Hills: A Book of Eskimo Poems* (Cleveland: The World Publishing Company), p. 7.
20. *Ibid.,* p. 8.
21. Day, *op. cit.,* pp. 42, 43.
22. Natalia Belting, *Calendar Moon.* (New York: Holt, Rinehart and Winston, 1964). "January," unpaged.

"February" includes the poetic story of the "moon-when-the-coyotes-are-frightened" which is by the Tewa Indians of the southwestern United States.[23] A poem about March by the Delaware Indians of the northeastern United States tells of the departing snow, the geese flying overhead, and speaks of the sugar moon as "the moon-when-the-juice-drips-from-the-trees."[24] Then Belting continues through the year with poetic words about each month and the name of a particular moon represented in the month.

Another book by Natalia Belting which has poetic interpretations related to the legends of the constellations is *The Stars are Silver Reindeer*. The Yuchi Indians have a tale about Spider being an ancestor of the stars and about how the Aleutian Indians think of the Milky Way as a river and Cygnus as the kayak, with its seal hunter. The Navajo Indians offer a night chant, prayers, and sand paintings to heal the sick. Designs on the gourds are figures of the North and South gods and a pattern of stars above. This volume also includes some poetic beliefs of the Indians of Matto Grosso, Brazil and some by the Talamancan Indians of Costa Rica.

Poetry and song accompanied by musical notation appear in *Songs and stories of the North American Indian* by Paul Glass. This volume includes stories and songs of five tribes of the North American Indians—the Yuma, Mandan, Teton Sioux, Pawnee, and Papago. Four specific categories of songs and stories are included. First of all, there is a sacred or religious song such as a sun dance song sung by the Teton Sioux or such songs as "I Bring the Rain" and "The Song of the Waters" sung by the Papago Indians praying for rain. A second category consists of songs about dreams, such as "The Horseman in the Cloud" or "The Bear is Pointing at the Sun." A third category has a song embedded in old legends which became a faith of a tribe, such as "The Travelling Deer," legend of the Yuma Indians. A fourth song type uses stories, games, and lyrics for fun and enjoyment. These include such a song as the one sung by the Mandan Indians entitled "The Kettle is Burning," a song which relates how an Indian brave gets rid of his carping squaw by indicating that the food is burning.

One of the more interesting stories included in the Glass book of songs and stories is "The Travelling Deer," which is a part of "The Deer Begins His Travels." Akwak, the deer, had a special power to make the other animals sing. Those who sang the song sat on three overturned baskets, with four singers to a basket. A leader of each group of singers struck a basket with willow sticks while other singers hit it with the

23. *Ibid.,* "February," unpaged.
24. *Ibid.,* "March," unpaged.

palms of their hands. It took an entire night to tell the story. A special song was sung for each part of the night and for each animal that the deer met. The deer moved through the night past what is now Indio, California. Finally, he came to a beach and saw a waterbug chasing a sunfish. Then a song was sung, "The Waterbug Stands on a Fish." Later, as the evening wore on and the shadows became darker, the deer knew that the waterbug brought darkness; so he sang his song, "From Daylight to Darkness." After there was much darkness, the deer met a spider who promised to build a road so that the deer could travel in the darkness. And as the spider wove his web, he sang "The Spider Makes a Road." Near the present city of Phoenix, the deer saw a flock of blackbirds while the morning sun was shining brightly on their feathers, and the blackbirds sang "The Song of the Blackbirds." So the long tale continued while the deer met the buzzards, a beautiful redbird, a hummingbird, an owl, and finally a night hawk. The Yuma Indians call these songs and chants "The Cycle of the Deer" because the deer returns to the place from which he originally started his journey.[25]

Singing for Power

Ruth Murray Underhill spent fourteen months in the desert corners of Arizona in 1931 and 1933 collecting some of the "song language" spoken by the Papago. Some of these songs are for mature readers, such as the ones connected with the drinking ritual. But songs sung in the chapter of "Singing Up the Corn" are appropriate for children and give some of the characteristics of the Papago culture. Corn with kernals of two colors was called "crazy corn," and that which had three colors was known as "laughing corn." Hunters sang when preparing to fight, hunt, or when they fasted. In the selections, "The Head Bearers" given in *Singing for Power: The Song Magic of the Papago Indians of Southern Arizona,* a beautiful drama is enacted with words by the hunter, the deer, the datura, and the lizard weed. Some of the beauties of the Arizona desert are enacted in words as the hunter speaks of finding the deer by the red ocotillo flower, near the yellow clamiso blossom, or climbing the mountain gap beyond the reeds. The relationship of poetry to life is beautifully expressed in this Underhill volume, and this particular selection could be enacted as a verse drama with performers wearing masks and enacting the play before desert scenes.

25. Paul Glass, *Songs and Stories of the North American Indians* (New York: Grosset and Dunlap, 1968), pp. 12-22.

Recent Indian Poetry Anthologies for Children and Adolescents

Several new poetry books including poems by the American Indians have been published recently for children and adolescents. *The Trees Stand Shining* includes poems selected by Hettie Jones for young readers. It samples poems from the oral tradition of various tribes of North American Indians, and the book is beautifully illustrated with fourteen color paintings by Robert Andrew Parker who was a 1970 Caldecott medal runner-up. Another anthology of American Indian Poems has been edited by John Bierhorst and is entitled *In the Trail of the Wind: American Indian Poems and Ritual Orations.* This volume includes native American Indian poetry translated from over forty languages. Richard Lewis, an anthologist of several poetry books for young children, has edited *I Breathe a New Song: Poems of the Eskimo,* with illustrations by Oonark and an introduction by Edmund Carpenter. Ninety examples of Eskimo chants, sacred songs, lullabies, and hunting and taunting songs are included in this anthology. Another somewhat different book of Indian poetry is one entitled *2 Rabbit 7 Wind: Poems from Ancient Mexico,* retold from Náhuatl texts by Toni De Gerez.

Most poetry of the various groups of American Indian people originated in songs since it was through chants and songs that Indian story tellers and dancers expressed the people's spiritual beliefs, problems, and needs. A valuable volume is *The Indian's Book,* which has been recorded and edited by Natalie Curtis. This book gives the story behind a song, as well as the recorded words, in both an Indian dialect and English. For instance, the "Korosta Katzina Song" of the Hopi people was composed and sung by Koianimptiwa. An explanation states that the song was sung in May, or "Corn Planting Time." (The katzinas wore masks with a rainbow symbolically painted on them.) This song was about the butterflies flitting over the cornfields and the beans: the butterflies seemed to be chasing each other and were beautified as they covered themselves with pollen while flying through the blossoms.[26]

A beautiful legend, "The Return of the Corn Maids," and a colored illustration of the Kau, or Corn Kachina, appear in *The Kachinas Are Coming: Pueblo Indian Kachina Dolls, with Related Folk Tales* by Gene Meany Hodge. The book *Hopi Kachina Dolls with a Key to Their Identification* has a description of Sakwap Mana, or the Blue Corn Maiden, who carries a basket of blue corn and the Sio Avachhoya, or Zuñi corn kachina.[27] The Takus Mana, or Yellow Corn Maiden, has a yellow half-

---

26. Natalie Curtis, ed., *The Indian's Book: An Offering by the American Indians of Indian Lore, Musical and Narrative, to Form a Record of the Songs and Legends of Their Race* (New York: Dover Publications, 1968), pp. 484-485, 508-516.
27. Harold S. Colton, *Hopi Kachina Dolls with a Key to their Indentification,* rev. ed. (Albuquerque, New Mexico: University of New Mexico Press, 1970), p. 59.

Indian sculptured paper mask.

mask with a feather beard and long hair hanging down the back.[28] Another excellent book about kachinas is *Dolls of the Indians* by Elsie V, Hanauer.

Another effective collection of poetry is *American Indian Poetry: An Anthology of Songs and Chants,* which has been edited by George W. Cronyn. This book was originally published under the title *The Path on the Rainbow.* This collection of poems enhances one's understanding of the reverence for nature shared by the Indians of almost any tribal group as well as one's innate sensitivity to all things beautiful.

Another volume which will be highly interesting to mature readers is *The Ghost Dance Religion and the Sioux Outbreak of 1890* by James Mooney. Some of the background which lies behind this religion appears in the chapter "The Peace Messiah" by Sharon S. and Thomas W. McKern

28. *Ibid.,* p. 50.

in the volume compiled and edited by Raymond Friday Locke entitled *The American Indian*. This chapter describes the origin of Wovoka, the Paiute "Peace Messiah," who managed to raise the aspirations and hopes of numerous tribes of starving Indians in 1888 after the disappearance of the buffalo from the American plains.

Locke explains that the Ghost dance songs are of important significance in the study of tribal mythologies and the Messiah religion. The songs sprang up by the hundreds. Every trance or state of hypnosis undergone by an Indian who believed in the Ghost Dance religion produced a new song. This volume offers songs by the Arapaho, the Cheyenne, the Comanche, the Paiute, Washo, and Pet River Tribes, the Sioux, the Kiowa and Kiowa Apache, and the Caddo and associated tribes. The scholar who collected these, James Mooney, includes songs in the native language with translations and explanations of the customs of the tribe and some of the mythological background behind the songs. For instance, among the Algonquian tribes of the East, such as the Sioux, Cheyenne, Arapaho, Kiowa, Comanche, and most prairie tribes, as well as among some of the tribes of the northwest coast and parts of Mexico, special beliefs arose concerning thunder and lightning. Both thunder and lightning were caused by a huge bird whose shadow was the thunder cloud and whose flapping wings made a thunderous sound. The eyes of the powerful bird which opened and closed his flashing eyes rapidly caused the lightning. Both the Cheyenne and Arapaho spoke of the thunder bird as Ba'a, a large bird who carried several arrows in his talons. When the loud rumble of thunder was heard, they said, "the thunder calls." In Indian pictography the symbols indicate the figure with zig-zag lines coming from the heart to represent lightning. Many powerful poems and chants by various American Indian tribes are created and sung in honor of Thunder who causes rain to fall on the parched earth.

Some mature secondary students and adults will enjoy studying the section entitled "Poetry and Music" appearing in *The Central Eskimo* by Franz Boas. Most of the tales told by the Eskimos are recitatives which commence with a musical phrase and continue as a rhythmical recitation with rhythmic phrases. Many onomatopoetic devices are used in the chants. Many Eskimo tales are poetic prose poems with a marked rhythm. At times an Eskimo jumps up and down to the right or the left with his legs bent and his hands hanging down while a song is recited. One of these old songs is "The Lemming's Song." Other songs have been created with such titles as "Summer Song," "The Returning Hunter," "Song of the Inuit Travelling to Nettilling," and many others.[29]

---

29. Franz Boas, *The Central Eskimo* (Lincoln, Nebraska: University of Nebraska Press, 1970), p. 241.

A recent book of poetry is *The Magic World: American Indian Songs and Poems* which has been compiled and edited with an introduction by William Brandon. A unique feature of this collection is the inclusion of a large number of Náhuatl poems including "Aztec Song," "Flower Song," "From the Aztec Ceremonial Calendar," "The Feast of the Great God Tezcatlipoca," "A Song of Nezahualcoyotl," and several song fragments. A humorous little poem by the Cochiti Indians is "Bird and Toad Play Hide and Seek." This poem is really a poetic drama which could easily be dramatized by young children.[30] Another Cochiti song "Coyote and Beaver Exchange Wives," could also be easily dramatized.[31]

A beautiful song of peacefulness is the Navajo poem entitled "The War God's Horse Song" which describes a horse with "a hoof like striped agate," a fetlock "like fine eagle plume," and legs "like quick lightning."[32]

A "Postface: The Sources" which appears on pages 143-145 of *The Magic World* gives some of the principal sources for the poems compiled in this volume.

American Indian Folk Literature

Another basic part of the character of the American Indian as an ethnic group is the traditional folklore of his particular tribal group. Some of the myths and legends of these tribal people were also expressed in beautiful words and songs which were usually included in the folktales of a particular people.

As long ago as 1633 some Jesuit fathers recorded American Indian tales in their *Relations,* and such folklore was reported later by travelers and explorers visiting Indians in various places of the North American continent. Perhaps the first systematic recording of Indian tales commenced during the second quarter of the nineteenth century when Henry Rowe Schoolcraft conscientiously reported the legends of the Ojibwa. In these stories he retold the myth of the Manabozho and gave him the Iroquois name of Hiawatha. Later, this legend was adapted by Longfellow, and the heroic story of Hiawatha became part of the literature of the United States.

Commencing around 1890, Professor Franz Boas encouraged scholars to collect Indian folklore on a scientific basis. Several universities and museums specialized in tales of certain tribes, and various scholars studied particular tribes. Stith Thompson, the noted folklorist, states that "no

---

30. William Brandon, *The Magic World: American Indian Songs and Poems* (New York: William Morrow & Co., 1971), pp. 50-53.
31. *Ibid.,* pp. 54-56.
32. *Ibid.,* p. 60.

other primitive people had such an extensive and accurate record of its myths, tales, and legends as the North American Indian."[33]

Most of this Indian folklore consists of mythological stories depicting the world and its beginnings which show something about the order of affairs. They explain origins of natural objects, the universe, ceremonies, animals, and tribes. The creation myth appears in such tribes as the Zuñi of the American Southwest, and in various California myths. The great Glooscap culture hero, so familiar to Nova Scotia residents, is an example of a culture hero who changed the topography of a land already in existence.

Stith Thompson classified many Indian tales, but states that published collections of such stories are often called "myths," "legends," or "tales." Usually tales depicting an earlier world, thereby explaining how things came to be in the present one, are known as myths.

Thompson classified a second major category of Indian tales as tricksters. Sometimes, as in those of the Manabozho cycle, the animal remains in the background. The trickster in these American Indian tales is not always beneficent. For example, Raven brings fire to shivering mankind, but he is also greedy and selfish.

A third class of Indian tales might be termed fairy tales, although little folks are not the heroes. Such stories concern transformations, magic journeys into another world, ogres, and beast marriages. Many of these are similar to the Grimm folktales in which motivations are weak, but some supernatural or magical force aids the characters. For instance, Cushing has recorded a Zuñi Cinderella-type tale taking place in Matsaki, or Salt City. In this story a very poor girl in her patched, tattered, and dirty clothes tends turkeys for a living. One day she hears about a festival, the Dance of the Sacred Bird. The maiden thinks that she can not attend this famous festival. Then her turkeys work magical feats and provide her with a beautiful cotton mantle, a lovely necklace, earrings, and other ornaments. As written in this volume, this tale has a beautiful style; one hears the song of the turkey as a part of the story. A recent book of Indian legends which has the characteristics of fairy tales is *American Indian Fairy Tales* by Margaret Compton. This includes such stories as "Snowbird and Water Tiger." This is a tale of Brown Bear and his wife, Snowbird, and their little papoose called Pigeon and how their happiness was disturbed by a wicked old squaw who was Brown Bear's mother. Snowbird graphically describes a kingdom below the lake with a grand lodge with walls "as blue as a blue jay's back" and "green like the first leaves of maize."[34] An-

---

33. Stith Thompson, comp. and ed., *Tales of the North American Indians* (Bloomington, Indiana: Indiana University Press, a Midland Edition, 1966), p. xvi.
34. Margaret Compton, *American Indian Fairy Tales* (New York: Dodd, Mead and Company, 1971), p. 17.

other magical tale is "The Star Maiden," a tale of the Ojibways, "a great nation whom the fairies loved" in the land which "was the home of many spirits."[35] Some of them lived in the moss near the roots or on the trunks of the trees and others hid under mushrooms and toadstools.[36] Here in this beautiful land came a Star Maiden who wanted to find a resting place from her worldly wanderings so she sought the land of the Ojibways with its colorful flowers, singing birds, flowing rivers, and green mountains. She searched for a dwelling place on the stem of a lovely flower but was frightened away by a buffalo herd; she discovered a mountain rose but she could not linger here as a mountain disturbed her view of the world; finally, she came to a beautiful white flower with a shining heart of gold. Here she could hide in its center and watch the stars. The fairy tales in this collection are told in a beautiful, pictorial style.

Numerous Indian folktales have certain basic similarities in various culture areas. In his volume *The Folk Tale,* Stith Thompson differentiates eleven cultures areas which describe folk tales according to geographical regions on the basis of the general cultures of various tribes of the North American Indians.

Alice Marriott has compiled *Winter Telling Stories for Children.* These tales feature Saynday, the culture hero, who was always coming along. He made the world as it is, placed the sun in the sky, fought a bobcat, filed off the deer's teeth so that they could munch grass, and issued an order that ants should be cut almost in two. These are tales of the Kiowa Indians, and most of them are written in a humorous style. A nonfiction book about the Plains Indians, by Alice Marriott, is *Indians on Horseback,* which depicts the customs and tribal ways of the Cheyenne, Arapaho, Comanche, and Kiowa.

A beautifully illustrated collection of mythological tales is *North American Indian Mythology* by Cottie Burland. This includes numerous illustrations and color plates. Burland speaks of such archetypal gods as Power Above, the Earth Mother, and the Curious Trickster. Besides these figures there are other powers, or spirits, such as Corn Maidens and the celestial beings like the Sun, Moon, the Twins, Morning Star, and Evening Star. Many drawings appearing in this volume are facsimiles of ones located in various museums. Several of these stories need to be retold for children, but the descriptions of the life and crafts of various tribal groups are particularly informative.

A valuable annotated bibliography is *Folklore of the North American Indians,* which has been compiled by Judith C. Ullom. This bibliography gives a brief discussion of primitive folktales and culture areas and gives annotated references for adults, lists of anthologies, and children's

35. *Ibid.,* p. 78.
36. *Idem.*

anthologies. Examples of illustrations appearing in many volumes are re-produced.

Another important source book is *American Indian Mythology* by Alice Marriott and Carol K. Rachlin. This volume includes both myths and legends of the American Indians. The authors define myths as actions of supernatural beings and the legend as a humanized counter-part with the deeds and doings of earthly heroes. These anthropologists have organized their tales into "Four World Corners." Part 1 includes "The World Beyond Ours"; Part 2, "The World Around Us"; Part 3, "The World We Live in Now"; and Part 4, "The World We Go To." The authors give interesting informational background to accompany each pub-lished tale. For instance, an intertribal story is "Bird of Power." These authors state that birds are supposed to have special power and a fast ac-cess to God's ears. Certain powerful birds are "the bald eagle, the prairie falcon and red-tailed hawks, the water turkey and the scissor-tailed fly catcher."[37]

Another wonderful collection of Indian folktales which has previously been mentioned in this chapter is *The Kachinas Are Coming: Pueblo Indian Kachina Dolls with Related Folktales* by Gene Meany Hodge. Jack F. Kilpatrick and Anna G. Kilpatrick have published two other volumes which will have interesting parts for children. One of these is *Friends of Thunder: Folktales of the Oklahoma Cherokees,* and the other one is *Run Toward the Nightland: Magic of the Oklahoma Cherokees.* These myths legends, and bits of folklore were tape-recorded.

Canadian Indian Folktales

In her chapter entitled "Indian Legends," in the *Republic of Child-hood: A Critical Guide to Canadian Childhood Literature in English,* Sheila Egoff offers a detailed discussion of certain Canadian collections of Indian tales written for children.

A culture hero of the Canadian Maritimes is known as Glooskap or Glooscap, the supernatural hero of the Micmacs of eastern Canada. Cyrus Macmillan has compiled a collection of these Indian legends in *Glooscap's Country and Other Indian Tales.* Glooscap was the son of Goodness; his twin brother Wolf was the son of Wickedness. Glooscap grew lonely for Man; so he made Fairies and Elves which peopled the meadows, streams, and caves. He shot the ash trees of the forest with his bow and arrows thereby making Indians. Then he called the animals into being. Beaver, Badger, and Bull Frog were his enemies and frequently planned to kill

---

37. Alice Marriott and Carol K. Rachlin, *American Indian Mythology* (New York: Thomas Y. Crowell Company, 1968), p. 177.

him. The story "How Summer Came to Canada" is beautifully written.

Kay Hill has compiled two volumes of Glooscap tales entitled *Glooscap and His Magic: Legends of the Wabanaki Indians* and *More Glooscap Stories: Legends of the Wabanaki Indians.* A foreword to the first volume explains that the Wabanaki, or Abenaki, were "those who live nearest the rising sun" and were "migratory tribes of the Eastern Woodlands speaking dialects of the Algonquin language."[38] These included the Micmacs and Malicetes in the Maritime Provinces of Canada, the Passamaquoddy and Penobscot tribes of Maine and Massachusetts, as well as a few others. Most of their mythology centered upon the trickster hero of Glooscap who was half god and half heroic man. Glooscap was surrounded by magical beings, such as cannibal ice giants; boöins; witches; wizards; Ableegumooch the rabbit; Keoonik the otter; the fun-loving badger, and the Megumoowesoos, or the Little People. In the story "Rabbit Calls a Truce" one learns about the trickster qualities of Ableegumooch the rabbit who played his antics with Keoonik, the otter.

In *More Glooscap Stories,* Kay Hill describes this culture hero more completely in "Glooscap, the Great Chief." He came down from the sky in a huge stone canoe with his twin brother, Malsum. These giants were twelve feet tall, but they could make themselves taller if they wished. Glooscap was a manlike being, but Malsum had the head of a wolf, and he was pushed from the sky for his evil actions.

Marion Robertson has published *Red Earth: Tales of the Micmacs,* which has an introduction to the customs and beliefs of the Micmac Indians. This collection gives many interesting myths and legends in addition to those of Glooscap. Some of these are about the "Little People."

Ella Elizabeth Clark has compiled *Indian Legends of Canada* which includes tales from various tribes of Canada and such language families as the Algonquins, Athapascan, Iroquoian, Kituahan, Salishan, Siouan, Skittagetan, Wakaskan, and Eskimo.

One of the best loved characters of folklore of the Canadian Westcoast Indians is the raven, who appears as the hero in a collection of tales by Robert Ayre entitled *Sketco the Raven.* He was known by different names among the various tribes, but he usually had the same attributes.

Indian Myths of the Northwestern United States and Canada

Several Indian stories of the Northwest and Canada have Raven as the culture hero. Some Raven stories which have been retold by Fran

38. Kay Hill, *Glooscap and His Magic: Legends of the Wabanaki Indians* (Toronto: McClelland and Stewart Limited, 1963), p. 6.

Martin appear in *Nine Tales of Raven.* These tales were originally told by the Alaskan Eskimos and Canadian Indians, and later reached the Washington and Oregon tribes. Two of the most picturesque tales in this collection are "How the Raven Stole the Stars" and "How He Stole the Moon and the Sun." Here one can meet Nassishig-ea-yalth who selfishly hides the stars in a pouch and the sun and moon in two boxes, one painted with silver paint and the other side gilded with gold. Raven has the ability of transforming himself into many different forms and succeeds in stealing the moon, the sun, and the stars for mankind.

Totem pole tales have always been popular with children. Totems were emblems which depicted the legendary history of the tribe and family. Such native characters as Thunderbird, Wolf, Killer Whale, Raven and Grizzly Bear were carved on large cedar houses and on chests, spoons, and war clubs. Five of the tales of mythical people depicted on totem poles appear in *Once Upon a Totem,* with woodcuts by John Frazer Mills. Hugh Weatherby has also told tales of the totem poles found in desolate parts of British Columbia in *Tales the Totems Tell.* This includes such stories as "The First Totem Pole," "The Raven and the Indians," and "How the Frog People Got Their Totem."

William Toye has retold a legend of the Tsimshian Indians of British Columbia entitled *The Mountain Goats of Temlaham* which has been colorfully illustrated by Elizabeth Cleaver. In the early times the hunters of the village of Temlaham hunted goats from the mountain peaks and killed only those which were needed for the skin, meat and horn. The hunters then turned greedy and wasteful and this story tells how the Indians of Temlaham suffered for their cruelty and greed; only the kindly young boy Raven Feather was saved.

Legends of the Ojibwa or Chippewa Indians

Dorothy M. Reid has told the story about a sleeping giant, a great creator magician in *Tales of Nanabozho.** In the waters of Lake Superior there is a rocky promontory which looks like a sleeping giant. The Ojibwa called him Nanabozho, a strong and wise culture hero but one who also made foolish mistakes and practiced trickery. Nanabozho was the son of Wenonah and the roaring West Wind. He won Minnehaha for his bride and saved his grandmother Nokomis from spirits through his courage and cunning. An interesting creation legend is one entitled "How Nanabozho Remade the Earth." This story depicts how the great giant rescued his people from a huge raft and how Nanabozho called upon the Beaver, Otter, and the Muskrat to assist him.

(*This word is sometimes spelled with an m.)

Students reading the *Tales of Nanabozho* may enjoy reading "The Song of Hiawatha" also. One version, *The Song of Hiawatha* by Henry Wadsworth Longfellow, has been illustrated with three hundred and eighty-seven illustrations by Frederic Remington. This is a facsimile reprint of a limited 1890 edition which has been out of print for some time.

Some stories appearing in *Legends of Green Sky Hill* by Louise Jean Walker retell a few of the legends of the Chippewa Indians. Manabozho appears in "How the Indians Received Tobacco," "Mackinac Island," "The Formation of South Fox and North Fox Islands," as well as others in this collection.

John Bierhorst has edited eight of the legends collected by School-craft and published them in *The Fire Plume: Legends of the American Indians*. Here are such stories as "The Red Swan," "The White Stone Canoe," and "Sheem," as well as "Three Chippewa Fables." An interesting single beautifully illustrated legend which has been edited by the same author is *A Shawnee Legend: The Ring in the Prairie*.

An unusual collection of Navajo tales is *Navajo Bird Tales,* told by Hosteen Clah Chee and arranged by Fran Johnson Newcomb.

A recent collection of tales and legends about other Indians of the Southwest is one by Harold Courlander entitled *People of the Short Blue Corn: Tales and Legends of the Hopi Indians*. These are stories of Hopis living in their stone villages in the American Southwest long before the arrival of the white man. One of their creation myths is recounted in "How the People Came from the Lower World" which tells about Spider Grandmother, an ancient one, who had been on earth since the beginning of life. Sometimes she was on old woman; at other times she transformed herself into the form of a spider. It is interesting to note that Mockingbird stood at the opening in the sky as people stepped into the upper world and gave each one of them a language such as Hopi, Navajo, Apache, Paiute, or Zuñi. Spider Grandmother also picked up a disk of cloth and carried it east, and it become the moon. It was not bright enough; so the medicine men painted a design of egg yolks on a disk of buckskin, and Spider Grandmother placed this in the sky so that the people had the sun. In "Coyote Helps Decorate the Night," Coyote found hundreds and hundreds of small shining objects which couldn't be eaten; so he tossed them away in disgust, and they became the stars. Stories in this volume are told in an interesting style, and "Notes on Hopi Oral Literature" add much helpful information. In the Hopi world the number four has ritual significance; so things come in fours—"four years, or four days, or four attempts, or four events, or four games, or four directions, or four messengers."[39]

39. Harold Courlander, *People of the Short Blue Corn: Tales and Legends of the Hopi Indians* (New York: Harcourt, Brace and Janonovich, 1970), p. 162.

Eleanor B. Heady has collected twenty-two of the tales of the Nimi-poo into a book for children entitled *Tales of the Nimipoo, From the Land of the Nez Percé Indians.* In her introduction to this book, Mrs. Heady explains that the land of the Nez Percé or Nimipoo people forms much of the country which is now known as northern Idaho, eastern Washington and Oregon, and a small part of western Montana. These Indians believed that before Indians came to the earth, all animals were governed by Itsayaya, the coyote. The first myth in the collection, "The Sun, The Moon, and the Stars," tells how pitch and wood were carried by the younger son from the east toward the west and how younger sister joined him carrying extra pitch wood so that the sun would be high in the sky for a longer time. In the tale "Itsayaya Frees the Salmon," one learns that Itsayaya the Coyote, had the power to transform himself into different forms similar to some of the transformations made by Raven in tales of the Indian cycle of the Northwest Indians.

Numerous collections of stories have been made of the California Indians. Two of the more popular ones are *Stories California Indians Told* by Ann B. Fisher and *Down from the Lonely Mountain,* retold by Jane Louise Curry. Most of the stories told by Ann Fisher were collected by Dr. C. Hart Merriam who recorded the tales as they were related by Indian storytellers.

An interesting creation tale in the Fisher book is "How California Was Made." The Great Spirit looked down from the sky and found no earth. He got the Turtle Brothers to carry tules and earth on their backs and planted trees on them. The giant Turtle Brothers quarreled and spread themselves around into the shape of California. Coyote is an important trickster hero in tales like "How Coyote Helped to Light the World" and "How Coyote Put Fish in Clear Lake." A humorous tale told by the Shasta Indians is "Why Women Talk More than Men."

The collection of tales, retold by Jane Louise Curry, offers a different California creation myth. It is entitled "The Beginning of the World and the Making of California." Coyote has an important role in this story as well as in "The Securing of Light" and "The Theft of Fire."

Legends of the Eskimos and the Pacific Northwest

One Eskimo legend, *The White Archer,* has been written and illustrated by James Houston. This is the tale of Kungo who became filled with the desire for revenge when raiding Indians killed his parents and sister. He makes a dangerous journey to Ittok in order to serve as his apprentice so that he can become a great bowman and kill his enemies.

Collections of Eskimo tales include: *The Day Tuk Became a Hunter and Other Eskimo Stories,* retold by Ronald Melzack; *The Rescue of the*

Sun and Other Tales from the Far North by Edythe W. Newell; *Shadows from the Singing House: Eskimo Folk Tales,* retold by Helen Caswell; *The Blind Boy and the Loon and Other Eskimo Myths* by Ramona Maher; and *Medicine Men of Hooper Bay* by Charles E. Gillham. Another recent collection of folktales of Alaska is *Alaskan Igloo Tales,* collected by Edward L. Keithahn, a curator and librarian of the Alaska Historical Museum and Library.

Emerson N. Matson has written *Longhouse Legends,* a book including stories which Indians of the Puget Sound enjoyed as they sat around the leaping flames of a potlatch fire. Chief Martin J. Sampson of the Swinomish tribe translated many of these tales along with an interpretation of carvings and dances to outline each one. Informative explanations also accompany each legend. For instance, an introduction to "The Boy and His Magic Robe" explains that this legend was taught as part of the childhood education of boys and girls of the Swinomish and Kikiallus.

Scholarly Volumes for Adults

There are scholarly volumes for adults which offer a tremendous amount of information about totem poles and stories behind tales told by the Tlingit, Haida, Tsimsyans, Kwakiutl, Nootka, and Salish Indians, and others. One example is *Totem Poles,* in two volumes, by Marius Barbeau. These volumes give a scholarly and thorough background of the people of the totem pole cultures. Marius Barbeau has also written *Tsimsyan Myths* for the National Museum of Canada, which usually includes a tale and the name and place, and date on which the informant related the story.

Another valuable scholarly collection published in Canada is *The Corn Goddess and Other Tales from Indian Canada* by Diamond Jenness. This collection includes Tales of the Iroquois, Ojibwa, Sarcee Tales, Sekani and Carrier Tales, those of the Coast Salish, and Eskimo Tales. In the title story of this volume a corn goddess comes to Gosadaya, the great hunter, and teaches his people the secrets of agriculture.

In his introduction to *Tales of the North American Indians,* Stith Thompson indicates that the Eskimos have poor explanatory myths and trickster tales, and such stories are usually concerned with the pursuit of animals and monsters.

Eskimos of Povungnituk, Quebec are known for their soapstone carvings which depict myths and legends in a way similar to tales of the totem poles. A valuable volume for adults is *unikkaatuat sanaugarngnik atyingualiit Puvirngniturngmit: Eskimo Stories from Povungnituk, Quebec,* illustrated in soapstone carvings. Povungnituk, which is situated on the east side of Hudson Bay, is one of the principal centers of contemporary

Eskimo carvings in Canada. Many of the stories connected with the carvings were collected on magnetic tape as well as in writing.

Values of Indian Myths and Legends

Indian myths and legends give the American Indian child pride in the Ancient Ones, those ancestors who have gone before him. Myths help persons to wonder about the origin of things—how things came to be. Indian myths have given names to geographic locations in Canada and the United States. These tales give a sense of commonality and unity in the traditions of a people. Morals, rituals, and tribal laws are frequently inculcated in the young people of a tribe through songs and tales. Many Indian myths offer a sense of spiritual satisfaction in an effort to help the Indian feel a sense of wholeness in his approach to three worlds: the white man's world, the Indian world, and the great unseen spiritual world. Children listening to tribal elders and gifted story tellers relating their tales gain an ear for rhythmical beauty and music in the spoken word. Other readers and listeners of Indian literature gain a respect for the cultural traditions of a people who were indigenous to this land long before the arrival of the Spaniard or white man. Persons can respect the nature lore of the Indian and some of his beliefs which make his world a place of beauty. Sometimes, this idyllic wholeness of beauty is distorted as the Indian finds adjustment to a modern urban society difficult.

Summary

This chapter has focused upon poetry, song, and folklore as one means of understanding the cultural traditions of various American Indian tribes living on the North American continent. As one reads poetry of the ancient Náhautl poets of Mexico and listens to the chants of *kachina* dancers, he realizes that some American Indians had a basic philosophical background of helping people follow the path of beauty away from the false accouterments and pressures of the white man's world and its repetitive technological change. Such poetry should help dim the stereotype of a hooting Indian letting out a war whoop and attacking wagon trains or American cavalrymen.

Folklore is basic in the moral fiber of a people, and the colorful myths and legends recounted by the wiser ones, the older ones of a tribe, helped younger children and the youth find their identity and place in a world of beauty.

Reaction—Questions and Projects

1. Select some poems of the American Indians which have refrains or a repetition of lines in them. Prepare some choral verse recitations.
2. Select some Indian poetry which might be particularly appropriate for children in the primary grades.
3. Find some recordings of Indian music and play them. Relate these recordings to poetry as well as to the ritual of Indian tribes.
4. Make a study of the poetry of the Indians of North America and determine certain characteristics of Indian poetry.
5. Many Indian children are brought to foster homes away from their parents and reservations. The Mormons have a project of keeping Indian children in their homes. Visit some of these children and record the songs and chants which they have learned from their people.
6. One way of sensing an identity of universal customs throughout the world is that of playing games enjoyed by persons in other cultures. Gordon C. Baldwin has written *Games of the American Indians* which is illustrated and has photographs. (New York: W. W. Norton & Company, 1969). Study some of these games and play them with a group of children or adults.
7. Study some folklore materials collected by such scholars as Barbeau, Jenness, or Schoolcraft. Read some of their descriptions of myths or legends. Adapt these stories for pupils in an elementary or junior high school and rewrite them in the form of a radio play.
8. Read several folktales in various collections which consider Coyote as a trickster character. Discuss Coyote and his role in these various tales. Some sources of Coyote tales are: *Nine Tales of Coyote* by Frances G. Martin with pictures by Dorothy McEntee (New York: Harper, 1950), and *When Coyote Walked the Earth: Indian Tales of the Pacific Northwest* by Corrine Running, illustrated by Richard Bennett (New York: Henry Holt, 1949). Fran Martin has also written *Nine Tales of Raven,* with pictures by Dorothy McEntee (New York: Harper & Row, Publishers, 1951).
9. Read some books about the Hopi and their *kachina* dancers. Write a few pages about a *kachina* dancing ceremony in a way which can be understood by elementary school pupils.
10. Write a story of the art of one group of Indians in relation to their folklore. This could be Eskimo stone carvings, Navajo blankets, Hopi kachina dolls, basketry or sandpainting, pottery bowls, silversmith work, or any other art. One valuable source is *Indian Art of the United States* by Frederic H. Douglas and Rene D'Harmoncourt (New York: The Museum of Modern Art, distributed by Simon and Schuster, 1941). Have children create some original *kachina* dolls.

A good source is *Dolls of the Indians: A Book of Kachina Effigies* by Elsie V. Hanauer (Cranbury, New Jersey: A. S. Barnes and Company, 1970).

BIBLIOGRAPHY
BOOKS FOR PRIMARY CHILDREN

BIERHORST, JOHN, ed. *A Shawnee Legend: The Ring in the Prairie.* New York: Dial Press, 1970.

COMPTON, MARGARET. *American Indian Fairy Tales.* New York: Dodd, Mead & Company, 1971.

JONES, HATTIE. *The Trees Stand Shining.* New York: Dial Press, 1971.

LEWIS, RICHARD. *I Breathe a New Song: Poems of the Eskimo.* New York: Simon and Schuster, 1971.

MARY-ROUSSELIERE, GUY. *Beyond the High Hills: A Book of Eskimo Poems.* New York: World Publishing Company, 1961.

TOYE, WILLIAM, retold by. *The Mountain Goats of Temlaham.* Toronto: Oxford University Press, 1969.

BOOKS FOR INTERMEDIATE GRADE CHILDREN

AYRE, ROBERT. *Sketco the Raven.* Toronto: The Macmillan Company of Canada, 1961.

BELTING, NATALIA. *Calendar Moon.* New York: Holt, Rinehart & Winston, 1964.

———. *The Stars Are Silver Reindeer.* New York: Holt, Rinehart & Winston, 1966.

BIERHORST, JOHN, ed. *The Fire Plume: Legends of the American Indians.* New York: Dial Press, 1969.

———. *In the Trail of the Wind: American Indian Poems and Ritual Orations.* New York: Farrar, Straus & Giroux, 1971.

CASWELL, HELEN. *Shadows from the Singing House: Eskimo Folktales.* Rutland, Vermont: Charles E. Tuttle Company, 1968.

COURLANDER, HAROLD. *People of the Short Blue Corn: Tales and Legends of the Hopi Indians.* New York: Harcourt, Brace & Jovanovich, 1970.

CURRY, JANE LOUISE. *Down from the Lonely Mountain: California Indian Tales.* New York: Harcourt, Brace & World, 1965.

FISHER, ANN B. *Stories California Indians Told.* Berkeley, California: Parnassus Press, 1957.

GILLHAM, CHARLES E. *Medicine Men of Hooper Bay: More Tales from the Clapping Mountains of Alaska.* New York: The Macmillan Company, 1955.

HARRIS, CHRISTIE. *Once Upon a Totem.* New York: Atheneum Publishers, 1963.

HEADY, ELEANOR B. *Tales of the Nimipoo: From the Land of the Nez Percé Indians.* New York: World Publishing Company, 1970.

HILL, KAY. *Glooscap and His Magic: Legends of the Wabanaki Indians.* New York: Dodd, Mead & Company, 1963.

———. *More Glooscap Stories: Legends of the Wabanaki Indians.* New York: Dodd, Mead & Company, 1970.

HOUSTON, JAMES. *The White Archer: An Eskimo Legend.* New York: Harcourt, Brace & World, 1967.

KEITHAHN, EDWARD L. *Alaskan Igloo Tales.* Seattle: Craftsman Press, a Robert D. Seal Publication, 1958.

LEWIS, RICHARD, ed. *Out of the Earth I Sing: Poetry and Songs of Primitive Peoples of the World.* New York: W. W. Norton and Company, 1968.

LONGFELLOW, HENRY WADSWORTH. *The Song of Hiawatha.* New York: Crown Publishers, Bounty Books, 1968.

MACMILLAN, CYRUS. *Glooskap's Country and Other Indian Tales.* Toronto: Oxford University Press, 1967.

MAHER, RAMONA. *The Blind Boy and the Loon and Other Eskimo Myths.* New York: John Day Company, 1969.

MARRIOTT, ALICE. *Wintertelling Stories.* New York: Thomas Y. Crowell Company, 1969.

MARTIN, FRAN. *Nine Tales of Raven.* New York: Harper & Row, 1950.

———. *Nine Tales of Coyote.* New York: Harper & Row, 1950.

MARY-ROUSSELIERE, GUY. *Beyond the High Hills: A Book of Eskimo Poems.* New York: World Publishing Company, 1961.

MATSON, EMERSON N. *Longhouse Legends.* Camden, New Jersey: Thomas Nelson & Sons, 1968.

MELZACK, RONALD. *The Day Tuk Became a Hunter and Other Eskimo Stories.* Toronto: McClellend and Stewart, 1967.

NEWCOMB, FRANC JOHNSON. *Navajo Bird Tales.* Edited by Lillian Harvey. Wheaton, Illinois: The Theosophical Publishing House, a Quest Book for Children, 1970.

NEWELL, EDYTHE W. *The Rescue of the Sun and Other Tales from the Far North.* Chicago: Albert Whitman & Company, 1970.

REID, DOROTHY M. *Tales of Nanabozho.* New York: Henry Z. Walck, 1963.

ROBERTSON, MARION. *Red Earth: Tales of the Micmacs with an Introduction to the Customs and Beliefs of the Micmac Indians.* Halifax, Nova Scotia: The Nova Scotia Museum, 1969.

WALKER, LOUISE JEAN. *Legends of Green Sky Hill.* Grand Rapids, Michigan: William B. Erdman, 1961.

WEATHERBY, HUGH. *Tales the Totems Tell.* Toronto: The Macmillan Company of Canada, 1962.

ADOLESCENT BOOKS

ASTROV, MARGOT, ed. *American Indian Prose and Poetry: An Anthology.* New York: Capricorn Books, 1962.

BOAS, FRANZ. *The Central Eskimo.* Lincoln, Nebraska: University of Nebraska Press, Bison Book printing, 1970.

CLARK, ELLA ELIZABETH. *Indian Legends of Canada.* Toronto: McClelland and Stewart, 1966.

CRONYN, GEORGE W., ed. *American Indian Poetry: An Anthology of Songs and Chants.* New York: Liveright, 1962.

DAY, A. GROVE. *The Sky Clears: Poetry of the American Indians.* New York: The Macmillan Company, 1951. Also reprinted as a Bison paperback book by the University of Nebraska Press, Lincoln, Nebraska, 1951.

DE GEREZ, TONI. *2 Rabbit 7 Wind: Poems from Ancient Mexico Retold from Náhautl Texts.* New York: Viking Press, 1971.

KILPATRICK, JACK F. and KILPATRICK, ANNA G. *Friends of Thunder: Folktales of the Oklahoma Cherokees.* Dallas: Southern Methodist University Press, 1964.

————. *Run Toward the Nightland: Magic of the Oklahoma Cherokees.* Dallas: Southern Methodist University Press, 1967.

KILPATRICK, JACK FREDERICK, and KILPATRICK, ANNA G. *Walk in Your Soul: Love Incantations of the Oklahoma Cherokees.* Dallas: Southern Methodist University Press, 1965.

RUNNING, CORRINE. *When Coyote Walked the Earth: Indian Tales of the Pacific Northwest.* New York: Henry Holt, 1949.

PROFESSIONAL BOOKS

ASTROV, MARGOT, ed. *American Indian Prose and Poetry: An Anthology.* Originally published as *The Winged Serpent.* New York: Capricorn Books, 1962.

BARBEAU, MARIUS. *Totem Poles.* Bulletin No. 119, Vol. I, *Totem Poles According to Crest and Topics.* Anthropological Series No. 30, National Museum of Canada, Ottawa, Canada: Queens Printer and Controller of Stationery, 1964.

————. *Totem Poles.* Bulletin No. 119, Vol. II, *Totem Poles According to Location.* Anthropological Series No. 30, National Museum of Canada, Queen's Printer and Controller of Stationery, 1964.

————. *Tsimsyan Myths.* National Museum of Canada, Bulletin No. 174, Anthropological Series No. 51. Illustrated by Arthur Price and with photographs. Department of Northern Affairs and Natural Resources. Ottawa, Canada: Queens Printer and Controller of Stationery, 1961.

BATEMAN, WALTER L. *The Navajo of the Painted Desert.* Boston: Beacon Press, 1970.

BRANDON, WILLIAM, ed. and comp. *The Magic World: American Indian Songs and Poems.* New York: William Morrow & Company, 1971.

CURTIS, NATALIE, ed. *The Indians Book: An Offering by the American Indians of Indian Lore, Musical and Narrative, to Form a Record of the Songs and Legends of Their Race.* New York: Dover Publications, 1968.

CUSHING, FRANK HAMILTON. "Zuñi Folk Tales." In *Tales of the North American Indians,* edited by Stith Thompson. Bloomington, Indiana: Indiana University Press, Midland Edition, 1966.

EGOFF, SHEILA A. *The Republic of Childhood: A Critical Guide to Canadian Children's Literature in English.* Toronto: Oxford University Press, 1967.

GLASS, PAUL. *Songs and Stories of the North American Indians.* New York: Grosset and Dunlap, 1968.

HANAUER, ELSIE V. *Dolls of the Indians: A Book of Kachina Effigies.* Cranbury, New Jersey: A. S. Barnes Company, 1970.

HANNUM, ALBERTA. *Spin A Silver Dollar: The Story of a Desert Trading Post.* New York: Viking Press, 1961.

HODGE, GENE MEANY. *The Kachinas Are Coming: Pueblo Indian Kachina Dolls with Related Folk Tales.* Flagstaff, Arizona: Northland Press, 1967.

JENNESS, DIAMOND. *The Corn Goddess and Other Tales from Indian Canada.* Bulletin No. 141, Anthropological Series No. 39, Ottawa, Canada: Queens Printer and Controller of Stationery, 1966.

NEWCOMB, FRANC JOHNSON. *Navajo Bird Tales.* Edited by Lillian Harvey. Wheaton, Illinois: The Theosophical Publishing House, a Quest Book for Children, 1970.

NUNGAK, ZEBEDEE, and ARIMA, EUGENE. *Unikkaatuat sanaugarngnik atyingualiit Puvirngniturngmit: Eskimo Stories from Povungnituk, Quebec.* Ottawa, Canada: The Queen's Printer, 1969.

THOMPSON, STITH, ed. *Tales of the North American Indians.* Bloomington, Indiana: Indiana University Press, Midland Book Edition, 1966.

————. *The Folktale.* New York: The Dryden Press, 1951.

TRASK, WILLARD R., ed. *The Unwritten Song: Poetry of the Primitive and Traditional Peoples of the World.* Vol. 2. New York: The Macmillan Company, 1967.

————, ed. *The Unwritten Song: Poetry of the Primitive and Traditional Peoples of the World,* Vol. 1, *The Far North, Africa, Indonesia, Melanesia, and Australia.* New York: The Macmillan Company, 1966.

TYLER, PRISCILLA, ed. "Writers in the World Tradition of English Literature" in *The University Review,* the University of Missouri, Kansas City, Winter number XXXVII: 108-117, December, 1970.

ULLOM, JUDITH C. *Folklore of the North American Indians: An Annotated Bibliography.* Washington, D.C.: Library of Congress, 1969.

UNDERHILL, RUTH MURRAY. *Singing for Power: The Song Magic of the Papago Indians of Southern Arizona.* Berkeley, California: University of California Press, 1968.

CHAPTER SEVEN

At the
Edge of
Two Worlds:
The Indian Way
and the Way
of the White Man

During the last century or so, the ways of the white man and of the Indian have been divergent. The American Indian has been maligned in history texts, in movies, and in television shows, and each generation of children has grown up with false stereotypes of American Indian tribal customs. The Indian has been represented as dirty, lazy, a lover of "fire water," and a thief. He supposedly attacked innocent wagon trains for no reason at all, and he celebrated his victories with grisly scalpings and war whoops. The American Indian was not ignored on the pages of history, but his image was distorted by Anglo-Saxon historians who presented history from the viewpoint of bureaucratic Washington officials, white immigrants who encroached upon soils of frontiers of the western states, and from the admirers of western folk heroes such as Kit Carson and Buffalo Bill.

A recent scholarly volume for adolescents and adults which rewrites history from the viewpoint of the American Indian is *Bury My Heart at Wounded Knee: An Indian History of the American West* by Dee Brown.

This is a nonfiction, historical book, but it gives considerable background which helps to interpret the schizophrenic feeling which many Indian children and youths suffer when they feel that they are standing at the edge of two worlds and can find no real identity in the old ways of the fathers or in the newer confusing customs of modernized man. The chapter "The Long Walk of the Navahos" gives a background for two or three fictional novels about the long walk which will be discussed in this chapter.[1] Chapter Ten of the Brown book, entitled "The Ordeal of Captain Jack," relates the story of the Modoc leader, nicknamed Captain Jack, who desperately hid out in the lava caves in northern California and confronted a large number of U. S. cavalry and infantry men in his Modoc stronghold. When his execution was threatened, Kintpuash, or Captain Jack of the Modocs, said:

> I am but one man. I am the voice of my people. Whatever their hearts are, that I talk. I want no more war. I want to be a man. You deny me the right of a white man. My skin is red; my heart is a white man's heart; but I am a Modoc.[2]

Captain Jack perhaps expresses the feeling of many an Indian who wishes to keep his individuality and identity in a small ethnic group but who wants to be recognized as a man—a human being whose heart is the same as a white man's heart.

The Philosophy of the New Indian

In recent years a new philosophy of the American Indians has united younger tribal members who feel that they want to be proud of their Indian heritage and to go their ways independently, not as wards of the white man. This philosophy of the new Red Power movement is expressed in a chapter, "Go in Beauty," in *The New Indians* by Stan Steiner.

As a representative of the Nez Percé tribe expresses it, his physical emotional, and spiritual involvement in a war dance makes him "mentally and physically refreshed" as well as "more human, more loving, and more peaceful."[3] Many negative stereotypes of the American Indian have appeared in literature for children and adults. Indians have fought the encroachments of newcomers to their land and have battled the continuous

1. Dee Brown, *Bury My Heart at Wounded Knee: An Indian History of the American West* (New York: Holt, Rinehart and Winston, 1970), pp. 14-36.
2. Quotation from an address of Kintpuash, (Captain Jack) of the Modocs, *Bury My Heart at Wounded Knee: An Indian History of the American West* (New York: Holt, Rinehart and Winston, 1970), p. 219.
3. Stan Steiner, *The New Indians* (New York: Dell Publishing Company, a Delta Book, 1968), p. 158.

pressures of submission and cultural assimilation. Federal bureaucracy has caused much suffering. Indians have felt alienated from white society and have been rewarded for rejecting their tribal language and customs. In some instances, according to Edgar S. Cahn, inhuman methods were used by government officials who reduced food rations if a family clan or tribal members were caught singing their native songs, doing tribal crafts, or speaking one of the 300 American Indian dialects or languages.

One way in which the Federal government tried to control Indians was through an establishment of Indian reservations which Carey Mc-Williams defines as "a government almshouse where an inconsiderable number of Indians are insufficiently fed and scantily clothed at an expense wholly disproportionate to the benefits conferred."[4]

No longer do many young "red nationalist" Indians want to be completely absorbed in a white urban culture. In some instances, tribal leaders who sell out to white business or government officials are derisively known as "Uncle Tomahawks."

As one listens to the rhythmical flow of language of tribal shamans and medicine men relating the myths of his people, or as one sees tapestries in sand expressing spiritual and emotional thoughts in beautiful artistry, he realizes that Indians should be accepted for their reverence of nature, their beautiful way of life where an individual takes time for beauty, and for the significance of Indian symbolism and spiritual beliefs, which help them to live life more effectively. A young Taos Indian girl expresses her feeling about the sacredness of life in her pueblo. If she had her dream, she would "want my people to hold on to our beautiful way of life. I would want my people to hold on to their ways, somehow, and yet be able to be on the same shelf, or level, as the white man. I would want my people to be able to compete with this white man and yet be able to come back to the pueblo, to live in our way."[5] In other words, she dreams that her people can have images of a beautiful way of life in a world in which the sacred Indian way of life is retained. Modern customs may be adopted as needed to raise the social and economic condition of the Indian, but new ways will be assimilated with the old.

Most persons speak of the Indian as having one identity, but there are many Indians. Two books by Ann Nolan Clark give the reader a sensitivity toward the Indian of the Southwest. These are *Journey to the People* and *Circle of Seasons*.

Clark feels that there are four Indian group concepts which differentiate an Indian group from those of white urban dwellers. These in-

4. Steiner, *The New Indians,* pp. 288-289.
5. Carey McWilliams, *Brothers Under the Skin,* rev. ed. (Boston: Little, Brown and Company, 1964), p. 71.

clude: (1) the Indian feeling about the land, (2) the Indian attitude toward work, (3) the concept of time, and (4) spiritual life.

Indian Concept of Land

A white Anglo-Saxon businessman feels that land is a salable commodity which can be owned individually or by a group under certain prescribed conditions. A white man can obtain land through seizure, treaty, grant, inheritance, purchase, or rent for a specified period of time. On the other hand, Indians feel that land belongs to their ancestors or the old people who burned their campfires or hunted and fished on it. Land does not belong to individuals but to the group. It should be as free as the air or the golden sunshine. Rigid boundaries should not be set by scientific surveyors; the boundaries of the Red Man are a distant peak, a dry wash, or the shores of a turquoise lake.

Indian Concept of Work

White exploiters have frequently classified the Indian laborer as shiftless, lazy, or ignorant. Traditionally, Indians in the past have not wished to hoard their dollars in a hidden bank account. Frequently, wealth is worn in the form or turquoise and silver ornaments on the person. An Indian works for his family or his community. Formerly, when an Indian needed his shoes, some moccasins were made; when he needed his hogan, relatives and clan members worked cooperatively to build it. Money was not exchanged, but people worked on the home until it was completed and then all of the laborers took a holiday or rest. The Indian objects to the ways of the white man who finishes one job and keeps on working day after day with no rest; he tries to beat his neighbor and takes more than he needs of food and luxuries.

The Indian Concept of Time and His Family Upbringing

The Indian has a different method of family upbringing and time concept than that of the white man. An Indian child in many households is considered in the group deliberations. Age is honored. An Indian suffers from the disapproval of his peers. Sometimes, if an Indian mother wishes to punish her child she refuses to speak to him for a long time. He suffers in silence.

The Indian turns to the sun and the moon as his clocks. He does not comprehend how time can be broken into little particles such as seconds, minutes, and hours. This is why such books as *Spin a Silver Dollar: The*

Story of a Desert Trading Post by Alberta Hannum, give episodes in which an Indian at a trading post grabs a clock and considers it a plaything.

The Indian Concept of Spiritual Life

Southwestern Indians are deeply reverent. Formerly, the Indian immersed himself in his whole environment and paid obeisance to Life Power. He made a sunrise call, asking that each new day be blessed. He scattered his thoughts in the evening. He prayed for good crops. He danced a sacred rain dance that he might have rain. He asked the Supreme Creator to bless his seeds. When an Indian netted a salmon or captured a deer or a bear, he gave thanks for his food. Man felt at ease in his spiritual life and lived in "beauty behind him, below him, around him'" as he traveled on the "beautiful trail of life."[6] *The Circle of Seasons* by Ann Nolan Clark offers more details about religious festivals such as "Day of the Dead," and such events as "Beginning of Long Winter."

A nonfiction book about the Navajo Indian by Walter J. Bateman is *The Navajo of the Painted Desert*. Chapter four is entitled "Making the Path of Life Beautiful." This explains many tasks of an Indian girl learning the craft of weaving and tells how some women left the design open without a border so that their personal spirit would not be lost in the rug. It also tells how Spider Man made the first looms and how Spider Woman taught weaving skills to the Navajo women. This Chapter also explains the ceremony called *Kinaalda* or *Hozhonigi* which honors the girl who becomes a woman; this is a means of "making the Path of Life Beautiful."[7]

The symbolism of *kachinas,* which offers a sense of spiritual significance is seen in *Book of the Hopi* by Frank Waters. *Kachinas* are not deities but symbolize intermediaries or spirits such as those of plants, birds, animals, minerals, clouds, people, planets, and stars which have not appeared in the sky. Some statistical anthropologists have classified 335 *kachinas,* but such an enumeration is "akin to measuring how many angels can be accommodated on the head of a pin. A star burns out, another is born."[8]

Kachinas appear on earth in some physical form, and masked male dancers impersonating them, known as *kachinas,* lose their personal identities as humans and become spirits. Dolls called *kachinas* are given

---

6. Ann Nolan Clark, *Journey to the People* (New York: Viking Press, 1969), pp. 18-26.
7. Walter L. Bateman, *The Navajo of the Painted Desert* (Boston: Beacon Press, 1970), p. 31.
8. Frank Waters, *Book of the Hopi* (New York: Ballantine Books, 1969), p. 205.

Masks made from ice-cream cartons.

to children to remind them of their significance. These small figures are made from soft cottonwood roots, and are painted and costumed to represent the masked impersonators. Waters gives a dramatic picture of *kachina* night dances performed in the kiva where dancers utter falsetto yells and shake rattles or stamp their feet. *Kachina* songs are sung, and the voice of the Crier Chief calls to the cloud people of the directions and sends his call to the four points of the compass: to the West, to the South, to the East, and to the North.[9] A beautiful book for adults is *Hopi Kachina Dolls* by Harold S. Colton. Another lovely book for adults and

9. *Ibid.,* p. 205.

children is *The Kachinas are Coming: Pueblo Indian Kachina Dolls with Related Folktales* by Gene Meany Hodge. This volume has a colored picture of a *kachina* and a folk tale related to this *kachina*. For instance, a colored plate shows Talwipi (Lightning) Kachina and the story "How the Twin War Gods Stole the Thunder-stone and the Lightning-shaft" accompanies the picture.[10]

Another sense of the spiritual heritage of many Indian tribes is seen in sand painting discussed in *Tapestries in Sand: The Spirit of Indian Sandpainting,* with paintings and interpretation by David V. Villaseñor. Sandpainting is a form of Southwest Indian Art in which a medicine man paints on the ground or on buckskin or cloth in such a way that the sand flow is controlled by the skill of his sensitive fingers. It is an art of many Indian people, including the Navajos, Zuñi, Hopi, Apache, Papagos, and Southern California Indians. Sandpainting is a ritual which can last from three to nine days and is accompanied by a chant or ritualistic prayer intoned as a series of incantations. Some paintings belong to the rhythm of the day, others to that of the evening. One interesting sand painting in this book tells the story of "Father Sky and Mother Earth," from whence came all life. The painting shows the sky and earth fused as one on the horizon, and it was believed that the physical earth and the spiritual sky should function together to bring forth new life. The symbolic representation of the stars, moon, and constellations is shown on the body of Father Sky. The zig-zags forming his arms and legs are part of the milky way. The bosom of Mother Earth radiates a life-giving force of the sun bringing fertility and the seed of all living things.

Another form of beauty is the Navajo rug woven in the old way before the invention of cheaper aniline dyes. Sara Hannum, in *Spin a Silver Dollar,* tells how she and her husband tried to renew older dye processes in the Indian trade by paying a premium at the Trading Post for rugs made this way. Some artists of the Navajo tribes have created over one hundred different colors using native materials. These include a brown dye from the Rocky Mountain juniper root, red rock, and ashes; black from sumac ochre and piñon pine; a soft light green from the sunflower; and pastel red from the prickly pear cactus fruit. Many other colors come from different roots, bushes, and berries growing in the environment of the weaver, or basket maker. More information about Indian ceremonies and crafts appear in *Masked Gods: Navaho and Pueblo Ceremonies* by Frank Waters.

Some of the classes in the San Francisco city schools have recently been studying the botanical plants growing in California and many of the various plants which were used for dyes, medicine, or for food. Pupils gathered acorns, and the teacher and children made acorn bread in a way

10. Gene Meany Hodge, *The Kachinas Are Coming: Indian Kachina Dolls with Related Folk Tales* (Flagstaff, Arizona: Northland Press, 1967), pp. 95-104.

similar to the method used by early California Indian women. Such experiences as these help both the Indian and the white child to understand some of the old ways of an Indian who lived at peace with his environment.

At the Edge of Two Worlds

Many short tales as well as more complex novels about various American Indian characters depict the Indian as being a person who is a confused, unhappy being trying to comprehend the white man's ways. He is often defamed, disembodied, or disparaged by many authors. Various mistruths about the white man's concept of the Indian are corrected in *Custer Died for Your Sins: An Indian Manifesto* by Vine Deloria, Jr.

Teachers in many schools, in their industrious zeal to make an Indian into a white, middle-class, economically independent person did many things to lower the self-image of their pupils and to alienate them from both their home and their people; and yet, they were not assimilated into the white man's world. Novels for older adolescents sometimes depict this alienation at such a level that the Indian feels degraded and turns to drunkenness and debauchery. Such a novel is the Pulitzer prize immortal Navajo love story by Oliver LaFarge entitled *Laughing Boy*. This novel gives a dramatic picture of an Indian man who has strayed from the life of beauty and of wholeness. He left his people and the accustomed way of life of his family for an intense love of a girl who became entrapped as a prostitute when she wanted to get even with the white man who wanted her to be ashamed of being an Indian. Unfortunately this novel will probably only be recommended for young adults due to the prostitution of Slim Girl, but the honest depiction of conflict between the ways of the Navajo and those of the urban city dweller is clearly portrayed, as is the unhappiness in those who have left the good life and come with many empty hearts having lost the trail of beauty and goodness.

Two rather mediocre books for young readers about Navajo children which present the problems of persons at conflict with the world of the Navajo and that of the white man at the city school are *Billy Lightfoot* by Richard B. Erno and *A Hogan for Bluebird* by Ann Crowell. Billy Lightfoot wants to become a young Navajo artist and is torn between the ways of his home in the reservation and his art experiences in an Indian boarding school. In *A Hogan for Bluebird,* a Navajo sheep herding girl faces many problems when she returns to her people. She wants to become a musician even though it means breaking tribal taboos. Another story of this same type is *My Name is Lion* by Margaret Embry. The old man cannot take care of the boy any more and the truant officer forces him back to the dorm at the school provided by the Bureau of Indian Affairs. The boy has many inner conflicts until he gains confidence in himself and scribbles the words "My Name is Lion. My Name is Lion."[11] Another story for older readers with a similar theme but of a different locale and tribe is *Waydah of the Real People* by William A. Steele. The grandfather of Waydah the Wolf, a Cherokee boy of Chota, says, "An Indian who takes the white man's way is like an oak tree split by lightning." He continues to explain that "as lightning splits the oak's trunk in two, so the white man's touch splits the red man. He is no longer one good tree, but two worthless ones, part white, part Indian, no good to either tribe."[12] Waydah attended the Brafferton School for Indians at Williamsburg in the colony of Virginia. The white man had promised the Chota lead and powder, knives and blankets, and trade with the Virginians if the Chota boy could remain at Brafferton for a year. In this story Wolf, or Waydah, suffers the taunts and prejudices of other boys at the school and is fearful until he finds the red garnet and the "winking magic stone," which becomes a talisman to him.

The Quest for Identity

Another major theme in many Indian novels is the quest for identity —the longing to find a place for oneself in the world.

The Light in the Forest by Conrad Richter is an unforgettable story about a white boy who was kidnapped by the Lenni Lenape Indians. He became known as True Son after he was renamed by the great warrior Cuyloga who reared him as his own boy. Then a treaty was signed and True Son had to return to his white parents as John Butler; yet he had learned to hate all white men in his Indian environment. Another story with a somewhat similar plot is *Shawnee Lance* by LeRoy Allen. Daniel, who is fourteen years old, has been hardened by life in the Ohio Valley wilderness. During a Shawnee raid, he kills a Shawnee because he witnesses the Indian killing his father with a hatchet. When Daniel is taken captive, he knows that he is either to be adopted in the tribe or killed. He suffers penalties and hardships as a white boy among them in order to keep alive. Here he struggles to overcome the hatred, jealousy, and ridicule of such tribal members as Buffalo Skull, the son of the Shawnee killed by Daniel. Most of the action is compressed into the short period of one moon, or a month.

Another novel for adolescents about an Indian youth fighting for his identity in two cultures is *No Moccasins Today* by Sharon Lockett. Jay Williams discovers that a Pacific College scout is at the high school, and he

---

11. Margaret Embry, *My Name Is Lion* (New York: Holiday House, Inc., 1970), p. 46.
12. William O. Steele, *Waydah of the Real People* (Williamsburg, Virginia: Colonial Williamsburg, 1964), p. 6.

is ashamed that he has worn his moccasins. He also resents the gaping tourists who visit his Chuala Indian reservation and thinks that his white classmates are laughing at the old Indian legends and customs of his people. He longs for a college education and a more prosperous future but has many difficulties in finding a solution to his problems.

Another novel which seems somewhat contrived is *Wigwam in the City* by Barbara C. Smucker. This considers the problem of the American Indian in a large city and tells the story of Susan Bearfoot who hates to leave the Chippewa Reservation and move to Chicago. She finds cruelty and hostility in the school, and she and her family have to make many painful adjustments to an urban culture.

A recent novel on a somewhat different theme is *Chief* by Frank Bonham. It concerns Henry Crowfoot who is the great-great grandson of Chief Buffaloboy, the hereditary leader of the Santa Rosa Indians. Henry wants better conditions for his people, but many of them are lazy, dejected, and discouraged. Henry accidently sets the chemistry laboratory at school afire and gets into difficulty with the law so he gets a down-at-the-heels attorney, Schackleford to be his lawyer. Some surprising things happen when Chief gives the attorney some old faded documents to examine which read:

> . . . Nor shall any white man be permitted to reside upon the land east of Santa Rosa Creek without permission and the paying of an amount of rent deemed fair.[13]

The characterization of Henry Crowfoot, Schackleford, and Joseph Whirlwind Horse, the Chief's uncle who is a Skid-Row wino, are cleverly developed. Events in the story show a different problem between the white man and the Indian, but it is still one of the chicanery of white men regarding treaties and legal papers.

Another extraordinary novel for adolescents is *When the Legends Die* by Hal Borland. As Tom is riding herd in the arena for a man who wins unfairly, he climbs into the empty stands and says, "Who Am I? Where Am I? Where Do I Belong?"[14] In the final part of the novel, when he goes back to the wilderness and tries to kill the bear, his throbbing pulse asked, "Why?" He answers to himself, "To be myself." But when he heard the words, "Who . . are . . you?" he could find no answer.[15] Finally, he comes to realize the behavior patterns which enhance the beauty of life. His penance journey up the mountain as man in search of himself and his identity is beautifully depicted.

13. Frank Bonham, *Chief* (New York: E. P. Dutton & Co., Inc., 1971), p. 43.
14. Hal Borland, *When the Legends Die* (Philadelphia: J. P. Lippincott, 1963), p. 118.
15. Hal Boland, *Legends Die,* pp. 207-208.

Documentary on Indian in Two Worlds

Land of the Four Directions is a photographed, documentary, nonfiction account of experience among the Passamaquoddy, Malisert, and Micmac Indian tribes of Maine and New Brunswick. In their own words and through their photographed faces these Indians reveal pride in their ancient heritage and resentment against the white man for his broken promises, outmoded policies, and the granting of only second-class citizenship to the Indian of Canada and the United States. An epilogue in this book states that the Indian can help the non-Indian to survive by teaching us "how to live in harmony with nature, our family, our community, and ourselves."[16]

The Place of the Indian in History

It is difficult to sift out truth from fiction in the Indian's contribution to the history of the United States. Another novel by Evelyn Sibley Lampman is sympathetic toward the action of the Indians in the tragic massacre of the Whitmans in 1848. This is *Cayuse Courage*. The "white-eyes" abandoned their trap in the bottom of a muddy pond and Samuel Little Pony caught his hand in it. It is mangled so badly that Dr. Whitman is forced to amputate it. The boy resents this loss of a hand and is bitter against all white men. However, he accepts some of the kindnesses of the Whitmans and tries to warn them of the time of an uprising against the mission. A note appended to the novel tells how an army pursued the Cayuses to bring the murderers of the Whitmans to justice. Finally, after two years of persecution, a trial was held in Oregon City, Oregon County, and five chiefs and braves were hanged for the murders at the Whitman Mission.

The Navajos as an Oppressed People

Two historical novels are based on some tragic events which took place in the history of the Navajo Indians between 1863 to 1865. The first of these is a less complex one entitled *Sing Down the Mountain* by Scott O'Dell. The story commences in the spring of 1864 at the Canyon de Chelly when the Navajo had a promising harvest and the sheep were lambing. Raiding is going on between Spanish land holders and the Navajos. Soldiers come to destroy the crops and force the Navajo on an arduous march of over 300 miles. This great journey known as "The Long Walk" was an historical event of much bitterness. Navajos were held as al-

---

16. Frederick John Pratson, *Land of the Four Directions* (Old Greenwich Connecticut: Chatham Press. Distributed by the Viking Press, 1970), p. 131.

most starving prisoners at Fort Summer until 1868 when they were set free and allowed to start afresh near Canyon de Chelly. Before this, however, nearly 1,500 Navajos died at Fort Sumner from smallpox, starvation, freezing cold, and other hardships. The story is told from the viewpoint of Bright Eyes, a young Navajo girl.

The second novel, *A Navajo Saga* by Kay and Russ Bennett, is written for older adolescent pupils and includes much more detail. In this account, the custom of raiding other tribes or the Mexican rancheros for women slaves is vividly depicted. This novel opens in 1846 with the episode of the raid of a Mexican hacienda by Gray Hat and his warriors in quest of women so that the population of the tribe might be increased. This novel depicts the Navajos as an oppressed people, hunted down like wild animals by American soldiers and settlers. They were starved into submission and marched mostly on foot to the Rio Grande, and then to the Pecos River. Here at Bosque Redondo they suffered many hardships until a peace treaty of 1868 permitted them to return to their homes to rebuild their hogans and replant their crops. A documentary account of this historical episode appears in the chapter "The Long Walk of the Navajos" in the book *Bury My Heart at Wounded Knee*.[17]

Custer's Last Battle

In one book, *Red Hawk's Account of Custer's Last Battle* by Paul and Dorothy Goble, one learns about warfare in which the Indian defeated the white man's army. It is in June 1876, and the combined bands of the Sioux and Northern Cheyenne Indians are camped at the Little Bighorn River under the leadership of Sitting Bull. Here General George Armstrong Custer and the Seventh U. S. Cavalry attack the camp. This is considered the most famous victory ever won by the American Indians. This book tells the story in the style of a fifteen-year-old Indian boy Oglala, or Red Hawk. The basic information has been obtained from first person accounts of both Sioux and Cheyenne warriors who participated in the Battle of the Little Bighorn. Illustrations are stylized from those seen on tipis and buffalo robes.

A more detailed documentary story about this episode appears in the chapter "The War for the Black Hills," which is included in the historical volume *Bury My Heart at Wounded Knee: An Indian History of the American West* by Dee Brown.[18] This same author has written *Showdown at Little Big Horn* which is based on contemporary reports, diaries, letters and testimonies of those who fought for either the Indians or Custer.

17. Dee Brown, *Bury My Heart at Wounded Knee: An Indian History of the American West* (New York: Holt, Rinehart & Winston, 1970), pp. 14-36.
18. Brown, *Wounded Knee*, pp. 276-313.

The Ordeal of Survival

Numerous novels of Indians of the United States outline the arduous fight for survival—the necessity of proving oneself in difficult circumstances either as man against his environment, against other persons, or against himself. One of the best survival novels for intermediate-grade children is *Island of the Blue Dolphins* by Scott O'Dell. This is the story of Karana, an Indian maiden, who had to fight her battle of survival on the island of San Nicholas where the blue dolphins and sea otters sported amongst the breakers. Here the Indian girl, who was later known as "The Lost Woman of San Nicholas," lived a Robinson Crusoe-like existence from 1835 until 1853.

Another story which does not portray this great intensity of courage is *Edge of Manhood* by Thomas Fall. This is the novel of a Shawnee boy, See-a-Way, who went with his family to the Indian Territory of Oklahoma but had to fight with the Pottawatomies for the land.

Poetry in the Novel

Some novelists have captured the rhythmical cadence of Indian poetry and song in their novels. Frequently, the poetry of the Indian becomes an integral part of the plot and reenforces the mood or tone of the novel. Two of these are *Waterless Mountain* by Laura Adams Armer and *Ishi— Last of His Tribe.* In the first book, the chapter "The Trail of Beauty" concludes with a poem which expresses an appreciation for beauty in the line "I travel a trail of beautiful thoughts."[19] Another chapter, "The Dance of the Maidens," concludes with the singing of a lovely Sky Song, as the Bearer of the Day comes "From the house made of dawn."[20]

Ishi—Last of His Tribe, by Theodora Kroeber, is written in cadenced prose which is poetic in many lines. In times of great stress Ishi utters a song or a poem such as the one sung when he peers over Black Rock and watches the feared saldu, or white enemy, in the distance and pleads for the manzanita, the chaparral, and the poison oak to punish the enemy. When the family had to flee their home, when Ishi put earth over the ashes of the fire pits, and when Elder Uncle blew smoke from his pipe over the empty village, a song was sung. Tuliyani, their former home, was being abandoned for a newer hiding place in Wowunupo. In a beautiful ceremony, they gave the empty village back to the ancestors with the hope that the "footmarks and handmarks" of the people would disappear into the

19. Laura Adams Armer, *Waterless Mountain* (New York: David McKay Co., Inc., 1931), p. 48.
20. *Ibid.*, p. 84.

earth.[21]   Theodora Kroeber has also written an adult biography on the same Indian entitled *Ishi in Two Worlds.*

The voice that beautifies the land is a song which reflects the day-to-day living and emotional intensity of significant moments in the life of a tribal Indian along with his innermost thoughts and images, and it causes him to feel at peace with himself and his personal heritage.

Projection Into Another World—A Raising of the Aspiration Level

Many novels about the American Indian glorify the leadership of a great Indian chief such as Tecumseh or Black Hawk. The fictionalized historical novel, such as *Indian America: The Black Hawk War,* is quite pitiful. This is a tale of the white man's lack of empathy for the Indian when settlers wanted their land and pushed Indian landowners to other less coveted property. In this novel Chief Black Hawk chooses to fight for his land, but he is finally defeated in the war waged in the Illinois-Wisconsin woods in 1832.

Unfortunately few biographies or novels give Indian boys and girls a chance to identify with successful roles of Indians in a modern society. Weyman Jones has created two biographies about Sequoyah, the talented Cherokee Indian, who developed a ramarkable syllabary in order that Indians could learn to read. One of these is a short little biography of ninety-six pages entitled *The Talking Leaf* which shows how this Cherokee Indian valued the written word. The second novel, *Edge of Two Worlds,* presents more excitement and conflict. Calvin, who is the sole survivor of a Comanche massacre, meets the old Cherokee, Sequoyah. The gradual development of a relationship of trust and friendship is clearly portrayed in a book which has received many notable literary awards.

A brief biography of only forty pages for primary grade children is *Maria Tallchief* by Tobi Tobias. This small book depicts Maria Tallchief as a famous ballerina. She is an Oklahoma Osage Indian who is a leading dancer in George Balanchine's American School of Ballet.

An interesting biography of an Indian Woman is *Sacajawea: The Girl Nobody Knows* by Nita Lohnes Frazier. There are numerous biographies of this courageous Indian scout who helped lead the Lewis and Clark expedition westward. This biography includes many quotations from the journals of Lewis and Clark and an afterward which contains interesting reflections concerning the last years of the life of Sacajawea. Another excellent biography of Sacajawea is *Winged Moccasins: The Story of Sacajawea* by Frances J. Farnsworth.

---

21. Theodora Kroeber, *Ishi: Last of His Tribe* (Berkeley, Calif.: Parnassus Press, 1964), p. 103.

A modern novel with an Indian boy, Roy Adams, as the principal character is *The Sea Pair* by Patricia Beatty. This relates the story of a Quilente Indian boy, Roy, who wants to become an automobile mechanic. An interesting additional facet of the novel is the arrival of two sea otters, a mother and a pup, on the off-shore waters of the Washington coast. Roy has considerable difficulty in adjusting to school. The struggle between the father and boy over the possible killing of the sea otters is a dramatic one.

A Way of Life

Several little books for primary age children are too brief to develop many conflicts or much characterization, but they build a background for understanding the way of life of persons in another minority culture. Usually such books are not dramatic, but young readers can look for some ideas which add to the study of people. In a nonfiction book, *The Hopi Way* by Mary Elting, the author tells us that anthropology is an adventure in two worlds; both the every-day, familiar one and a life which is different. Such strangeness gradually reveals that "through understanding others, we can grow wiser about our own feelings and beliefs. As we grow wiser, we come to value not just our uniqueness, but also that of others."[22] This book discusses much of Hopi life in a simple language and includes special Hopi customs such as the washing of their hair with the leaves and the crushed root of the yucca. It also explains "The Butterfly Dance" and the use of *pahos*, or message sticks.

Another poetic book which describes life of the Indian child is *In My Mother's House* by Ann Nolan Clark. This author has also written *Blue Canyon Horse*, which is beautifully illustrated by Ellen Houser. In this little story, the boy's mare hears the call to freedom and joins a herd of wild horses. Later she returns with her colt to the safety of her village. Another book by Ann Nolan Clark which is more non-fictional is *The Desert People*, which describes the past history of the Papago Indians of the Southwest.

David, Young Chief of the Quilentes: An American Indian Today by Ruth Kirk is a small book which is illustrated with many photographs by the author. The eleven-year-old son of chief David Hudson is the principal point of focus. The story is not too exciting, but much information about the Quilente Indians is given.

Salt Boy by Mary Perrine, a book for younger children which contains only thirty-one pages, tells about a small Navajo Indian boy who is re-

---

22. Mary Elting, *The Hopi Way* (New York: M. Evans and Company), unpaged and untitled preface.

buked for roping one of his mother's sheep; he regains favor when, later, he saves a drowning lamb.

Kemi: An Indian Boy Before the White Man Came by Mary and Conrad Buff is a slight tale of the California Indians in which Kemi breaks his mother's cooking pot and begs to accompany his father on a trading expedition.

One beautiful poetic book about a prehistoric group of Indians is *One Small Blue Bead* by Byrd Baylor Schweitzer. The story commences with Boy who has a dream in his eyes, and a band of his people who are huddled in a cave thinking about the wonder of a land beyond on the other side of the world. The Boy wants to go on the search. As he goes out into the world he meets other people and hears the cry of danger. He meets a strange boy who gives him one small turquois bead tied in a reed. The book is a simply written one but rich in beauty and symbolism.

A small primary-grade picture book is *The Sunflower Garden* by Janice May Udry. This is the story of a young Algonquin Indian girl, Pipsa, who lives with her five brothers and is generally unnoticed by her father. He directs his attention to the feats of her brothers, such as how they can gather wood, fish, and swim, or how they can snare rabbits and birds. She learns to make clothes out of deerskin and obediently hoes the weeds and plants corn, beans, and squash in her mother's garden. Then, Pipsa grows sunflowers, the magic plant which is used for Indian beauty preparations for hair oil, for good-tasting cakes, and even sometimes as tobacco for smoking. When Pipsa becomes a heroine and her father follows a different path to her garden, she is finally noticed. The book has universal values for children in all cultures since all persons long to be recognized and appreciated.

Eleanor Clymer has written *The Spider, the Cave, and the Pottery Bowl.* This is another book about Indian life in two worlds—the urban life where Kate's family could find work and the mesa where grandmother, the beautiful potter, lived. Kate succeeded in discovering a new bed of clay so that Grandmother could get the good clay which she loved to use.

N. Scott Momaday has written a poetic book for adults entitled *The Way to Rainy Mountain,* an epochal journey of the Kiowa Indians made over three hundred years ago when they early acquired Tai-me, the sacred Sun Dance doll which became a symbol of their spiritual well-being. In his prologue the author states that the journey evokes three things: "a landscape that is incomparable, a time that is gone forever, and the human spirit which endures."[23] In following the path of beauty, Indians both old and new will quest an enduring human spirit.

---

23. N. Scott Momaday, *The Way to Rainy Mountain* (Albuquerque: The University of New Mexico Press, 1969), p. 4.

Summary

American Indian literature has been discussed as one type of literature, but the term is misleading. There are hundreds of different American Indian tribes and villages which extend from southern Mexico to Alaska and northern Canada. There are also many dialects and languages spoken. Federal bureaucracy, with broken treaties and unfulfilled promises, is a frequent theme of both fiction and nonfiction books about American Indian heroes.

As one reads examples of poetry by such Indian groups as the Hopis and the Navajos, he realizes that the Hopi and the Navajo customs, such as the worship of the old ones and the old way of life, helped children and youth to maintain their self-identity.

Many tribal persons and modern Indians have adapted some of the white man's way of life, but historically most tribal Indians have differed because of their feelings concerning land ownership and time, as well as peculiar attitudes toward work. Most Indians think differently about their spiritual salvation than do modern white men.

Kachina dolls had a part in educating the young Hopi child, and *kachinas* helped in interpreting his tribal heritage. Indian sand painting also had much spiritual significance. Legends and myths were interwoven with art, music, and poetry, and a young child in a Navajo or Hopi family learned to speak in phrases which were rhythmical and musical.

Several anthologies of Indian poetry which have been discussed in the previous chapter include poems from various tribal groups. The most well-known anthologies are probably *The Sky Clears: Poetry of the American Indians* by A. Grove Day and *American Indian Prose and Poetry: An Anthology* by Margot Astrov. Two more recent anthologies which include quite an intensive collection of poems are *In the Trail of the Wind: American Indian Poems and Ritual Orations,* edited by John Bierhorst, and *The Magic World: American Indian Songs and Poems,* selected and edited by William Brandon.

Many novels about Indians are written in poetic words. Much American folk literature is narrated in a rhythmical and pictorial style. The folklorist, Stith Thompson, has written a noted classification of Indian myths and legends which appear in *Tales of the North American Indian.*

The Indian is often depicted as a person standing at the edge of two worlds, one which is dominated by the white man and the other which has his own different values. Many novels for young children discuss some of the traumatic fears of an Indian child who is compelled to attend the white man's government school with its many restrictions and different codes of conduct. Much inner conflict arises when an Indian child leaves the free and open life of the tribe living in the wide-open spaces and later is forced into the constricted living conditions of urban life. Frequently Indians have resented being relegated to the position of second-class citizens or wards of the government.

Several novels, such as *Sing Down the Mountain* by Scott O'Dell and *A Navajo Saga* by Kay and Russ Bennett, reenact certain historical episodes such as "The Long Walk of the Navahos." A documentary book, *Bury My Heart at Wounded Knee: An Indian History of the American West* by Dee Brown, places a different interpretation of many historical novels using Indians as the principal characters. Some novels show the bravery of individual persons who have battled for survival.

A few biographies and novels help the young reader to project himself into another world from the one in which he lives. Some biographies of Indians who have succeeded in life may raise the aspiration level of those who are ashamed of their tribal heritage.

Many books for young children illuminate the way of life of persons living in a different culture from their own. This ethnic group has contributed much to the culture of majority groups or white Anglo-Saxons who frequently long for the path of beauty seen by these early people.

Reaction—Questions and Projects

1. Select an episode from *Bury My Heart at Wounded Knee: An Indian History of the American West* by Dee Brown. Read the episode carefully. Then get a traditional United States history book and read about the same episode as written by an earlier historian. Compare the difference in viewpoint.

2. Select two characters which have opposite roles in an episode related in *Bury My Heart at Wounded Knee*. Create an imaginary dialogue showing biases or "blind spots" of the speakers. For instance, in "The Ordeal of Captain Jack" one person could be Hooker Jim and the other would be Captain Jack, or one speaker could be General Canby and the other would be Captain Jack.

3. The Association on American Indian Affairs is located at 432 Park Avenue South, New York, New York 10016. It is in the process of compiling bibliographies of children's books relating to the American Indians. In 1969 this group published "A Preliminary Bibliography of Selected Children's Books about American Indians." This association selected only a sixty-three-book list out of over two hundred books read. A larger bibliography was published in 1970. Select three books which are not listed in this Indian bibliography or in the bibliography in this chapter, annotate them, and give reasons why they should be included in such a list.

4. Discuss some negative stereotypes of the American Indian and illustrate them by using some books for children.

5. Discover some modern Indian personages who might be good biographical sources, such as Indians who have succeeded in modern business, agriculture, or education. Collect materials about these people.

6. Develop a docudrama or a play using music, documents, and narration about the Lewis and Clark expedition and the role of Sacajawea. Use two or three biographies of Sacajawea and present the play by relying on journals and eyewitness accounts.

7. Find examples of peoples of other ethnic groups such as the Japanese, Turkish, or Latvian people who find difficulty in adapting to strange ways of an urban white culture in the United States.

BIBLIOGRAPHY
BOOKS FOR PRIMARY CHILDREN

BUFF, MARY (Marsh). *Kemi: An Indian Boy Before the White Man Came.* Los Angeles: Ward Ritchie Press, 1966.

CLARK, ANN NOLAN. *In My Mother's House.* New York: The Viking Press, 1941.

————. *Blue Canyon Horse.* New York: The Viking Press, 1954.

CLYMER, ELEANOR. *The Spider, the Cave, and the Pottery Bowl.* New York: Atheneum Publishers, 1971.

ELTING, MARY. *The Hopi Way.* Philadelphia and New York: J. P. Lippincott Company, 1967.

EMBRY, MARGARET. *My Name is Lion.* New York: Holiday House, 1970.

JONES, WEYMAN. *The Talking Leaf.* New York: Dial Press, 1965.

SCHWEITZER, BYRD BAYLOR. *One Small Blue Bead.* New York: The Macmillan Company, 1965.

TOBIAS, TOBI. *Maria Tallchief.* New York: Thomas Y. Crowell Company, 1970.

UDRY, JANICE MAY. *The Sunflower Garden.* Irvington-on-Hudson, New York: Harvey House, 1969.

BOOKS FOR INTERMEDIATE GRADE CHILDREN

ARMER, LAURA ADAMS. *Waterless Mountain.* New York: David McKay Company, 1966.

BEATTY, PATRICIA. *The Sea Pair.* New York: William Morrow and Company, 1970.

BENNETT, KAY and ROSS. *A Navajo Saga.* San Antonio, Texas: Naylor Company, 1969.

CLARK, ANN NOLAN. *The Desert People.* New York: The Viking Press, 1962.

CROWELL, ANN. *A Hogan for Bluebird.* New York: Charles Scribner's Sons, 1969.

ERNO, RICHARD B. *Billy Lightfoot.* New York: Crown Publishers, 1969.

FALL, THOMAS. *Edge of Manhood.* New York: Dial Press, 1964.

FARNSWORTH, FRANCES J. *Winged Moccasins: The Story of Sacajawea.* New York: Julian Messner, 1954.

GOBLE, PAUL and DOROTHY. *Red Hawk's Account of Custer's Last Battle: The Battle of the Little Bighorn, June, 1876.* New York: Pantheon Books, a division of Random House, 1969.

GURKO, MIRIAM. *Indian America, the Black Hawk War.* New York: Thomas Y. Crowell Company, 1970.

JONES, WEYMAN. *Edge of Two Worlds.* New York: Dial Press, 1968.

KIRK, RUTH. *David, Young Chief of the Quilentes: An American Indian Today.* New York: Harcourt, Brace & World, 1967.

LAMPMAN, EVELYN SIBLEY. *Cayuse Courage.* New York: Harcourt, Brace & World, 1970.

O'DELL, SCOTT. *Sing Down the Mountains.* Boston: Houghton Mifflin Company, 1970.

————. *Island of the Blue Dolphins.* Boston: Houghton Mifflin Company, 1960.

PERRINE, MARY. *Salt Boy.* Boston: Houghton Mifflin Company, 1968.

SMUCKER, BARBARA C. *Wigwam in the City.* New York: E. P. Dutton, 1966.
STEELE, WILLIAM O. *Wayah of the Real People.* Williamsburg, Virginia: Colonial Williamsburg, 1964. Distributed by Holt, Rinehart & Winston.

ADOLESCENT BOOKS

ALLEN, LEROY. *Shawnee Lance.* New York: Delacorte Press, 1970.
BENNETT, KAY and ROSS. *A Navajo Saga.* San Antonio, Texas: Naylor Company, 1969.
BONHAM, BARBARA. *The Battle of Wounded Knee: The Ghost Dance Uprising.* Chicago: Reilly & Lee Books, a division of the Henry Regnary Company, 1970.
BONHAM, FRANK. *Chief.* New York: E. P. Dutton & Co., 1971.
BORLAND, HAL. *When the Legends Die.* New York: Bantam Books, Pathfinder Edition, 1969.
BROWN, DEE. *Bury My Heart at Wounded Knee: An Indian History of the American West.* New York: Holt, Rinehart & Winston, 1970.
————. *Showdown at Little Big Horn.* New York: Berkeley Publishing Company, Medallion Edition, 1971.
CLARK, ANN NOLAN. *Journey to the People.* New York: The Viking Press, 1969.
————. *Circle of Seasons.* New York: Farrar, Straus & Giroux, 1970.
DELORIA, VINE, JR. *Custer Died for Your Sins: An Indian Manifesto.* New York: Avon Publishers, a division of the Hearst Corporation, 1970.
FRAZIER, NETA LOHNES. *Sacajawea, The Girl Nobody Knows.* New York: David McKay Company, 1967.
KROEBER, THEODORA. *Ishi—Last of His Tribe.* Berkeley, California: Parnassus Press, 1964.
————. *Ishi in Two Worlds: A Biography of the Last Wild Indian in North America.* Berkeley: University of California Press, 1963.
LAFARGE, OLIVER. *The American Indian: Special Edition for Young Readers.* New York: Golden Press, 1969.
LOCKE, RAYMOND. *The American Indian.* Los Angeles: Mankind Publishing Company, 1970.
LOCKETT, SHARON. *No Moccasins Today.* New York: Thomas Nelson, 1970.
LAMPMAN, EVELYN SIBLEY. *Half-Breed.* Garden City, New York: Doubleday & Company, 1970.
MOONEY, JAMES. *The Ghost Dance Religion: Sioux Outbreak of 1890.* Chicago: University of Chicago Press, 1970.
RICHTER, CONRAD. *The Light in the Forest.* New York: Bantam, Pathfinder Editions, 1953.

PROFESSIONAL BOOKS

BROWN, DEE. *Bury My Heart at Wounded Knee: An Indian History of the American West.* New York: Holt, Rinehart & Winston, 1970.
CAHN, EDGAR S. *Our Brother's Keeper: The Indian in White America.* New York: New Community Press, 1969.
COLTON, HAROLD S. *Hopi Kachina Dolls with a Key to Their Identification.* Albuquerque, New Mexico: University of New Mexico Press, 1970.

HODGE, GENE MEANY. *The Kachinas Are Coming: Indian Kachina Dolls with Related Folk Tales.* Flagstaff, Arizona: Northland Press, 1967.

LAFARGE, OLIVER. *Laughing Boy.* New York: Pocket Books, 1959.

LONGFELLOW, HENRY WADSWORTH. *The Song of Hiawatha.* New York: Crown Publishers, Bounty Books, 1968.

MARRIOTT, ALICE, and RACHLIN, CAROL K. *American Indian Mythology.* New York: Thomas Y. Crowell Company, 1968.

MCWILLIAMS, CAREY. *Brothers Under the Skin.* Rev. ed. Boston: Little, Brown and Company, 1964.

MOMADAY, N. SCOTT. *The Way to Rainy Mountain.* Albuquerque, New Mexico: The University of New Mexico Press, 1969.

PRATSON, FREDERICK JOHN. *Land of the Four Directions.* Old Greenwich, Connecticut: The Chatham Press, distributed by the Viking Press, 1970.

STEINER, STAN. *The New Indians.* New York: Dell Publishing Company, a Delta Book, 1968.

VILLASEÑOR, DAVID V. *Tapestries in Sand: The Spirit of Indian Sand Painting.* Rev. ed. Healdsburg, California: Naturegraph Co., 1966.

WATERS, FRANK. *Book of the Hopi.* New York: Ballantine Books, 1969.

———. *Masked Gods: Navaho and Pueblo Ceremonialism.* New York: Ballantine Books, an Intext-Publisher, 1970.

CHAPTER EIGHT

The Eagle
and the
Serpent:
Mexican-American
Literature

The eagle and the serpent were the ancient symbols of the Aztecs which have been incorporated into the coat of arms of Mexico. This chapter will be principally concerned with literature of the Mexican-Americans in the United States which consist of nearly five million persons. Many Mexican-Americans cluster together in *barrios,* or neighborhood regions, where conditions of living are poor and the people are poverty-stricken. Leaders in these *barrios* are militant in their call for a sense of unity, a change in their way of life, better education, more civil rights, and improved economic conditions. During the past few years people of this minority group have indicated resentment at being considered hyphenated Americans. They see the need for a new type of American who is proud of his lineage, his language, his culture, "his *raza,*" and one who is "ready to take his share of U. S. prosperity."[1] When they are shout-

1. Dial Torgerson, " 'Brown Power' Unity Seen Behind School Disorders," in *Mexican-Americans in the United States: A Reader,* edited by John H. Burma (Cambridge: Schenkman Publishing Company, distributed by Canfield Press, a department of Harper & Row, Publishers, 1970), p. 280.

ing such slogans as "Viva la Raza," they are honoring their race or people. However, these Spanish-speaking Americans have splintered themselves into many groups. Some of the militant youth are calling themselves the Brown Berets and demand Brown Power unity as they seek their identity with Mexican cultural traditions. Another group of Mexican-Americans led by Reies Tijerana, or "El Tigre," speaks of the *Alianza,* or Alliance of the Indian-speaking peoples of northern New Mexico, and they prefer to be Indio-Spanish in name. Residents of much of Colorado, New Mexico, and Texas often use the term Spanish-Americans. Some Mexican-Americans in California and other states call themselves Chicanos. Regardless of name, most of these people have two traits in common: they are bilingual and bicultural.

Many Mexican-American students resent the fact that their splendid Mexican culture and heritage is neglected. Stereotyped images of Mexicans "mercilessly slaughtering brave Texans at the Alamo" persist. Rosalinda Mendez says "we never hear about the child heroes of Mexico who courageously threw themselves from the heights of Chapultepec rather than allow themselves and their flag to be captured by attacking Americans."[2] Mexican-Americans resent the negative stereotype of a dirty, unshaven Mexican man carrying a tequila bottle in one hand and a tortilla in the other. He usually has a serape dropping from his shoulder and a tilted sombrero sliding down his head. Some Easterners think of Mexican-Americans as "wet backs" or "braceros" following the crops northward. However, many of these people are also working as hod carriers, bus drivers, and at other jobs in such cities as Los Angeles and San Diego. In "A Minority Nobody Knows," Helen Rowan discusses some of the purposes of Cesar Chavez who has successfully organized many Mexican immigrants and farm workers and uses the appeal of "combination of religious pageantry, evocation of the heroes of the Mexican Revolution, and nonviolent civil rights techniques—"[3]

Nonfiction Books—Mexican-Americans

Three books for young adolescents on the subject of Mexican-Americans is *The Mexicans in America: A Students' Guide to Localized History* by Carey McWilliams, *Mexican-Americans, Past, Present and Future* by Julian Nava, and *South by Southwest: The Mexican-American and His Heritage* by John Tebbel and Ramón Eduardo Ruiz. Part 6, "The Mexican-

2. Charles A. Ericksen, "Uprising in the Barrios," in *Mexican-Americans,* ed. Burma, p. 291.
3. Helen Rowan, "A Minority Nobody Knows," in *Mexican-Americans,* ed. Burma, p. 299.

American Today," by Nava includes brief biographies and pictures of Mexican-Americans with whom their youth might identify. These are such persons as Rudolpho P. Hernández who won the Medal of Honor; Cesar Chavez who has championed farm workers; Vicente T. Ximenes of New Mexico, a chairman of the President's Cabinet Committee—Mexican-American affairs; and Armando Rodríguez, a coordinator of the Educational Program for the Spanish-speaking in the U. S. Office of Education, as well as many others.

The third book, *South by Southwest: The Mexican-American and His Heritage* by John Tebbel and Ramón E. Ruiz, gives adolescents some background of the term "Mexican-Americans" and the fight for independence in Mexico by the Mexican people.

Professional Books for College Teachers and Students

Several recent books which give information on Mexican-Americans are *La Raza: Forgotten Americans,* edited by Julian Samora, and *La Raza: The Mexican Americans* by Stan Steiner. The Steiner book has a chapter about the Chicano which is quite informative.

Marjorie Fallows has written a chapter entitled "The Mexican-American Laborers: A Different Drummer?" which appears in *The Aliens: A History of Ethnic Minorities in America,* edited by Leonard Dinnerstein and Frederic Cople Jaher. According to Fallows: "The Mexican-American sees status in the Anglo world as something to be bought or seized. In his own world it is something to be won through adherence to the ideals of the group: loyalty to one's own, devotion to the family, and a dignified acceptance and appreciation of things as they are because this is the way God has planned it."[4]

A chapter, "The Indians in Mexico," appears in *Minorities in the New World: Six Case Studies,* which gives an interesting background concerning the Indian minorities of Mexico.

Oscar Lewis has been developing a type of ethnological reportage which records all possible observations of the day-to-day life of family households in Mexican communities. Three of his volumes are *Five Families: Mexican Case Studies in the Culture of Poverty, The Children of Sánchez: Autobiography of a Mexican Family,* and *Pedro Martínez: A Mexican Peasant and His Family.* These three volumes offer some sociocultural backgrounds which help readers to understand something about the Mexican cultural patterns.

4. Leonard Dinnerstein, and Frederic Cople Jaher, *The Aliens: A History of Ethnic Minorities in America* (New York: Appleton-Century-Crofts, Meredith Corporation, 1970), p. 316.

Another book, one of a series of case studies in cultural anthropology, is *Mexican-Americans of South Texas* by William Madsen. Chapter three, entitled "La Raza," explains that the concept of *La Raza* implies a "splendid and glorious destiny" and Mexican people who have a strong religious impulse, a belief in "machismo" or manliness, a pride in their ancient heritage, and a belief in the strength of the family circle.[5]

A helpful book by Ernesto Galarza, Herman Gallegos and Julian Samora is *Mexican-Americans in the Southwest* which gives the problems of the minority group and some of the relations between the "Anglo" and the Mexican-American. A second recent useful book is *Emerging Faces: the Mexican-Americans* by Y. Arturo Cabrera.

A recent adult novel is *Chicano* by Richard Vasquez. This story gives a panoramic view of some Mexican-Americans who follow jobs northward and who try to improve their socio-economic condition by accepting Anglo-white middle-class traditions. The depiction of Chicanos as new-comers in restricted housing areas, the struggle to be educated in a second language, and police persecution in the *barrios* of Los Angeles are events which are graphically portrayed. Also there is the Anglo-American sociology student, David Stiver, who wants to fraternize with Chicanos. He tries to understand their families and customs but cannot face the social ostracism of his white Anglo-Saxon parents by marrying the Chicano girl, Mariana, after he has made her pregnant.

Latin American Bibliography and Sources About Mexican Literature

Readers of Mexican-American literature should note the negative stereotype of a Mexican-American and should avoid a book in which an author uses a stereotyped, condescending style with an artificial Spanish-Mexican dialect. Books which offer propaganda favoring a particular religious faith should be avoided. For instance, life of Mexicans and Indians in Franciscan missions is idyllic in many children's books focusing on the mission era in California history. Mexican-American books should not give the impression that life is one continuous round of fiestas and bull-fights. For instance, *Nine Days to Christmas* by Marie Hall Ets and Aurora Labastida is a beautifully illustrated picture book about the Mexican custom of breaking a piñata, but young children should understand that Mexican-American children celebrate both ancient Mexican party ways and modern customs and holidays in the United States.

A rather extensive bibliography on Mexican literature appears in *Latin America: An Annotated List of Materials,* selected by a Committee

5. William Madsen, *The Mexican-Americans of South Texas* (New York: Holt, Rinehart & Winston, 1964), pp. 15-23.

of librarians, teachers, and Latin American specialists in cooperation with the Center for Inter-American Relations which is published by the Information Center on Children's Cultures, the United States Committee for UNICEF. Annotated lists of children's books appear under such classifications as Pre-Conquest, The Conquest and After; The Struggle for Independence; The Early 20th Century; History and People from Past to Present; Games, Dances, Arts and Crafts; Present Day Stories and Pictures; Mexicans in the U. S.; Folklore; and other categories.

An article by Gloria T. Blatt entitled "The Mexican-American in Children's Literature" discusses the depiction of cultural information in a correct, unstereotyped, truthful manner. A bibliography of some Spanish-American books is included.

David K. Gast indicates that recent children's literature frequently stereotypes the Spanish-American minority in primary grade books which are mostly picture ones. Mexican-Americans wear serapes and sombreros as well as sloppy leather sandals and enjoy numerous traditional Mexican holidays. Gast also says that many books about the Spanish-Americans depict them as isolated and alien to Anglo-Americans living in a different economic strata.

Toni de Gerez in "The Way of Quetzalcóatl" presents background for giving the Mexican-American child some roots in the old world so that he can remember the greatness of his heritage. Aztec traditions and Náhuatl literature give a framework of the wise teachers of long ago, the *tlamatineme*. Quetzalcóatl was the Great God, or the Most High Priest. He was the "Feathered Serpent," the God of Learning, the God of the Priesthood, the God of the Wind, and also the God of the Evening Star. No one knows his origin, but he performed heroic deeds for his people. Once he transformed himself into an ant and stole the " 'first grain of corn' or the sustenance of the gods."[6] This article includes excerpts of poetry which have been translated and interpreted by Dr. Angel Maria Garibay, a great Náhuatl scholar. The transience of life is expressed by King Nezahualcoyotl, who lived from 1407 to 1472. He symbolically speaks of life on earth as a broken piece of jade, or crushed gold—an existence so transient it can be torn asunder like the quetzal feather.[7]

Toni de Gerez has also written another article entitled "Three Times Lonely: The Plight of the Mexican Child in the Southwest." Mrs. de Gerez indicates that a whole mythology is built around the word *corn*. *Maiz* is planted in a cornfield, or *milpa*. When the plant is young it is a *jilote;*

---

6. Toni de Gerez, "The Way of Quetzalcóatl," *Hornbook Magazine* 43 (April 1967): pp. 171-175.
7. *Ibid.*, p. 175.

when it is ready to be gathered, it is known as *elote*. Some of this appreciative feeling for corn is seen in various books for young children as well as in folktales. Gerez states that the Mexican-American child in the United States suffers a triple loneliness, "his cultural background, his Mexican heritage, his language."[8]

Books for Miguel

One of the finest bibliographies for Spanish-speaking children is one listing books for the Spanish-speaking population by Toni de Gerez entitled "Books for Miguel." This bibliography considers migrants coming to America from Latin America, Cuba, and Puerto Rico and includes many Spanish books which will be of interest to Mexican-American children in the southwest. This has an extensive list of bilingual books listed under such categories as Dictionaries and Encyclopedias; Easy Reading; Bilingual Picture Books; Books on Legends, Heroes, and Folklore, Spanish Versions of Fairy Tales and Classics; Biographies, Books on Science and Nature; and Stories. Many of these books may have to be obtained in Mexico, Spain, and other Latin-American countries.

More Books on Migrant Workers

A book on migrant workers which has been popular for some time is *Blue Willow* by Doris Gates, which is easily read by most pupils in the sixth grade. In this story Janey Larkin manages to gain a permanent home for her family and herself. The blue willow plate, a cheap heirloom, makes her proud of her family possessions. This story depicts a family of Mexicans as being better off financially than the Larkin family. A book for teen-agers about Mexican-American argicultural workers is *A Long Time Coming* by Phyllis Whitney. This novel tells how young people want to help the Mexican-American migrant workers in their town. Positive changes are only brought about through struggles against prejudice, tension, and ill feelings. Another book about the poor agricultural workers is *Migrant Girl* by Carli Laklan. This story relates how Dacey Cotter and her family, including Grandma and little Gaither, follow the crops to work in the fields from Florida to New York. They pull corn, pick tomatoes, and chop cabbage. Each year Dacey dreams that things will be better. She meets Juan, a Mexican-American, who bravely and determinedly fights to improve the conditions of migrants. Dacey and her family

8. Toni de Gerez, "Three Times Lonely: The Plight of the Mexican Child in the American Southwest," *Hornbook Magazine* 46 (February, 1970):66-73.

suffer many hardships, but most of their problems are caused by a cheating crew boss, or labor contractor. Juan bravely causes the migrants to think about *La Causa* even though Miguel and others are fearful of being called agitators and of losing their jobs when bullied by the labor boss.

A brief biography, *Cesar Chavez* by Ruth Franchere, is about the well-known leader of the struggle to improve the conditions and pay of the Chicano laborer. This is one of a series of biographies being edited by Susan Bartlett Weber. These biographies are brief, but they give some of the accomplishments of representatives of minority peoples. Another biography of Cesar Chavez is *Mighty Hard Road: The Story of Cesar Chavez* by James J. Tarzian and Kathryn Crones. An ironic bitter depiction of the Mexican-Americans shouting words of revolution and working on the railroads, on the cotton fields, and in the canneries is "Goodbye Revolution—Hello Slum" by Octavio I. Romano-V.[9]

Myths, Legends, and Folktales As A Heritage

Myths, legends, and folktales of Mexican Indians and Spaniards are part of the cultural heritage of Mexican-Americans in the United States. One good collection of tales is *Star Mountain and Other Legends of Mexico,* which was written by Camilla Campbell. Two popular legends included in this collection are "Our Lady of Guadalupe" and "China Poblana." Our Lady of Guadalupe is a shrine honored by Mexican Indians. The legend tells the story of poor Juan Diego who had a vision and saw the Virgin and the miracle of blooming December roses. (A child's book on the same legend is *A Miracle for Mexico* by Josefina Niggli.) "China Poblana," as told in the Camilla Campbell book, is a story concerning the miraculous appearance of riotous flowers on the white blouse and skirt of Catarina, who was known for her many kindnesses to the sick and the poor. The same legend is retold in *Pirate's Doll* by Eula Long.

Some Mexican folktales appear in *Latin American Tales: From the Pampas to the Pyramids of Mexico* by Genevieve Barlow. Two stories in this collection are "The Cuckoo's Reward" and "Bird Cu." In this second story, the bird, feeling dispirited because of his ragged, gray feathers, complains to the eagle who suggests that each bird of the forest donate a feather from its own brilliantly colored plumage. The story continues until the little bird becomes beautiful but vain. Later, it is punished for both its vanity and laziness.

9. Octavio I. Romano-V, "Goodbye Revolution—Hello Slum," in *El Espejo—The Mirror: Selected Mexican-American Literature,* edited by Octavio Ignacio Romano-V. (Berkeley, California: Quinto Sol Publications, 1969), pp. 76-82.

Paper bag puppets used while telling Mexican story.

Two books by Anita Brenner containing much Mexican folklore are *The Boy Who Could Do Anything & Other Mexican Folktales* and *A Hero by Mistake*. The first book includes Mexican-Indian legends with some Spanish traditions interwoven in them. The second book is about Dioniosio, a Mexican-Indian boy who frequently suffers from fear but manages to perform brave deeds in spite of himself.

A newer version of an old Mexican creation legend appears in *The Creation of the Sun and the Moon* by B. Traven, which is dramatically illustrated by Alberto Beltram.

Carlton Beals has collected a group of folktales entitled *Stories Told by the Aztecs Before the Spaniards Came*. In "The Four Destructions of Mankind," Nahui Ocelotl is displaced by the Plumed Snake who hurls him into the sea. The Black God turns into the constellation in the form of a jaguar known as "The Great Bear." There are other world destructions mirrored by such catastrophes as floods, hurricanes, earthquakes, and volcanic eruptions. In "Wise Man of the Toltecs," the Plumed Serpent comes to the Toltecs to teach the art of the silversmith and stonecutter. People learn to use beans for *chocolatl*. The Plumed Serpent becomes the supreme ruler and lives in the House of Feathers. In "The Flight of the Plumed Serpent" and other legends of the Feathered Snake, the religious and political views of the Toltecs are portrayed. "The Flight of the Plumed Serpent" is really a story of the dispersal of the Toltecs. These legends are

Life-size Mexican stick puppet.

closely related to the ascendancy and fall of most of the Aztec Gods until the final chapter, "Conquest," explicates the mingling of history, magic and legend. This book of legends is for teen-agers.

An illustrated book which presents one special legend for younger children is *When the Monkeys Wore Sombreros,* which has been written by

Mariana Prieto and illustrated by Robert Quackenbush. This is a tale about Andres and Francisco, two brothers who live in Mexico. They wear the traditional sombreros woven by their mother from *paja trigaza,* or wheat straw. One day the boys go on a journey on their burros piled high with sombreros. In the evening they stop for rest, and wasps sting their burros. The sombreros become untied, and chattering monkeys gather up the hats. The boys toss pebbles at the monkeys and the animals throw oranges at the boys. This is an amusing tale which has other complications.

A Folklore Volume for Mature Adolescents

A valuable resource for older adolescents who are studying folk-tales of many different cultures is *Folktales of Mexico,* a volume which has been edited and translated by Américo Paredes. This is quite an extensive collection of folktales which are a part of the oral tradition of the Mexicans. These are categorized under such classifications as Legendary-Narratives, Animal Tales, Ordinary Folktales, Jokes and Anecdotes, and Formula Tales. Richard M. Dorson who has written a foreword to the collection, mentions that over half of the people live "folkloric lives."[10] Most Mexican folklore has a Spanish-Indian synthesis. The foreword gives much valuable information about Mexican folktales.

A book for older adolescents and adults is *Mexican and Central American Mythology* by Irene Nicholson. This volume is illustrated with beautiful color plates and photographs. In "How music was made" one learns that Quetzalcoatl is helped to reach the sun by Cane and Conch, Water Woman, and Water Monster. When Quetzalcoatl reaches the sun, he asks it for musicians who can return to earth to give pleasure to man. A sixteenth-century Nahua manuscript describes this incident in poetic form. Here Tezcatlipoca, god of heaven, cries from the depths of the four quarters "Come, O Wind!"[11] Tezcatlipoca tells the wind that the earth is sick from silence and wants music. Father Sun is surrounded by music makers attired in four colors who sweetly play their flutes. The Sun's musicians are dressed in four colors. White represents cradle songs, red the epics of love and of war, sky-blue is for "the troubadors of wandering cloud," and gold was milled by the Sun from the peaks of the World.[12] Some of the symbolism characteristic of the gods of Mexican and Central American mythology is beautiful in poetic form.

10. Américo Paredes, ed. and trans., *Folktales of Mexico* (Chicago: The University of Chicago Press, 1970), p. xi.
11. Irene Nicholson, *Mexican and Central American Mythology* (London: Paul Hamlyn, 1967), p. 31.
12. *Ibid.,* p. 33, 34.

Quetzal Feathers and Eagle Shields—Mexican Poetry

Some Mexican-American poetry is indebted to many traditions of the Spanish poets who brought their songs to the New World. Other poets look back to beautiful tunes sung by ancient Náhuatl people prior to the arrival of the Spanish conquistadors.

Flowers and Song

In recent years, several scholars have become interested in ancient Náhuatl poetry due principally to the noted scholarship of Angel María Garibay K*. One of the foremost American scholars of Mexican and Mexican-American cultures, Rafael Jesús González, has written "Symbol and Metaphor in Náhuatl Poetry"[13] which lucidly interprets some of the significance of beautiful words and flowers and song written by gifted Náhuatl poets. González selects such words as *centzontli,* or mocking bird, and shows that this is literally a "bird of four hundred voices."[14]

According to González, four of the most frequently used Náhuatl metaphors are flowers, quetzal plumes, jade, and hearts. Miguel León-Portilla states that Xochipilli, the spring god of the Náhuas is known as the Prince of Flowers. Xochipilli symbolizes a new sun, or a spring and the rebirth of a land after winter. His weeping tears are the rainfall giving new green growth to the parched land. The god wears flowers in his sandals. These too represent a form of birth since flowers arrive before fruit which sustains life. Monseñor Garibay states that the words "flower and song" symbolizes poetry as the Prince of Flowers is the god of poetry and song.[15]

The *quetzal* plume was another significant symbol of the Náhuas. The *quetzal* was precious; so *quetzalxochitl* was a "precious flower," or a "flower of plumes." Feathers were highly prized by the Aztecs who fashioned crowns, sceptres, and capes out of them and symbolized their gods as wearing feathered clothes. When the Spaniards conquered the Aztecs they greedily grabbed gold from their shields and ensigns and stripped away the *quetzal* feathers which were much more highly prized by the Aztecs. An ancient poem from *Poesía Indígena* by Garibay speaks of the poet walking with a "flowered tambourine ringed with quetzal plumes" and "adorned with flowers of gold."[16] A novel, *The Prince of*

---

*This author speaks of Angel María Garibay K; Toni de Gerez speaks of Dr. Angel María Garibay as the greatest Náhuatl scholar.
13. Gerald W. Haslam, *Forgotten Pages of American Literature* (Boston: Houghton Mifflin Company, 1970), p. 231.
14. *Ibid.*
15. *Ibid.,* p. 232.
16. *Ibid.,* p. 233.

Aztec masks made by 5th grade children.

Mexico by Federica De Cesco, which has been written for young adolescents, depicts Montezuma and the young Prince Guatemoc in the feathered
glory of many birds. In chapter three of the novel, Montezuma is clothed
in a magnificent cloak of flamingo and humming-bird feathers which covered a white tunic adorned with "pearl-embroidered butterflies."[17]

A third sacred symbol of Náhuatl poetry was jade, which was the
sacred gem of Tlaloc. A bead of jade was supposedly swallowed by the
mother of Quetzalcoatl. Jade was the token of both nobility and sacredness. The Náhuas symbolized the greenness and new life of spring through
the use of jade in their songs, and the god Tlaloc kept the rain in huge
jade urns. When a man died, a valuable piece of jade was placed over his
lips to replace his silent heart. Gold was only a setting for jade, which
symbolized the "noble, beautiful, and esteemed," and an ancient Otomí
poet spoke of a song being "polished jade and molded gold."[18] Jade of-

17. Federica De Cesco, *The Prince of Mexico* (New York: The John Day Company
1970), p. 21.
18. Rafael Jesús González, "Symbol and Metaphor in Náhuatl Poetry," in *Forgotten
Pages,* by Haslam, 234.

fered a greater sense of permanence than did flowers which withered and died.

The fourth significant symbol of ancient Náhuatl poetry was the heart. The spring god of the Náhuas, or Xochipilli, carried the flower, and the quetzal plume and wore a jade collar but he also had a heart on his baton. The human heart was the greatest sacrifice which the Aztecs offered to their gods as it symbolized feeling, knowledge, and courage. According to the Náhuas, a teacher's responsibility was to "humanize people," or he makes the hearts strong."[19] The jade-heart symbol represented a dualistic image of the significance of Quetzalcoatl, the plumed serpent. González states: "In Náhua mythology the serpent is identified with the Mother goddess (Coatlicue), the earth; the bird with masculinity (Huitzilopochtli), the sky, the heroic."[20]

Rafael Jesús González has translated a few "Brief Songs" of pre-Hispanic Mexican poetry which illustrate the metaphorical use of several of these symbols. A beautiful poem, "To Tlacohuepan," speaks of one who goes to the kingdom of the dead hiding in Seven Caverns as a "fire-tinted quechol bird." This is the world where acacia blossoms give golden beauty and where the ocelot growls and the eagle screeches.[21]

Many Náhuatl songs, most of them written by Monseñor Garibay, appear in the volume *The Unwritten Song: Poetry of the Primitive and Traditional Peoples of the World,* edited and in part translated by Willard R. Trask. One of the poems in this collection, "War Song," illustrates the metaphors previously interpreted by González. The poet speaks of the "flowers of battle, the clattering shields, and a bonfire which seethes and coils like a serpent. Flowers of the Tiger and shield mix with the dust and the tinkling of ankle bells, and where "Quetzal-feather shields" clash "with standards of green and yellow feathers."[22]

Another different type of poem (and a beautfiul one) is the "Song: The Bird and the Butterfly" which depicts the trilling "red bird of the god" and a beautiful butterfly with outspread wings which lands on the flowers and sups the nectar.[23]

The poem "The Poet's Mission" explains the significance of song and poetry in the Náhuatl Culture. The poet pours out song and refreshes his fellow man as does the rain which brings forth fresh things to the world. The poet must also "polish a song like a turquoise."[24]

19. *Ibid.,* p. 235.
20. *Ibid.,* p. 236.
21. Rafael Jesús González, trans., "To Tlacohuepan" in Haslam, *Forgotten Pages,* p. 237.
22. Willard R. Trask, ed. and trans., *The Unwritten Song: Poetry of the Primitive and Traditional Peoples of the World, volume 2* (New York: The Macmillan Company, 1967), p. 280.
23. *Ibid.,* p. 281.
24. *Ibid.,* p. 281.

An unusually beautiful poem is "The Origin of Songs," a song of great beauty and one which could help the Náhuatl people face death. The poet goes to the green hummingbird, the "emerald flycatcher," and the "golden butterfly" and begs to have the birds help him to discover the fragrantly-scented flowers. The birds then lead him to the mountains where the poet enjoys the precious, fragrant flowers which are to be given to noblemen and friends.

A large number of Náhuatl poems appear in *The Magic World: American Indian Songs and Poems,* which has already been mentioned in the previous chapter on the American Indian literature. Here the Náhuatl "Flower Song," adapted from *Ancient Náhuatl Poetry* by Daniel G. Brinton, speaks of flowers in a rhythmical, chanting style as the poet talks about the beautiful *poyomatl,* a narcotic rose which can be mixed with tobacco and smoked.[25]

The rather lengthy poem "From the Aztec Ceremonial Calendar" is rather gruesome when viewed from the light of the Christian culture, but it explains much about the ceremonial rites and rituals practiced by the Aztecs. On the first month little children were sacrificed so that their hearts could be offered to the gods of water in order to make rain come. In the second month many captives were dragged to the temples by their hair and slain at the base of the pyramid. A feast of the third month was held and the earliest blooming flowers were offered to the god. On the fourth month reeds were sprinkled with blood from the ears or the calves of the legs of people who were sacrificed to the god. On the most important feast of Easter, the feast of Tezcatlipoca, a special youth who had been trained as a god for a year was slain. On the sixth month priests brought reeds, people hid themselves for fear of destroying the sacredness of the ceremony, and captives were dressed in ornaments worn by the god Tlaloc and slain at a feast. A woman who resembled *Uixtociuatl,* Tlaloc's elder sister, was slain on the seventh month as girls and old women danced with garlands of flowers. On the eighth month a woman was slain in honor of the goddess of maize while other men and women feasted and danced for eight days. The god of war was honored on the ninth month and the people feasted on dogs, tamales, and fowls, and the statues of the gods were garlanded with flowers. The poet continued to reenact rites and ceremonies through the eighteenth month, and other feasts were held on other significant dates of the Aztec calendar.[26]

25. William Brandon, sel. and ed., *The Magic World: American Indian Songs and Poems* (New York: William Morrow & Company, 1971), p. 7.
26. Adapted from the Náhuatl Song "From the Aztec Ceremonial Calendar" which was adapted from Book II of Fray Bernardino de Sahagun, *General History of the Things of New Spain, the Florentine Codex* translated by Charles E. Dibble and Arthur J. O. Anderon and appearing in *The Magic World: American Indian Songs and Poems,* selected with and an introduction by William Brandon (New York: William Morrow & Company, 1971), pp. 9-14.

Other Mexican and Latin-American Poetry

Two volumes of Mexican poetry have been selected and edited by Octavio Paz and others. The first one is *An Anthology of Mexican Poetry* and the second one is *New Poetry of Mexico,* selected with notes by Octavio Paz, Ali Chumacero, José Emilio Pacheco, and Homero Aridjis.

Octavio Paz has written a lengthy introduction to the first volume. He states that poetry of Mexico is "distinguished from that of Spain by its absence or scarcity of medieval features,"[27] which makes it more universal in scope. Readers interested in the Oriental *haiku* style of poetry will recognize little verses by José Juan Tablada which were written in a similar style.

A series of *haiku* verses appear in this volume, such as "Haiku of a Day" and "Haiku of the Flowerpot." The imagery is fresh and beautiful. For instance, in one *haiku* verse the poet speaks of a dragonfly which fastens "its transparent cross/to the bare and trembling bough."[28] This poet also experimented with "ideographical" poems. Poems by such Mexican poets as Manuel Guitérrez Nájera, Francisco A. de Icaza, Luis G. Urbina, Amado Nervo, Ramón López Velarde, and many others appear in this volume.

The second bilingual volume edited by Mark Strand on the newer poetry of Mexico commences with poetry by Homero Aridjis and concludes with poems by José Juan Tablada. Here appear several different *haiku* verses, such as "The Peacock," which is about a bird shimmering in a procession in a "democratic henyard."[29] In "The Toads," the toads are hopping down an "unlighted path."[30]

Poems by Mexican-Americans as well as ones by Puerto Ricans appear in the volume *American Ethnic Writing: Speaking for Ourselves* by Lillian Faderman and Barbara Bradshaw. The poet, Omar Salinas, in "Aztec Angel" speaks of himself as being both an angel and an outcast of society. He is a Mexican-American of the Pachuco type. Josef Rodriguez has written two lovely poems of belief entitled "Smoke" and "Prayer." These appear also in this anthology.

Richard Lewis has edited *Still Waters of the Air: Poems by Three Modern Spanish Poets.* These three poets were born in Spain and present the vision, attitude, and poetic spirit of Spanish thought and feeling. Here human experience and nature are intermingled. Poems are printed in both

27. Octavio Paz, comp., *Anthology of Mexican poetry,* translated by Samuel Beckett (Bloomington, Indiana: Indiana University Press, 1969), pp. 24-25.
28. *Ibid.,* p. 152.
29. José Juan Tablada, "The Peacock" and "The Toads" in *New Poetry of Mexico,* edited by Octavio Paz et al. (New York: E. P. Dutton Co., 1970), p. 205.
30. *Ibid.,* p. 207.

English and Spanish. Antonio Machado depicts Spring with "halle-lujahs of flowering brambles!" Juan Ramón Jiménez speaks of "the golden children" who are climbing poplars toward the sky with "their eyes like pure dreams" and the blueness of their eyes and the sky are one.[31] Federico García Lorca looks at an insignificant little animal in "Snail." He tells how the snail sings a "map-green ocean," and causes the poet to feel kindness toward small brown and silver fish.[32] Antonio Machado beautifully depicts the sun as a "globe of fire" and the "moon as a purple disk." He gives an image of a small dove perched in a high centennial cypress in his poem, "The Sun Is a Globe of Fire." These poems are for the Spanish and Mexican child, but their colorful pictorial images are a de-light to all persons enjoying the beauty of nature embedded in song.

Some of these same poems in an imagist style appear in *Juan Ramón Jiménez: Three Hundred Poems, 1903-1953,* translated by Eloïse Roach, and in *The Selected Writings of Juan Ramón Jiménez,* translated by H. R. Hays. The poems of Jiménez are pictorial and filled with clear images of passing oxcarts weeping on the road to Pueblo Nuevo and of stars that "tremble, tremble in the sky." Also, Jiménez speaks of the "blue titmouse in the poplar" and a "green greenfinch" which "sweetens the sunset hours."[33]

Unstill Life: An Introduction to the Spanish Poetry of Latin America, edited by Mario Benedetti, also has many beautiful poems in both the Spanish and English languages. Pablo Neruda is considered to be one of the greatest poets writing in Spanish today. His poems utilize a luxurious-ness of words as well as a human sensitivity and compassion toward people. In "Poem 20," which appears in this volume, he speaks poignantly about the love of a poet for a lost maiden who belongs to another. Octavio Paz, the Mexican poet, writes about silence and solitude in shadowy dreaming waters and in his horse's eyes which "tremble in the night."[34] This volume gives a brief biography as well as a selection of poetry created by some of the leading Spanish poets of Latin America.

Another selection of Latin American poetry is *Young Poetry of the Americas,* published by the General Secretariat of the American States. This volume includes the work of five Mexican poets who speak of tor-tured times with a feeling that the current period of history is transitory.

31. Richard Lewis, ed., *Still Waters of the Air: Poems by Three Modern Spanish Poets* (New York: The Dial Press, 1970), pp. 15, 17.
32. *Ibid.,* p. 27.
33. Eloise Roach, trans., *Juan Ramón Jiménez: Three Hundred Poems, 1903-1953* (Austin, Texas: University of Texas Press, 1962), pp. 18, 23.
34. Octavio Paz "Nocturne," in Mario Benedetti, ed., *Unstill Life: An Introduction to the Spanish Poetry of Latin America,* translated by Darwin J. Fladkoll and Claribel Alegría (New York: Harcourt, Brace & World, 1969), p. 69.

They express themselves in the depths of the human spirit: new men will arise and newer poets will create joyous poems of liberty. "Nocturne" and "Visitors" by Octavio Paz are included. Joaquín Sánchez MacGregor, who is a professor of philosophy at the University of Vera Cruz, speaks of horror, panic, and continents turning to ashes in "Fallout Shelter." Homero Aridjis, in "The Hatching," depicts magnicide with the assassination of thousands of tyrants until all are killed. José Emilio Pacheco has a selection here which is a fragment of "Awakening Day." Jaime Ausgusto Shelley writes in "Occidental Sax," the poem of Edgar Blackie, a Negro contrabassist who is plodding up and down endless staircases looking for work. Poems in this collection are better for more mature secondary pupils who are interested in relevant poetry of social protest.

Seymour Resnick has written two volumes of bilingual Spanish poetry. One is *Selections from Spanish Poetry.* One poem appearing here is "The Hen that Laid the Golden Eggs" by Félix María de Samaniego. One learns about an owner who was not satisfied with the hen that laid a golden egg each day; so he killed it to obtain the gold mine in its stomach. Another book of a similar type is *Spanish-American Poetry: A Bilingual Selection.* Many poems in these two volumes are simple enough to be understood by elementary-school pupils and will be interesting to older readers also.

Some secondary-school pupils will enjoy certain selections in *The Selected Poems of Federico García Lorca,* edited by Francisco Garcia Lorca and Donald M. Allen. Many poems appearing here have been translated into English by various translators. Some of the poetry like "Half Moon" is simple enough to be understood by elementary pupils. This is almost in the style of images reflected in an Oriental *haiku* poem. Here the moon goes scything slowly through the river waters and a young frog chooses her for a mirror.

Another book of poems by Federico Garcia Lorca, *Poet in New York,* includes poems that are much more enigmatic and difficult; so they should probably be reserved for sophisticated readers of poetry at the high-school or college level.

Another Latin-American poet, Pablo Neruda, has written a long poem, *The Heights of Macchu Picchu,* which is a journey to the ruins at Inca City, high in the Andes.

Mexican-American students who are turning to Spanish-American traditions as part of their racial heritage may enjoy *An Anthology of Spanish Poetry from Garcilaso to García Lorca in English Translation with Spanish Originals,* which has been edited by Angel Flores.

A book which includes many examples of Mexican-American poetry is *El Espejo—The Mirror: Selected Mexican-American Literature,* edited by Octavio Ignacio Romano-V. Selections appear in this volume in both Spanish and English. One poem written in such a dramatic style that it could be spoken as choral work or dramatized as a play is "Mosaico Mexicano" by Octavio I. Romano-V. This is a poem which reaches back into the Mexican heritage in which a mother comes from Tamaulipas, home of the cardinals and tarantulas, where a grandfather fights bravely against the Apaches, and where señora Consuelo Sánchez speaks of a father and two brothers who have been killed by Villa's Troops.[35] Here also is a "Song of Immigrant Despair" and a "Song of the Barrio."[36]

Another interesting bilingual poetry book is *Modern Poetry from Spain and Latin America,* translated by Nan Braymer and Lillian Lowenfels. Most of these poems cause students to look at humanity with different eyes. For instance, Victoriano Crémer writes "Blessed are the Poor," and Enoch Cancino Casahonda speaks of the light of the people coming to the eyes of a blind man in "Cuba," and of the foolishness of a drunkard trying to maintain his equilibrium in a dispossessed neighborhood in a poem "The Drunkard."

Books for Younger Children

Numerous picture books are available for young pupils but many of them are rather slight. In *Benito* Clyde Robert Bulla depicts a Mexican-American boy, Benito, who suffers loneliness, shyness, and speech difficulties until he becomes acquainted with an artist, Manuel, and decides to become a professional artist in spite of cruel lashings by Uncle Pedro.

Two little stories for girls are *Maria* by Joan M. Lexau and *Two Pesos for Catalina* by Ann Kirn. In *Maria* a girl suffers great disappointment when her grandmother gives her a doll which is too beautiful to touch. This child might be Puerto Rican instead of Mexican, but the message is universal. In the second story a little girl receives two pesos from a tourist and has difficulty in selecting a proper purchase. Another little book for boys, entitled *Johnny Lost* by Juanita Perdido, is about a Cuban refugee child. This little boy has the fear of all small children who become lost in a strange, large city; in this case, the child gets lost at his first parade.

In *The Corn Grows Ripe* by Dorothy Rhoades, one learns about the significance of corn in the life of the Mayas. This is the story of Dionesio Tigre who learns to help his father clear his land for growing corn. An accident happens to his father; so Tigre assumes the duties of manhood

35. *Ibid.,* p. 85.
36. *Ibid.,* pp. 91-92.

suddenly and makes *milpa.* As he chops away the brush in sunburning heat he mutters "Mi Milpa," (My Corn).

Books by Leo Politi are beautifully illustrated, and although some of the stories seem a little bit stereotyped, there is currently such a small number of books for the young Mexican-American child that some of them can be used if they are balanced out with other books. One of his popular ones is *The Angel of Olvera Street,* which is the story of a famous street in Los Angeles, California where Mexican wares are sold to tourists. Another tale by Politi is *Song of the Swallows,* a story of the Mission San Juan Capistrano in the Spring.

Jan Balet has created a clever picture book for children, entitled *The Fence,* which has some of the characteristics of a folk tale. It is the story of a rich family which has many luxuries, but the children and parents are unhappy. An extremely poor family lives next door. The mother of the poor family sends the children to the fence to savor the rich aroma of cooking food which is being prepared by the maid of the rich family. The wealthy man takes the father to court to try him for stealing the smell of the food. A clever solution to the dilemma is provided at the trial.

Bilingual Books in Spanish and English

An interesting book for young children is *Ramón Makes a Trade/Los cambios de Ramón,* which is written by Barbara Ritchie and illustrated by Earl Thollander. This book is written in both Spanish and English and tells how Ramón compares his bowl with the beautiful pottery fashioned by his father Sandino. He decides to make a trade rather than compete against his father's craft.

Children who are eager to find more books written in the Spanish language will enjoy reading *¿ Que será?,* or *What Can It Be?* This is a book of traditional Spanish riddles collected and arranged with English translations by Loretta Burke Hubp. Some riddles are a little confusing as printed in this text, and some of the experiences may seem odd to modern Anglo-American children, but many of the little verses are amusing.

A bilingual book written in both Spanish and English for Spanish-speaking pre-school and kindergarten children is *Welcome, Roberto!,* or *¡ Bienvenido, Roberto!,* which has been written by Mary Serfozo, with photographs by John Serfozo. This is a slight little book with little plot which is designed to prepare the pre-school Spanish-speaking child for school. It includes photographs of many kindergarten experiences such as the playing of instruments in a rhythm band or role playing in using a telephone.

Ernesto Galarza has written *Zoo Risa* [Fun at the Zoo], which is a picture and rhyme book designed to entertain beginning readers who speak Spanish. A picture index comes at the front of the book giving the picture of an animal and the page where a rhyme will be found about it. A *diccionario* with words in both Spanish and English is at the back of the book. A companion book with the same pictures which is written in English is *Fun at the Zoo*.

Several little books are being written which help the Spanish-speaking child feel more at ease in reading. One of them is a science book dealing with the shape of the moon, its gravitational pull, and the fact that no life is on it. This is *¿ Como es la luna?* Many little books of this type are being published by Harper and Row, Publishers. These are designed for instructional purposes for young children who are learning Spanish or for those whose native tongue is Spanish. These have been translated from the English by Pura Belpré. Three of these are: *Danielito y el dinosauro* [Danny and the Dinosaur] by Syd Hoff, *Osito* [Little Bear] by Else Homelund, and *Teresita y las orugas* [Terry and the Caterpillars] by Millicent E. Selsam.

Another interesting book for young children in Spanish is *Mother Goose in Spanish,* with translations by Alastair Reid and Anthony Kerrigan. It is delightfully illustrated by Barbara Cooney.

Books for Puerto Rican Children

Although this chapter is principally concerned with Mexican-American children, some Puerto Rican students attending a primary-grade class may wish to read a Spanish or English book with a Puerto Rican theme. A teacher who has mostly Mexican-American children in her classroom may wish to use a few Puerto Rican folk tales for contrast. One good collection is *The Three Wishes: A Collection of Puerto Rican Folktales,* selected and adapted by Ricardo E. Alegría and translated by Elizabeth Culbert. A foreword to the collection indicates that the Puerto Ricans represent three great races of humanity, namely, the Mongolians or the Tainos, who were conquered by the Spanish explorers; the Negroes, or Africans, who were formerly slaves from the West Coast of Africa; and the Spaniards, who represented Hispanic cultural traits. Some popular tales which appear in the collection are "Pérez and Martina," "Juan Bobo and the Calderón" and "The Witch's Skin."

Perez and Martina is the story of a little cockroach Martina and her courtship by Perez, the mouse. The poor little mouse married Martina, but one day he fell into the cooking pot and was drowned.

The tale of Perez and Martina in a pictorial form has been translated by Pura Belpré and published in a book entitled *Perez y Martina: Un cuento folklórico puertorriqueño.* Pura Belpré (White) lives in New York and has translated many small books into Spanish for the Puerto Rican and Spanish-speaking child.

Another story for the Puerto Rican child which is written in English but which gives the pronunciation of the words and many Spanish words and names is *A Story of Puerto Rico: Ramón and the Pirate Gull* by Robert Barry. Ramón is quite excited when he sees a red sea gull stealing a fish from a pelican just like a pirate, but his mother and others will not believe his strange tale and this causes many adventures.

Spanish Aristrocracy in California

Two novels about the Spanish aristocracy living in California are *Treasures of the Medranos* by Elizabeth Howard Atkins and *Tomás and the Red Headed Angel* by Marian Garthwaite. In the first story Felisa Medrano, daughter of a Spanish ranchero in Old California, listens to tales of *banditos*. The secret role of Miguel Carlos Rodríguez, or *El Senor,* adds adventure to the story. The second novel is for young adolescents and concerns the cruelty and pride of Don Luis de Marenga who coldly accepts Angelita into his home but not into his heart. Tomás is only an Indian slave, and he feels the slashing cut of the lash frequently, but he is faithful to Angelita and becomes enmeshed with her in her clandestine love affair.

Another book by Marian Garthwaite is *Mario: A Mexican Boy's Adventure*. Much of this novel depicts the plight of the "wetbacks" who illegally cross the Mexican border into the United States.

Three books set in the terrain of Baja, California are *Three Without Fear* by Robert C. DuSoe, *The Black Pearl* by Scott O'Dell, and *Vagabundos* by Frank Bonham. The first story is one about an American boy and two orphaned Indian children who live by their wits to survive off the perilous Baja, California countryside before they succeed in their journey back to civilization. *The Black Pearl* is a novel about Ramón Salazar who hears superstitious tales about Manta Diablo, the monster of the sea. He bravely obtains the Pearl of Heaven and gains the enmity of the Sevillano, the finest diver of the pearl fleet. *The Black Pearl* is a tale of greed, avarice, and superstition as well as one of faith, courage, and compassion. In the third novel, *The Vagabundos* by Frank Bonham, Eric Hanson follows his father to Baja, California and learns that "El Rojo" Hanson is respected by the local fishermen, or *vagabundos*. Eric has many adventures catching up with his father and finds that both Mexicans and Californians have vitality, friendship, and human dignity.

Another book for older adolescents is *The Tilted Sombrero* by Evelyn (Sibley) Lampman which commences with the beginning of the Mexican War of Independence in 1810. Nando learns from his older brother that he has an Indian grandmother. He is a proud Creole who looks back to his

Spanish forbears and down upon the Mestizos, or Spanish Indians. He resents his Indian grandmother. Later he and his brother become connected with the popular cause the War for Independence. Father Miguel Hidalgo y Castilla, the priest who led the first Indian revolt, is prominently portrayed in this novel.

A rather unusual book for children is *Charro: Mexican Horseman* by James Norman which gives considerable information about the traditions of cowboy life and culture.

Music Books

Numerous folk song books of Mexico and Latin America are available. One of these is *A Fiesta of Folk Songs from Spain and Latin America,* edited by Henrietta Yurchenco.

Viva Chicano

Few novels are available for children and adolescents which depict the story of Mexican-American immigrants in an urban setting. The adult novel *Chicano* by Richard Vasquez presents Mexican-Californians as migrants through several generations.

A book for adolescents is *Viva Chicano* by Frank Bonham. In this novel Kenny Duran is a Mexican-American delinquent who wants desperately to reform. His mother is constantly screaming and berating him by threatening to send him back to the reform school. Her current, unemployed husband offers the boy little understanding or companionship. Kenny fights drugs, a fight which helps him face up to his difficulties, and he tries to keep out of active gang warfare. The boy would like to attend school more regularly but he loses out because he cannot stand the "screaming madhouse" of his home. Ken dimly remembers his Chicano father who offered pride in *la Raza,* but he lost his father at the age of six. Much of his problem comes from his negative attitude toward Americans. He is proud of being a Chicano and hates to be called a "greaser." The author, Frank Bonham, depicts this youngster with a sensitive understanding of his difficulties and says: "Common sense tells one that adolescents, white or black, will always be uncertain, impassioned, idealistic, sensitive, as well as often crude, cruel, and impulsive."[37]

Documentary Photographs of Chicanos

A documentary type of photography book on the Chicanos is *Small Hands, Big Hands: Seven Profiles of Chicano Migrant Workers and Their*

37. Frank Bonham, *Viva Chicano* (New York: E. P. Dutton & Company, 1970), p. 179.

Families, by Sandra Weiner. The profiles in this book were collected by the author from taped interviews held during the fall of 1969 with Chicano workers in California. She used this same procedure in writing a book about a pathetic Negro Ghetto child entitled *It's Wings That Make Birds Fly.* Weiner states that the labor of the migrants is not as inhuman as factory work in assembly plants with noises and foul smells, but the annual income of a family of four only amounts to about fourteen hundred dollars; so many members of this group live in inadequate housing with poor sanitary facilities.

One of the profiles is of Albert Reyes who goes to Mexico part of the year and lives in California in farm labor camps the rest of the time. He speaks of picking prunes, apricots, and cucumbers.

Antonio Lopez is a contrast to Albert. He was born in Bachimba, Mexico in 1897 where he formerly picked a hundred or more boxes of oranges daily. He also picked cotton in Corpus Christi, Texas. Wages were so poor that his wife made clothes for the children out of cattle-feed sacks. Doria Ramirez tells the story of her family working for a labor contractor. Nine people in the family got seven dollars for working twelve hours. These are not bitter statements but ones made with a feeling that this is the way things are. These and other profiles included in this book present migrant Chicano workers struggling against poverty, starvation, and illness.

A New Day by Don Bolognese presents a different version of the typical nativity story. José and Maria are migrant workers following the crops from harvest to harvest until one night their baby is to be born. The parents can find no room at the motels and hotels, but a gas station attendant allows them to stay in his garage. The baby was born as the sun rose and the villagers and workers joined together in a festival honoring the birth of the child.

Mexican Novels for Intermediate Grade Readers

A rather unusual novel about a boy in a Mexican orphanage is *Juan* by Mary Stolz. Juan is a little boy who is hurt and angry; he often tells lies and does unpredictable things. He dreams that he is not an orphan but was deposited at the doorway of Casa María after having been stolen by bandits. He thinks that his parents are on a lengthy trip and will come for him soon. Juan is a highly imaginative child. For instance, one day he sits on his mattress on the floor studying the wall painting. He thinks it would be fun to ride on a cloud behind the Lord Jesus if he wouldn't have to die first. He also wonders if Pablo, who died the year before, might be riding on a pink cloud driven by the Lord. Strange events happen to Juan until he gets his own bright boots which he refuses to take off even after he has gone to bed. Juan is a delightfully drawn character who will be enjoyed by children in any culture.

Another novel about Mexico by the same author is a fantasy entitled *The Dragons of the Queen.* Two American tourists and their Mexican chauffeur can find no room in a little inn; so they stay with an old woman in an ancient hacienda building. This building is generally known as a castle, and she is called a queen. It is a wierd fantasy which has an unusual ending.

The Mexican-American and Spanish Traditions

Two aspects of Mexican-American life portrayed in several novels are sheepherding and bullfighting. In the novel by Joseph Krumgold, *And Now Miguel,* the storyteller Miguel Chavez, relates that his grandfather and members of the Chavez family had proudly raised sheep long before the coming of the Americans and the formation of a United States. The Chavez family lives in New Mexico and Miguel longs to grow up rapidly into a man so that he can go with the men of the family to the Sangre de Cristo Mountains.

Shadow of a Bull by Maia Wojciechowska takes place in Spain, but it is a novel which is also concerned with the problem of becoming a man. Manolo Olivar was the son of the greatest bullfighter of all Spain, and therefore he is expected to follow his father's footsteps as a great toreador, but he has no *afición* for the bullring. Manolo tries to keep his fears and doubts to himself, but the titled Alfonso Castillo understands his inner struggles. He realizes that Manolo has fought hard to find his place as a man, and he tells the boy that a man's life must have time for loving as well as for fighting: "A man's life is many things. Before he becomes a man, he has many choices; to do the right thing, or to do the wrong thing; to please himself, or to please others; to be true to his own self; or untrue to it."[38]

The Pearl by John Steinbeck

Many Mexican-Americans, as well as Anglo readers, can identify with the characters portrayed in *The Pearl* by John Steinbeck. This is based upon an old Mexican folktale of the great pearl. The novel relates the simple tale of Kino the fisherman, and his wife, Juana, who dearly love the boy, Coyotito. It is the story of persons who are avaricious and cruel and those who are friendly and kind. A song is sung throughout the story.

38. Maia Wojciechowska, *Shadow of a Bull* (New York: Atheneum Publishers), p. 145.

The song of the family is interrupted by a Song of Evil which "is a savage, secret, dangerous melody."[39] A scorpion bites Coyotito. When Kino discovers the great pearl with its "silver incandescence" he looks forward to a better world, but the pearl causes much evil and tragedy in his family life.[40] This short novel is a good one to teach symbolism to pupils who need to see beneath the surface layer of the plot of a novel.

Books of Romance in Problems of Mexican-American Relations

Three books of romance which may help young adolescents to understand some of the problems faced by misunderstandings between Mexicans or Indians and white Anglo-Saxon Americans are *Crossroads for Chela* by Dorothy Witton, *Across the Tracks* by Bob and Jan Young, and *Buenos días, Teacher* by Ruth MacLeod.

Crossroads for Chela is a novel about a Tarascan Indian girl who meets Lorrie Kimberly, the American son of a geologist. A conflict in loyalties exists as Uncle Jaime and her father consider all foreigners as *gringos*. There is also a conflict between the old and new ways when modern industrial manufacturing methods replace the old methods used by the lacquer workers in Uruapan, a center for exquisite lacquer-encrusted bowls and trays. Also in festivals a new orchestra from Mexico City plays modern tunes, but the *Danza de los Viejitos,* or the comic dance of the little old men, was still popular. Some of the traditions of the Tarascan people are beautifully outlined in the novel. When a fire starts in the forest, Chela bravely supports the Kimberlys against the suspicious, prejudiced *Tarascans* who mistrust all *gringos* and strangers.

Across the Tracks by Bob and Jan Young is a novel about the breaking of barriers between white Anglo-Saxon adolescent teen-agers and Mexican-American students who are considered inferior. Betty Ochoa is a popular senior at Bellamar High, but she feels hurt when she loses the election as President of the Girl's League. An arrogant Mexican boy, Pete Flores, accuses Betty of losing some of her Mexican identity because she lives on the better side of the tracks and has many American friends. Betty wants to bring understanding and friendship between Anglo and Mexican students. The president of the student council, Dick Ackerman, makes conditions better when he nominates Betty Ochoa as activities commissioner. Even Pete Flores campaigns for Betty, and all of the Mexican-American teen age pupils vote at the school election at Bellamar High School for the first time in the history of the school.

In *Buenos días, Teacher* by Ruth MacLeod, one meets a dedicated

---

39. John Steinbeck, *The Pearl* and *The Red Pony* (New York: The Viking Press, a Compass Book edition, 1965), p. 6.
40. *Ibid.,* p. 20.

Anglo teacher, Jennifer Meade, whose first teaching position is at the Del Rio School. Here she teaches a third grade class in which over half of the pupils are Mexicans and many of them can not speak English. Jennifer meets David Wyman who is working on material for his master's thesis. Her handsome fiancé, Frank, belittles her crusading zeal. Some of the problems of interrelationships and distrust even among Mexican-Americans themselves are outlined in this career-romance novel. Mr. Garcia discusses the many controversies of their strikes and boycotts and the little farmers who suffer as well as the corporate landowners. The La Raza movement is discussed. He states that some Mexican-Americans call him a "Taco Tio" which is the *Chicano* version of Uncle Tom. He indicates that many Mexican-Americans living in the *barrios* mistrust others who have succeeded in the white man's world. He also mistrusts militant students who are shouting *"Viva La Revolución."*[41]

Gang Warfare Problems

Frank Bonham, who has written many young novels for teen-agers which have focused mostly upon boys and their teen age gangs of the street-corner society, has written *Durango Street*. This is a novel principally about Rufus Henry, chief of the Moors, and Alex Robbins, who tries to help the boys to lead a cleaner life in spite of their clashes with gangs like the Gassers.

Books for Older Adolescents and Mature Readers

The chapter entitled "Viva la Raza!: Latino-American Literature," appearing in *Forgotten Pages of American Literature* by Gerald W. Haslam, has several Spanish-American stories which are by Puerto Rican and Mexican authors. In an introduction to this section, Haslam states that Hispanic- and Portuguese-Americans trace some of their heritage back to early settlers in the "New World" and through their Indian ancestors are linked with the indigenous cultures of the Western Hemisphere. Many Mexican-Americans also trace their roots to a Central or South American nation.[42] "Mala Torres" by Amado Jesus Muro, which appears in this section, speaks of Mexican characters in their typical Mexican settings. In this story a picture is seen of hungry, suffering men coming to Pozolera's puesto. They have suffered many hardships and have lived on "mesquites, quelites, and sabandijas."[43]

---

41. Ruth MacLeod, *Buenos días, Teacher* (New York: Julian Messner, a division of Simon & Schuster, 1970), p. 171.
42. Gerald W. Haslam, *Forgotten Pages of American Literature* (Boston: Houghton Mifflin Company, 1970), pp. 165-166.
43. Amado Jesus Muro, "Mala Torres," in Haslem, *op cit., Forgotten Pages*, p. 225.

"The Legend of Gregorio Cortez," which appears in *American Ethnic Writing, Speaking for Ourselves,* is by Americo Paredes, a Mexican-American. He taped different versions of it from people living on both sides of the Mexico-Texas border. Gregorio Cortez was a legendary figure who was celebrated by the border ballad, or *corrido.* He was born on a ranch between Matamoros and Reynosa on the Mexican side of the border. In this tale Gregorio Cortez and his brother, Ramón, move North and do many jobs such as picking cotton, riding as vaqueros, or clearing land. Gregorio is really a popular folk hero who has many problems with the sheriff and the law.

Several poems and stories by Mexican-Americans appear in the collection *Latin American Writing Today,* edited by J. M. Cohen. A mystical, strange story is "Aura" by Carlos Fuentes. It is an odd fantasy written in the Henry James style, one in which the narrator, Señor Montero, comes to an old woman to write the memoirs of her husband, General Llorente for a large sum of money. He is cut off from his former life and has fantastic dreams about Aura. Strange happenings such as a pet rabbit running about the house and a nest of rats near the trunk of old-yellow manuscripts add to the atmosphere of the story.

Three novels by this popular Mexican author for mature young adults are *The Good Conscience, The Death of Artemis Cruz,* and *Where the Air Is Clear.*

The Good Conscience takes place in Guanajuato, Central Mexico, in the center of a wealthy mining district. The Ceballos family is in power and Jaime Ceballos struggles between the realistic beliefs of his weak father and powerful uncle and the idealism of youth. Many of his uncle's actions are not consistent with his beliefs, but Jaime fights to emerge as a man with a "good conscience."

The Death of Artemio Cruz is a novel of modern Mexico, one in which a political boss tells his story in retrospect from his death bed.

Where the Air Is Clear is the first novel by Carlos Fuentes and is written from the viewpoint of Ixca Cienfuegos who was born and lives in Mexico City, but this is a place where "old gods and devils struggle to overcome the new."

Pedro Páramo by Juan Rulfo is a strange, original novel which has been translated by Lysander Kemp. This is an odd, brooding tale in which the history of a long-dead political boss, Pedro Páramo, is depicted through the voices of ghosts talking to ghosts. In spite of his life of cruelty, the sympathies of the readers are aroused because of his hopeless devotion to Susana.

An Anthology of Chicano Stories

A recent collection of short stories for older adolescents is *The Chicano: From Caricature to Self-Portrait,* which has been edited by

Edward Simmen. These stories are often ones of pathos, humor, and poignancy about those Mexican-Americans who are emerging as an active minority group on the American scene. They want to be recognized for their individuality and human dignity and for the cultural contributions of their race. "Sánchez" by Richard Dokey is a poignant picture of Juan Sánchez who can not endure the sight of his son working at the Flotill Cannery in Stockton as he lives in a cheap skid row section. "Señor Garza" by Mario Suárez reflects a vivid section of the happy and seamy side of life in a barber shop. In "Cecelia Rosas" by Amado Múro a love-sick Mexican youth is infatuated with a señorita who wishes to discard her Mexican ways for those of the white Anglos. The story "To Endure" by Robert Granat depicts the tragic death of little Arcelia who is crushed by a coffin. "The Wonderful Ice-Cream Suit" by Ray Bradbury is a humorous revealing story about several men who purchase one suit. It is both amusing and sad in that these Mexican-Americans want to rise above their social caste by wearing a white suit. Another similar type of book is *The Chicanos: Mexican American Voices,* edited by Ed Ludwig and James Santibañez. These editors have selected articles, fiction, and poetry to depict a picture of Chicano life in the current scene.

A Novel About the Pochos

José Antonio Villarreal wrote a young adult novel, *Pocho,* over ten years before the *Chicano* movement became strong. *Pochos* are persons born of Mexican parents in the United States. They retain some of the cultural ways of their parents, but they struggle to adapt or assimilate themselves into the white Anglo-Saxon way of life. In the process they suffer from a mixture of Mexican and American cultural ways. Richard Rubio is born from Mexican parents in the Imperial Valley of California. He lives in the Santa Clara Valley and tries to adopt Anglo ways. At one time, when pressured by the police, he even denies his Mexican heritage and becomes a "tió Taco," or an Uncle Tom. Clashes inevitably occur between prejudiced Anglos and the *Pochos.* This novel should probably be read by college students rather than by unsophisticated adolescent readers.

With the Ears of Strangers

A comprehensive book which discusses the image of the Mexican in American literature is *With the Ears of Strangers: The Mexican in American Literature* by Cecil Robinson. Part 1 includes four chapters under the general title of *"Criollo* Mexico and Frontier America," and Part 2 concerns Mexico and the Hispanic Southwest in Modern American Literature.

This volume gives a good historical and cultural background for scholars who wish to specialize on Mexican-American literature or literature of Mexico.

Emerging Faces—The Mexican-Americans

In his book *Emerging Faces: The Mexican-Americans* Y. Arturo Cabrera discusses the current scene in which Mexican-Americans are in different stages of acculturation in America. In this book Cabrera traces the history of Spanish-speaking persons living in the southwestern section of the United States and the two basic stereotypes which have emerged. One of these is of dark, comely señoritas with roses in their hair, and of handsome Spanish gentlemen, riding spirited horses, performing heroically in bullfights, or managing their haciendas as in the courtly style of members of the Spanish aristocracy. The second stereotype is one of the *indio* or *peón* who was victimized by a feudal system inherited from Europe or from the feudal lord who was part of the warrior-priest hierarchies of the Mexicans.[44] Cabrera points out that Mexican-Americans have such ties as the Spanish language, the Catholic religion, the unifying quality of a large Mexican family which extends its circle to other relatives, as well as that of parents and children. A Mexican-American family man also values certain social amenities explained in the words *bien educado* (well-reared.) The Mexican-American of today is fighting the same discrimination and prejudices faced by other ethnic groups, such as poverty and unemployment, poor housing, an inadequate education, and a lack of a voice in the political power.

People who live in the poverty-stricken *barrio* complain that "accultured Mexican-Americans lose their Mexicanism" as newer, better-educated persons lose contact with the old community.

Chapter 2 of the Cabrera book entitled "Treatment in the Literature" points out that Mexican-Americans are almost like the "invisible man" depicted by Ralph Ellison. Many accounts of contemporary publications being used in American public schools omit the contributions of the Mexican-American to history.

The Mexican-American person wants to find his self identity as a member of a minority group in the culture of the United States. He longs to be free to make choices for those things which he wants to retain from his great Mexican heritage. He also desires to select carefully certain threads from the fabric of the Anglo-American cultural serape which he can weave into the pattern of his true being. Then he will no longer be thought of as a hyphenated American; he will be a whole person.

---

44. Y. Arturo Cabrera, *Emerging Faces: The Mexican-Americans* (Dubuque, Iowa: William C. Brown Company, Publishers, 1971), p. 3.

Summary

Although much Latin-American or Spanish-American literature is available, this chapter focuses mainly upon the Mexican-American whose population is principally clustered in New Mexico, Arizona, Texas, Colorado, and other regions of the United States. Cuban refugees, and Puerto Ricans who are living mostly in New York City and other urban centers also represent a Spanish-speaking minority group.

Numerous nonfiction books have been written concerning the place of the Mexican-American minority person, and several sources such as *Mexican-Americans in the United States: A Reader,* edited by John H. Burma, and *The Aliens: A History of Ethnic Minorities in America* by Leonard Dinnerstein and Frederic Cople Jaher are helpful.

Myths, legends, and folk tales offering a cultural heritage for Mexican-American children have been reviewed, as well as a book *Folk Tales of Mexico* by Américo Paredes, which is for more mature readers.

A section entitled "Quetzal Feathers and Eagle Shields" and one entitled "Flower and Song" survey much of the Indian and Mexican poetry which is available in either English translation or in bilingual editions. An article by Rafael Jesús González entitled "Symbol and Metaphor in Náhautl Poetry," which appears in *Forgotten Pages of American Literature,* helps to illuminate the significance of much beautiful Náhautl poetry.

Reaction—Questions and Projects

1. Read some references cited in this chapter on the cultural, sociological, and aesthetic background of the Mexican-American immigrant to the United States. Indicate how some of this background relates to the literature of the Mexican-American person.

2. The Mexican-American minority group does not concern the Puerto Ricans and Cubans who are also migrants. Find some literature about Puerto Ricans or Cubans which might help these persons to become accepted as newcomers.

3. Select some Mexican-American or Spanish-American poems which may be appropriate for children in grades four, five, and six of an elementary school. Practice reading these with expression and present them to young children.

4. Start a scrap book of current news articles about Mexican-Americans, Indians, or Black Americans. Study these articles to determine what basic needs these persons have in finding their own identities

Some illustrated books for younger readers in English as well as a few ones in either Spanish or bilingual editions are briefly reviewed. One problem is that few books for young children lack negative stereotypes of Mexican or Mexican-American characters.

A few novels on the Spanish aristocracy in California, as well as ones with a setting in Baja, California are mentioned.

Viva Chicano by Frank Bonham, which is for young adolescents, is reviewed, as well as a few intermediate grade novels for young children. Three books of romance on the problems of Mexican Indians or Mexican-American relations between young adolescents are discussed, as well as another novel by Frank Bonham entitled *Durango Street*. A few other novels for intermediate grade readers and young adolescents are mentioned.

One concluding section of the chapter is concerned with poetry, stories, and novels which have been mostly written for young adults or adult readers. The image of the Mexican-American in literature has been traced by Cecil Robinson in his volume *With the Ears of Strangers: The Mexican-American in Literature*. The Mexican-American has an emerging face, one which will not become invisible in a majority culture. He will emerge as a human being of some stature, a person who will no longer be a hyphenated American but a whole person with a proud heritage and culture which will add to the cultural pluralism of our American Society.

in the Anglo-Saxon culture. Relate these news articles to some of the discussions of literature in this chapter.

5. Go to a large, city book store or a library and make an annotated bibliography card list of at least five books which are in both the Spanish and English language or ones which are written in Spanish for children.

6. Study differences between the terms Spanish-speaking American, Mexican-American, Chicano, Indio-American, and others being used to distinguish persons with Spanish surnames.

7. Make a list of Mexican-American persons who have made significant contributions to the United States, such as artists, sports heroes, senators, or inventors. Study their lives in encyclopedias for children. Use the *Children's Catalog* or other basic guides to children's literature to determine if biographies have been written about these persons which might raise the self-image of Mexican-Americans.

8. Discover ways in which Mexican-American cultural traditions have added to the culture of Anglo-Americans in the United States.

These might be such things as music, art, foods, languages, architecture, and names of streets, rivers, lakes, or cities.

9. The Lerner Publications Company of Minneapolis, Minnesota has published several books in the In America Series. Virginia Brainart Kunz has written *The French in America* (Minneapolis: Lerner Publications Company, 1966), and Frances Butwin has written *The Jews in America* (Minneapolis: Lerner Publications Company, 1969). Each book gives historical data, customs and achievements of the minority group being discussed. Others are *The Czechs and Slovaks in America, The Dutch in America, The East Indians and Pakistanis in America, The English in America, The Germans in America, The Greeks in America, The Hungarians in America, The Irish in America, The Italians in America, The Japanese in America, The Negro in America, The Norwegian in America, The Poles in America, The Scots and Scots-Irish in America, The Swede in America,* and others. Read one of these books. Design an outline for a book on *The Mexicans in America,* or one for *The Cubans in in the United States,* or *The Puerto Ricans in the United States.* Collect newspaper and magazine pictures and articles which depict people who might make children of this minority group more proud of their lineage and culture. Use encyclopedias and other sources to write miniature biographies.

10. Use the tape recorder to record original stories of Mexican-American persons in a school or home situation. Read stories with Mexican-American heroes in them. Have children listen to stories by other children of their minority group. Use some Mexican music as a background.

11. Listen to the music of the highly acclaimed Mexican folk dancers on the recording, "Ballet Folklórico de México," produced by Musart D 618. This group presents concerts both in the opera house of Mexico City and in various cities of the United States. Choreography and program notes of these dances give much of the folklore and culture of Mexico. Obtain one of the records of this touring group, listen to it, and relate the music and dance to literature.

12. Some teachers may want to correlate Mexican folk art with Mexican folktales. An interesting book is one by Gerd Dörner entitled *Mexican Folk-Art* (with 28 colour plates; translated by Gladys Wheelhouse. Munich: William Andermann Verlag, 1962). Color plates included in this book depict pieces of Mexican pottery, earthenware figures for a Christmas candelabra, a censer from Oaxaca, an earthenware figure of death from Metepec, a moneybox pig from Tonala near Guadalajara, various samples of pre-Hispanic *huipils,* serapes, handwoven skirt material, cross-stitch embroidery on a rebozo,

lacquer work, silverware, and other interesting art objects. Have children look at these illustrations and create some designs which might be used for embroidery or art pieces. Another helpful art book is *Mexican Art* by Justino Fernández with photographs by Constantino Reyes-Valerio.

BIBLIOGRAPHY

BOOKS FOR PRIMARY CHILDREN

BALET, JAN. *The Fence.* New York: Dell Publishing Company, 1969.

BARRY, ROBERT. *A Story of Puerto Rico: Ramón and the Pirate Gull.* New York: McGraw-Hill Book Company, 1971.

BELPRÉ, PURA, trans. *Pérez y Martina: Un cuento folklórico puertorriqueño.* New York: Frederick Warne & Co., 1966.

BOLOGNESE, DON. *A New Day.* New York: Delacorte Press, Dell Publishing Company, 1970.

BRANLEY, FRANKLIN M. *¿Cómo es la luna?* Translated by Richard J. Palmer. A Spanish edition of *What the Moon is Like.* New York: Thomas Y. Crowell Company, 1968.

BULLA, CLYDE ROBERT. *Benito.* New York: Thomas Y. Crowell Company, 1961.

ETS, MARIE HALL, and LABASTIDA, AURORA. *Nine Days to Christmas.* New York: Viking Press, 1959.

FRANCHERE, RUTH. *Cesar Chavez.* New York: Thomas Y. Crowell Company, 1970.

GALARZA, ERNESTO. *Zoo Risa* [Fun at the zoo]. Santa Barbara, California: McNally and Loften, Publishers, 1968.

HOFF, SYD. *Danielito y el dinosauro* [Danny and the Dinosaur]. Translated by Pura Belpré. New York: Harper & Row, Publishers, 1970.

HUBP, LORETTA BURKE, trans. *¿Qué será?/ What Can It Be?* New York: John Day Company, 1970.

KIRN, ANN. *Two Pesos for Catalina.* Chicago: Rand McNally and Company, 1968.

LEXAU, JOAN M. *Maria.* New York: Dial Press, 1964.

MINARIK, ELSE HOMELUND. *Osito* [Little Bear]. Translated by Pura Belpré. New York: Harper & Row, Publishers, 1970.

PERDIDO, JUANITA. *Johnny Lost.* New York: John Day Company, 1969.

POLITI, LEO. *Pedro, the Angel of Olvera Street.* New York: Charles Scribner's Sons, 1946.

———. *Song of the Swallows.* New York: Charles Scribner's Sons, 1949.

PRIETO, MARIANA. *When the Monkeys Wore Sombreros.* Irvington-on-Hudson, New York: Harvey House, 1969.

REID, ALASTAIR, and KERRIGAN, ANTHONY, trans. *Mother Goose in Spanish/ Poesias de la Madré Oca.* New York: Thomas Y. Crowell Company, 1968.

RITCHIE, BARBARA. *Ramón Makes a Trade/Los cambios de Ramón.* Translated by Kenneth Edwards. Berkeley, California, Parnassus Press, 1959.

SELSAM, MILLICENT E. *Teresita y las orugas* [Terry and the Caterpillars]. New York: Harper & Row, Publishers, 1970.

SERFOZA, MARY. *Welcome Roberto! ¡Bienvenido, Roberto!* Chicago: Follett Publishing Company, 1969.

WEINER, SANDRA. *Small Hands, Big Hands: Seven Profiles of Chicano Migrant Workers and Their Families.* New York: Pantheon Books, a division of Random House, 1970.

————. *It's Wings that Make Birds Fly: The Story of a Boy.* New York: Pantheon Books, 1968.

BOOKS FOR INTERMEDIATE CHILDREN

ALEGRÍA, RICARDO E., ed. *The Three Wishes: A Collection of Puerto Rican Folktales.* Translated by Elizabeth Culbert. New York: Harcourt, Brace & World, 1968.

ATKINS, ELIZABETH HOWARD. *Treasures of the Medranos.* Berkeley, California: Parnassus Press, 1957.

BARLOW, GENEVIEVE. *Latin American Tales: From the Pampas to the Pyramids of Mexico.* Chicago: Rand, McNally and Company, 1966.

BEALS, CARLETON. *Stories Told by the Aztecs Before the Spaniards Came.* London, New York, Toronto: Abelard Schuman, 1970.

BRENNER, ANITA. *The Boy Who Could Do Anything and Other Mexican Folktales.* New York: William R. Scott, 1942.

————. *A Hero by Mistake.* New York: William R. Scott, 1953.

CAMPBELL, CAMILLA. *Star Mountain and Other Legends of Mexico.* 2d. ed. New York: McGraw-Hill Book Company, 1960.

DuSOE, ROBERT C. *Three Without Fear.* New York: David McKay Company, 1947.

GARTHWAITE, MARIAN. *Tomás and the Red-Headed Angel.* New York: Julian Messner, 1966.

————. *Mario: A Mexican Boy's Adventure.* Garden City, New York: Doubleday & Company, 1960.

GATES, DORIS. *Blue Willow.* New York: Viking Press, 1940.

KRUMGOLD, JOSEPH. *And Now Miguel.* New York: Thomas Y. Crowell Company, Apollo Edition, 1970.

LONG, EULA. *Pirate's Doll.* New York: Alfred A. Knopf, 1956.

NIGGLI, JOSEPHINA. *A Miracle for Mexico.* New York: Graphic Society, 1964.

NORMAN, JAMES. *Charro: Mexican Horseman.* New York: G. P. Putnam's Sons, 1970.

O'DELL, SCOTT. *The Black Pearl.* Boston: Houghton Mifflin Company, 1967.

RESNICK, SEYMOUR. *Selections from Spanish Poetry.* Irvington-on-the-Hudson, New York: Harvey House, 1962.

————. *Spanish-American Poetry: A Bilingual Selection.* Irvington-on-the Hudson, New York: Harvey House, 1964.

RHOADS, DOROTHY. *The Corn Grows Ripe.* New York: Viking Press, 1969.

STOLZ, MARY. *Juan.* New York: Harper & Row, Publishers, 1970.

————. *The Dragons of the Queen.* New York: Harper & Row, Publishers, 1969.

TRAVEN, B. *The Creation of the Sun and the Moon.* New York: Hill and Wang, 1968.

WOJCIECHOWSKA, MAIA. *Shadow of a Bull.* New York: Atheneum Publishers, 1964.

BOOKS FOR ADOLESCENT READERS

BONHAM, FRANK. *Durango Street.* New York: E. P. Dutton & Company, 1965.
————. *The Vagabundos.* New York: E. P. Dutton Company, 1969.
————. *Viva Chicano.* New York. E. P. Dutton Company, 1970.
BRANDON, WILLIAM, ed. *The Magic World: American Indian Songs and Poems.* New York: William Morrow & Company, 1971.
BRAYMER, NAN, and LOWENFELS, LILLIAN. Trans. by *Modern Poetry for Spain and Latin America.* New York: Corinth Books, 1964.
COHEN, J. M. *Latin American Writing Today.* Baltimore: Penguin Books, 1967.
DE CESCO, FEDERICA. *The Prince of Mexico.* Translated from the German by Frances Lobb. New York: John Day Company, 1970.
FERNÁNDEZ, JUSTINO. *Mexican Art.* rev. ed. London: The Hamlyn Publishing Group Ltd., 1967.
FLORES, ANGEL, ed. *An Anthology of Spanish Poetry from Garcilaso to García Lorca in English Translation with Spanish Originals.* Garden City, New York: Doubleday & Company, Incorporated, Anchor Books, 1961.
GENERAL SECRETARIAT OF THE ORGANIZATION OF AMERICAN STATES, Washington, D. C. *Young Poetry of the Americas.* Volume I, n.d. Cultural Themes, Argentina, Brazil, Chile, Costa Rica, Ecuador, El Salvador, Haiti, Mexico, Panama, Uruguay.
LAKLAN, CARLI. *Migrant Girl.* New York: McGraw-Hill Book Company, 1970.
LAMPMAN, EVELYN (SIBLEY). *The Tilted Sombrero.* Garden City, New York: Doubleday & Company, 1966.
LEWIS, RICHARD, ed. *Still Waters of the Air: Poems by Three Modern Spanish Poets.* New York: Dial Press, 1970.
LORCA, FEDERICO GARCIA. *Poet in New York.* Translated by Ben Belitt. New York: Grove Press, Inc., 1955.
LORCA, FRANCISCO GARCIA, and ALLEN, DONALD M., eds. *The Selected Poems of Federico García Lorca.* New York: New Directions Publishing Corporation, 1955.
MACLEOD, RUTH. *Buenos días, Teacher.* New York: Julian Messner, 1970.
MCWILLIAMS, CAREY. *The Mexicans in America: A Student's Guide to Localized History.* New York: Teachers College, Columbia University, 1969.
NAVA, JULIAN. *Mexican Americans—Past, Present, and Future.* New York: American Book Company, 1969.
NERUDA, PABLO. "Poem 20." In *Unstill Life: An Introduction to Spanish Poetry of Latin America,* edited by Mario Benedetti. Translated by Darwin J. Flakoll and Clarabel Alegría. New York: Harcourt, Brace & World, 1969.
————. *The Heights of Macchu Picchu.* Translated by Nathaniel Tarn. New York: Farrar, Straus & Giroux, 1966.
————. *Alturas de Macchu Picchu* New York: Farrar, Straus & Giroux, 1966.
PAZ, OCTAVIO. "Mexico." In *Naturaleza viva: Introducción a la poesía hispano Americana Edita lo por Mar,* edited by Mario Benedetti. Illustraciones de Antonio Frasconi. New York: Harcourt, Brace & World, Inc., 1969. Mario Benedetti Traduccion de Darwin J. Flakoll y Claribel Alegría. 58
————. comp. *Anthology of Mexican Poetry.* Translated by Samuel Beckett. Bloomington, Indiana: Indiana University Press, 1969.
————. OCTAVIO, et al. *New Poetry of Mexico.* New York: E. P. Dutton & Co., 1970.

ROACH, ELOISE, trans. *Juan Rámón Jiménez: Three Hundred Poems, 1903-1953.* Austin, Texas: University of Texas Press, 1962.

STEINBECK, JOHN. *The Pearl.* In *The Pearl* and *The Red Pony.* New York: Viking Press, a Compass Book, 1965.

TABLADA, JOSÉ JUAN. "The Peacock" and "The Toads." *New Poetry of Mexico,* edited by Octavio Paz, Ali Chumacero, José Emilio Pacheco, and Honero Aridjis. Bilingual edition edited by Mark Strand. New York: E. P. Dutton & Co., 1970.

TARAZIAN, JAMES P., and CRAMER, KATHRYN. *Mighty Hard Road: The Story of Caesar Chavez.* Garden City, New York: Doubleday & Company, 1970.

TEBBEL, JOHN, and RUIZ, RAMÓN EDUARDO. *South by Southwest: The Mexican-American and His Heritage.* Garden City, New York: Doubleday & Company, Zenith Books, 1969.

WEINER, SANDRA. *Small Hands, Big Hands: Seven Profiles of Chicano Migrant Workers and Their Families.* New York: Pantheon Books, a division of Random House, 1970.

WHITNEY, PHYLLIS. *A Long Time Coming.* New York: David McKay, 1954.

WITTON, DOROTHY. *Crossroads for Chela.* New York: Washington Square Press, an Archway Paperback, 1969.

YOUNG, BOB AND JAN. *Across the Tracks.* New York: Washington Square Press, 1969.

YOUNG-ADULT BOOKS

FUENTES, CARLOS. *The Good Conscience.* New York: The Noonday Press, a division of Farrar, Straus & Giroux, 1970.

———. *The Death of Artemis Cruz.* Translated from the Spanish by Sam Hileman. New York: Farrar, Straus & Giroux, 1964.

———. *Where the Air is Clean.* Translated by Sam Hileman. New York: Farrar, Straus & Giroux, Noonday Press Edition, 1971.

LUDWIG, ED, and SANTIBAÑEZ, JAMES, ed. by. *The Chicanos: Mexican-American Voices.* Baltimore: Penguin Books, 1971.

RULFO, JUAN. *Pedro Páramo, A Novel of Mexico.* Translated by Lysander Kemp. New York: Grove Press, Evergreen Black Cat Edition, 1969.

SIMMEN, EDWARD, ed. *The Chicano: From Caricature to Self-Portrait.* New York: New American Library, a Metro Book, 1971.

VILLARREAL, JOSE ANTONIO. *Pocho.* Garden City, New York: Doubleday & Company, Anchor Books, 1970.

PROFESSIONAL BOOKS

BLATT, GLORIA T. "The Mexican-American in Children's Literature." *Elementary English* 45, April 1968. pp. 446-451.

CABRERA, Y. ARTURO. *Emerging Faces: The Mexican-American.* Dubuque, Iowa: William C. Brown Company, Publishers, 1971.

CARLSON, RUTH KEARNEY. *Literature for Children: Enrichment Ideas.* Dubuque, Iowa: William C. Brown Company, Publishers, 1970.

DE GEREZ, TONI. "The Way of Quetzalcóatl." The *Hornbook Magazine* 43 (April 1967): pp. 171-175.

———. "Three Times Lonely: The Plight of the Mexican Child in the American Southwest." *The Hornbook Magazine* 46 (February, 1970): 66-73.

————. "Books for Miguel." *School Library Journal,* December 1967, pp. 45-47, 51.

DINNERSTEIN, LEONARD, and JAHER, FREDERIC COPLE. *The Aliens: A History of Ethnic Minorities in America.* New York: Appleton-Century-Crofts, Educational Division, Meredith Corporation, 1970.

ERICKSEN, CHARLES A. "Uprising in the Barrios." Edited by John H. Burma. In *Mexican-Americans in the United States: A Reader.* Cambridge Massachusetts: Schenkman Publishing Company, distributed by Canfield Press, a department of Harper & Row, Publishers, 1970, p. 299.

FADERMAN, LILLIAN, and BRADSHAW, BARBARA. *American Ethnic Writing: Speaking for Ourselves.* Glenview, Illinois: Scott, Foresman and Company, 1969.

GALARZA, ERNESTO; GALLEGOS, HERMAN; and SAMORA, JULIAN. *Mexican-Americans in the Southwest.* Santa Barbara: McNally & Loftin Publishers, 1970.

GAST, DAVID K. "Minority Americans in Children's Literature." *Elementary English* 44, January 1967, pp. 12-23.

HASLAM, GERALD W. *Forgotten Pages of American Literature.* Boston: Houghton Mifflin Company, 1970.

HAYS, H. R., trans. *The Selected Writing of Juan Rámon Jiménez.* Edited by Eugenio Florit. New York: Grove Press, 1957.

Latin America: An Annotated List of Materials, selected by a Committee of Librarians, Teachers and Latin American specialists in cooperation with the Center for Inter-American Relations, 331 East 38th Street, New York, New York 10016. Information Center on Children's Cultures, United States Committee for UNICEF, 1969.

LEWIS, OSCAR. *Five Families: Mexican Case Studies in the Culture of Poverty.* New York: New American library, a Mentor Book, 1959.

————. *The Children of Sanchez: Autobiography of a Mexican Family.* New York: Vintage Books, a division of Random House, 1961.

————. *Pedro Martínez: A Mexican Peasant and His Family.* New York: Vintage Books, a division of Random House, 1967.

MADSEN, WILLIAM. *Mexican-Americans of South Texas.* New York: Holt, Rinehart & Winston, 1964.

NICHOLSON, IRENE. *Mexican and Central American Mythology.* London: Paul Hamlyn, 1967.

PAREDES, AMÉRICO, ed. and trans. *Folktales of Mexico.* Chicago: University of Chicago Press, 1970.

ROBINSON, CECIL. *With the Ears of Strangers: The Mexican in American Literature.* Tempe, Arizona: The University of Arizona Press, 1969.

ROMANO, OCTAVIO I.-V. "Goodbye Revolution—Hello Slum." In *El espejo— The Mirror: Selected Mexican-American Literature,* edited by Octavio Ignacio Romano-V. Berkeley, California: Quinto Sol Publications, 1969.

ROWAN, HELEN. "A Minority Nobody Knows." In *Mexican-Americans in the United States: A Reader,* edited by John H. Burma. Cambridge Massachusetts: Schenkman Publishing Company, distributed by Canfield Press, a department of Harper & Row, Publishers, 1970, p. 299.

SAMORA, JULIAN, ed. *La Raza: Forgotten Americans.* Notre Dame and London: University of Notre Dame Press, 1969.

STEINER, STAN. *La Raza: The Mexican-Americans.* New York: Harper & Row, Publishers, 1970.

TORGERSON, DIAL. " 'Brown Power' Unity Seen Behind School Disorders." In *Mexican-Americans in the United States: A Reader,* edited by John Burma. Cambridge, Massachusetts: Schenkman Publishing Company, distributed by Canfield Press, a department of Harper & Row, Publishers, 1970, p. 280.

TRASK, WILLARD R., ed. and trans. *The Unwritten Song: Poetry of the Primitive and Traditional Peoples of the World, Volume 2,* Micronesia, Polynesia, Asia, North America, Central America, South America. New York: The Macmillan Company; London: Collier Macmillan, 1967, p. 280.

VASQUEZ, RICHARD. *Chicano.* Garden City, New York: Doubleday & Company, 1969.

VILLARREAL, JOSÉ ANTONIO. *Pocho.* Garden City, New York: Doubleday & Company, Anchor Book, 1970.

WAGLEY, CHARLES, and HARRIS, MARVIN. *Minorities in the New World: Six Case Studies.* New York: Columbia University Press, 1964.

YURCHENCO, HENRIETTA, ed. *A Fiesta of Folk Songs from Spain and Latin America.* New York: G. P. Putnam's Sons, 1967.

INDEX

239